marriage
MINISTRY
in the 21st Century:
The Encyclopedia of Practical Ideas

Group

Loveland, Colorado
www.group.com

Group resources actually work!

This Group resource helps you focus on **"The 1 Thing®"**—a life-changing relationship with Jesus Christ. "The 1 Thing" incorporates our **R.E.A.L.** approach to ministry. It reinforces a growing friendship with Jesus, encourages long-term learning, and results in life transformation, because it's:

Relational
Learner-to-learner interaction enhances learning and builds Christian friendships.

Experiential
What learners experience through discussion and action sticks with them up to 9 times longer than what they simply hear or read.

Applicable
The aim of Christian education is to equip learners to be both hearers and doers of God's Word.

Learner-based
Learners understand and retain more when the learning process takes into consideration how they learn best.

Credits
Editor: Brad Lewis
Project Manager: Amber Van Schooneveld
Senior Developer: Roxanne Wieman
Chief Creative Officer: Joani Schultz
Copy Editor: Ann Jahns
Art Director/Cover Art Director: Jeff A. Storm
Designer: Pamela Poll Graphic Design
Cover Designer: Samantha Wranosky
Illustrator: Matt Wood
Production Manager: Peggy Naylor

Unless otherwise indicated, all Scripture quotations are taken from the *Holy Bible*, New Living Translation, copyright © 1996, 2004. Used by permission of Tyndale House Publishers, Inc., Carol Stream, Illinois 60188. All rights reserved.

Library of Congress Cataloging-in-Publication Data
Marriage ministry in the 21st century : the encyclopedia of practical ideas.
    p. cm.
  ISBN 978-0-7644-3567-6 (pbk. : alk. paper) 1. Church work with married people--Handbooks, manuals, etc. 2. Marriage--Religious aspects--Christianity--Handbooks, manuals, etc. I. Group Publishing.
  BV4012.27.M37 2007
  259'.1--dc22
                              2007034813

10 9 8 7 6 5 4 3 2 1   17 16 15 14 13 12 11 10 09 08
Printed in the United States of America.

contents

section **one: 20 nights out and weekends away** **15**

10 DATE NIGHT IDEAS

5 GETAWAY IDEAS

5 SPIRITUAL RETREAT IDEAS

section **two: 20 ideas for growing together spiritually** **31**

5 PRAYER IDEAS

section **six: movie nights** **121**

15 MOVIE NIGHTS FOR COUPLES

section **seven: 20 ideas for connecting with other couples** **139**

10 SMALL GROUP IDEAS

10 OUTREACH IDEAS

section **eight: 20 ideas to care for marriages** 155

10 IDEAS FOR STARTING MARRIAGES RIGHT

5 IDEAS FOR HELPING COUPLES THROUGH ROCKY TIMES

5 IDEAS FOR MINISTERING TO COUPLES GOING THROUGH DIVORCE

section **nine: 15 ideas for later-in-life marriages** 173

5 TRANSITION IDEAS

contributors

Thanks to the following men and women who have provided the ideas contained in this volume.

Linda Bever
Stephanie Carney
Dave Embree
David Frisbie
Lisa Frisbie
Dave Gallagher
Cheri Gillard
Cheryl Gochnauer
Linda Holloway
Jeanette Littleton
Keith Madsen
Robin Martens
Jim Miller
Pat Mitchell
Les Parrott
Leslie Parrott
Kristi Rector
Dean Ridings
Doyle Roth
Larry Shallenberger
Jason Tarka
Molly Wright

how to use this resource

Welcome to *Marriage Ministry in the 21st Century: The Encyclopedia of Practical Ideas*!
If you're a pastor, counselor, marriage ministry director, or a layperson in charge of a marriage ministry program in your church, this book is for you! It's packed full of ideas on caring for marriages, family-building, retreats, date nights, outreach, events, and much more. In addition, the last few sections of the book cover some big topics you need to consider in marriage ministry, such as the importance of a marriage mentoring ministry, the challenges of working with second marriages and blended families, and some important counseling disciplines that can help you keep your sanity. In fact, we've asked some leading experts to contribute these sections, so look for their bylines.

Whether you want to build or already have a thriving marriage ministry in your church, you probably realize that marriage ministry differs from many programs or ministries. While you might plan activities, retreats, Bible studies, and special events for couples, you also minister to marriages in many other ways. For example, you probably work with engaged couples in your church before their weddings take place. You likely offer counseling and maybe even support groups for couples going through difficult times or considering divorce. Further, a big part of marriage ministry involves equipping all couples to maintain and grow healthy relationships in their homes, with their families, and of course, with each other. The ideas in this book hit on all of these areas, too.

In fact, while some of the ideas address what to do in a marriage ministry program setting in the church, many of the ideas cover what you might encourage couples to do in their homes and with their families. Thinking this way actually expands your marriage ministry—instead of looking at it as a program that some of the couples in your church take part in, you can think of marriage ministry as equipping all the couples in your church to have thriving marriages all the time—and that will certainly result in strengthening your whole church!

This book is a collection of practical ideas. While you can read it from cover to cover, it's designed as a reference tool. In the Contents listing, look up the area of marriage ministry where you need tips and ideas, and go from there.

We pray that this tool will help you build an effective marriage ministry as you serve Christ. May God bless you and your group!

—Brad Lewis, Editor

The Desperate Need for Effective Marriage Ministry

by Drs. Les and Leslie Parrott

Whether you know it or not, some people in your congregation are desperate for help. While they might not look particularly needy, countless couples on any given weekend file into churches across the country, looking their "Sunday best," while quietly keeping their marriage problems to themselves. They might need help, but they feel too ashamed to ask for counseling. They might feel all alone, thinking no one else can understand what they're going through. Or maybe they just have no one to talk to. Their marriages are hurting, and they're not getting the help they need.

Truth be told, some of these couples are going down.

You've probably witnessed couples go through painful divorces where trouble was never suspected. You've certainly seen a newlywed couple, full of promise, experience a short-lived marriage because they didn't get a solid start. And think of the numerous couples in your church who are stuck in a rut, not reaching their full potential.

How can you meet the needs of these couples? Chances are, you already do a lot: recommend good marriage books, facilitate couples' support groups, sponsor marriage retreats or seminars, preach sermons on marriage, conduct marriage counseling, and make counseling referrals. Maybe you've even launched a marriage mentoring ministry to link seasoned and experienced couples with less-experienced couples in your congregation.

In other words, you're probably already doing a great deal to meet the demanding needs of couples in your care. But if you're like most pastors and marriage ministry leaders, you still scratch your head and ask: "Why isn't this working better?" After all, the divorce rate in the church is no different than it is outside the church.

Why Typical Marriage Ministry Doesn't Work

Why do so many couples have difficulties when your church does so many things to help them? Let's look at two major reasons that the average marriage ministry efforts of local churches fall short.

First, pastors, marriage ministry leaders, and counselors are often overwhelmed with too many couples who need help. You have limited time to work with couples, and that means you need to place a limit on how many couples you can see. Whether you serve in a megachurch or a smaller church, your time is limited.

Second, pastors, marriage ministry leaders, and counselors don't know which couples need help, because many couples in trouble won't seek counseling. This second reason might be the more disheartening of the two, because the couples who need help the most are the least likely to ask for it. If you knew which couples to ask, they'd list a variety of excuses.

But most likely, they feel embarrassed. The shame and disgrace of needing help with marriage keeps far too many needy couples from allowing you to effectively minister to them.

That's why we're excited to present *Marriage Ministry in the 21st Century*. This resource is chock-full of new and innovative ways to minister to and meet the needs of today's couples.

For example, you'll find dozens of practical ideas for ministering to engaged couples and newlyweds, building stronger family relationships, helping couples find purpose and ways to meet each other's needs, reaching out to new couples, leading couples' Bible studies, planning marriage retreats, encouraging date nights, and much more.

Discovering What Your Marriage Ministry Needs

We've all heard the startling statistics of divorce—almost anyone can tell you that "almost half of all marriages end in divorce." We're nearly immune to the numbers. But if you ask the people in your church to raise their hands if someone in their family or a close friend has suffered a divorce, almost every hand goes up. We all know something needs to be done.

We're here to say that something *can* be done! You can start by taking a quick inventory of the needs of people your current marriage ministry serves—as well as those it isn't reaching. Why? Because this raises your level of awareness, and awareness is a big part of the solution.

Every church, no matter how effective overall, does some things well and some things not so well. That's a way of saying that every church has plenty of room to improve. This certainly rings true in the area of marriage ministry.

So, take a moment to consider how well your church is doing to meet the needs of couples in your care. We've listed the top 15 issues couples look for help with from their churches. Simply place a check in front of those that the marriage ministry in your church provides.

We have concrete ways, readily known to people in our congregation, for helping couples:

- ❑ Conquer frequent conflict
- ❑ Move beyond financial pressures
- ❑ Dismantle power struggles
- ❑ Cope with busy schedules
- ❑ Ease work pressures that impact the home
- ❑ Find hope when struggling with infertility
- ❑ Navigate tumultuous relations with extended family
- ❑ Overcome sexual unfulfillment
- ❑ Cultivate spiritual intimacy
- ❑ Turn around communication meltdowns
- ❑ Triumphantly make it through a major illness
- ❑ Work through the devastation of an addiction
- ❑ Rebuild trust and love after infidelity
- ❑ Remain "husband and wife" while being "mom and dad"
- ❑ Balance the roles and responsibilities on the home front

So, how do the efforts of your church stack up? Can you check off most of these? Not if your church is like most churches. In fact, in one cycle of the typical church calendar, most churches squarely address only a small minority of these issues. Sure, we can all say that we let people know about our counseling program, for example. But will a couple simply trying to cope with busy schedules, parenting, and a lack of spiritual intimacy seek counseling in your church? Unlikely. So what should our churches do?

It's Time We "Do Something"

One morning, near the turn of the 20th century, Bramwell Booth visited his elderly father, William Booth, founder of The Salvation Army.

"Bramwell, did you know that men slept out all night on the bridges?" William had arrived in London very late the night before from a town in the south of England and had to cross through the capital to reach his home. What he'd seen on his late-night journey prompted his question.

"Well, yes," Bramwell replied, "a lot of poor fellows, I suppose, do that."

"Then go and do something!" William said. "We must do something."

"What can we do?"

"Get them shelter."

"That will cost money."

"Something must be done. Get hold of a warehouse and warm it, and find something to cover them!"

That was the beginning of The Salvation Army shelters.

If William Booth were alive today, he might just have the same passion for "doing something" about the state of marriage.

Because you're reading these words, we know you have this kind of passion for marriage ministry. And we're thrilled to help you "do something" about it through the tips, suggestions, plans, and ideas of *Marriage Ministry in the 21st Century*.

Drs. Les and Leslie Parrott are co-founders of RealRelationships.com and the Center for Relationship Development at Seattle Pacific University. Their best-selling books include *Love Talk, Your Time-Starved Marriage,* and the award-winning *Saving Your Marriage Before It Starts.* Their work has been featured in The New York Times and USA Today, and they have appeared on *CNN, Good Morning America,* and *Oprah.* The Parrotts live in Seattle, Washington, with their two sons.

twenty nights out
AND WEEKENDS AWAY

Most married couples need more fun in their lives. As they go through the daily, weekly, monthly, and lifetime grind of dealing with work, family, and other relationships, they simply need time to reconnect.

Again, remember that marriage ministry is much more than a program you establish, maintain, and grow at church. Your ministry also includes equipping all married couples in your church to build and strengthen their relationships with each other, with their families, with God, and beyond the walls of their home.

The ideas in this section are written directly to couples, so you can talk about them in a Sunday school class or during a sermon on marriage. Or you can reprint them in your church newsletter. Just be sure to use them to help married couples have more fun, reconnect, and remind themselves of why they fell in love and got married in the first place!

10 DATE NIGHT IDEAS

Start simple! Encourage couples in your church to establish a regular date night once every week or two, or even once a month. Their goal? Have fun and rediscover each other—and do something besides "dinner and a movie."

DATE 1
literary picnic

Most of us seldom have time to read more than daily paperwork, newspaper headlines, and e-mails. So enjoy a break from the norm and spend an evening reading together. Browse *The Sunflower* by Richard Paul Evans (Simon & Schuster) or *Dinner with a Perfect Stranger* by David Gregory (WaterBrook Press) for short book ideas.

Then pick a place where you can enjoy your evening of reading. Choose a park, a romantic overlook, a lakeshore, or a place that holds special meaning just for the two of you. Pick a date and make arrangements for child care.

When the day arrives, pack a large blanket, a flashlight or lantern for reading, comfortable clothes, cups, a Thermos of hot cocoa (enter "hot cocoa" in a search engine for thousands of variations), and a yummy dessert. To get beyond conversations of daily details, think of questions to ask each other on your way to the picnic. Questions can be serious or humorous.

> ### no kids allowed!
> If couples can't afford child care, combine these ideas with "Child Care Solutions" on page 145 or "Footloose and Fancy Free" on page 148.

At your picnic, focus on relaxing together with a good book, savoring your time and treats, and leaving the noise and demands of daily life behind you, even if only for a few hours.

If you need to stay closer to home, picnic in your backyard, or set up in your living room with a large blanket, candles to imitate starlight, and music for ambience. Soundtracks of the ocean, rainstorms, or mountain streams add to the atmosphere.

DATE 2
hide and seek

Hide and Seek has amused children for centuries—because it's fun! You don't have to be a kid to appreciate this rollicking pastime. Tweak the rules a bit, and you've got a playful game for you and your spouse.

Divide your home into "his" and "her" sections. These can be inside/outside, upstairs/downstairs, west wing/east wing—you get the idea. Each section is "off limits" to the other spouse until the hunt begins.

Hide secret treasures for your spouse in your section. These gifts can be as simple as handwritten coupons offering romantic rewards, like a jaunt in the Jacuzzi or dancing barefoot in the backyard. Or you can purchase several small tokens of your affection to stash throughout your area.

If you decide to buy some of your surprises, make sure you're both operating on the same budget and have agreed on the same number of tokens. Think like a kid: It bugged you to get three gifts when your brother got six, even if yours cost more! Also, make sure the items you select are something your mate will enjoy.

Once the presents are planted, the party begins. Decide who goes first, and invite your mate into your section. As you search, point each other in the right direction by providing subtle or not-so-subtle clues: "You're getting warmer…colder…*hot!*" When you find a hidden gift or note, open and act upon it immediately. This isn't the time to offer a coupon for a candlelit dinner—unless, of course, you've already got it made and waiting!

The one way you can act like grown-ups is by savoring each discovery. Alternate turns back and forth to search for gifts. If something sparks discussion, a sentimental moment, or giddy passion, let your hearts be your guide.

> **treasure ideas**
> Wondering what to give? These ideas can kick-start your imagination:
> • Piggyback ride
> • Ice cream cone
> • Pedicure
> • CD or DVD
> • Sponge bath
> • Yo-yo

DATE 3
playful palettes

Add color and vibrancy to your relationship by learning to appreciate art. Explore a nearby art exhibit or museum.

Too stuffy? Don't worry. Art encompasses so many themes and takes on so many forms that you can find something to appeal to your personalities. Art is also widely available. Nearly every community features some sort of art exhibit, from huge displays in Chicago's Museum of Contemporary Art to student self-portraits displayed in hometown libraries.

Contact your chamber of commerce to see if any local organizations are hosting touring exhibits. Or hunt online by entering your city and state plus the words "art museums and festivals" in a search engine. Also check out Museums in the USA (www.museumca.org/usa/), an expansive Web site with links to the home pages of major museums in all 50 states.

When you arrive at the exhibit or museum, take a close look at intriguing images and objects, and allow plenty of time to pause, interpret, and absorb the messages a piece of art projects. How does it strike you? What does your spouse think? What pieces speak to you as a couple, reflecting positive aspects of your marriage? By the way, there are no right or wrong answers!

When you get home, express your own creativity. Clear off the kitchen table or another large, flat area. Fashion your own masterpiece, using your unique artistry and inspiration to express how you feel about your spouse. Use matte board and paints, poster board and watercolors, or construction paper and markers, or simply tear off a big sheet of white butcher's paper and scribble with crayons. If you feel especially adventurous, bring out the finger paints!

DATE 4
name that tune

Husbands, if you want your wife to adore you, set aside the flowers and chocolates. Instead, simply take her by the hand and say, "Shall we dance?"

Ballroom dancing is romantic, and most women love it. When your wife tells her friends that you've invited her to take lessons, you can almost count on their response being, "I wish *my* husband would do that!"

So pick up the beat, fellas. You can salsa, swing, rumba, or line dance. Or perhaps you'd like the foxtrot, waltz, merengue, or country two-step. Whatever dance you choose, stay on your toes by following these tips:

• *Practice fancy footwork.* Every dance has a basic step. Once you learn it, you build levels of expertise off that step.

• *Frame up.* Your "frame" is your body position. It provides connection to your dance partner, making leading and following possible.

• *Focus.* Give your spouse your total attention. Don't look at other dancers, the ceiling, or the floor. It's just you two, swirling and twirling in your own world.

Dance classes are relatively inexpensive. Typically, an hour-long group class costs less than $10 per dancer. Enroll in weekly classes or pay as you go.

If you and your spouse prefer being in the audience to stepping out on the dance floor, get tickets to see a professional traveling dance troupe as it passes through town. Call the theater department of a college within driving distance, and see if their performance schedule includes any musicals. Support local students by cheering their attempts at amateur dance productions. Patronize community theater and church musicals. And don't overlook events like concerts in the park, jazz fests, summer street dances, and holiday presentations of *The Nutcracker*.

Of course, the most romantic dance of all can take place when you're alone with your mate, swaying under the stars in a private meadow, tap-dancing among the trees, churning up sand on a secluded beach, or gliding across your own living room. Just kick up your heels and make your own music.

DATE 5
love languages

You've probably heard the song "Fifty Ways to Leave Your Lover." This date could be called "Fifty Ways to *Lead* Your Lover."

The pursuit begins with something simple, like a text message: "Look inside your planner, on page 48." This just happens to be a calendar page with your anniversary date circled. Taped to this page is a note inviting your spouse to a special date this evening, at a place yet to be revealed. Challenge him or her to watch for more messages—clues you'll provide throughout the day.

The note would include directions to the next hint, such as "Stand in front of our house, and look toward the garage." That leads to another clue, perhaps written in sidewalk chalk on the driveway. Think up outrageous ways to convey your messages,

clue ideas

Some creative ways to guide your spouse to the end of the journey:

• Float a note in a bottle in the bathtub.
• Frame instructions and post them on a wall.
• Spell out a clue with pebbles.
• Run a classified ad.
• Tie a helium-filled balloon (with a clue inside) to your spouse's car.
• Scroll a message across your mate's computer screen.
• Ask a local DJ to air the next clue, along with your favorite song.
• Write it on an Etch A Sketch.
• Slip a note inside your pet's collar.
• Burn directions on a CD.
• Freeze a clue (sealed in a plastic bag) in a block of ice.
• Post a yard sign.
• Send a singing telegram.

presenting each clue in a different way. It pays to be practical as well as romantic, so include a phone call early in the process to confirm that your spouse received the original message and is actually on the way!

To add a little flair, leave a Hershey's Kiss, a flower, or some other small token along with every clue. Choose a rendezvous spot that affords you some privacy, and greet your mate with a poem or love letter. Read selections together, and then share what you love about each other. Find a specific way to compliment your spouse: how she interacts with others, how he cares for your children, how she feels about herself, or how he makes you feel.

How do I love thee? Let me communicate the ways!

DATE 6
be a sport

Heading out to the ballpark for a regular date with your mate? Ah, the whiff of tangy tailgate barbeque. Roaring with the crowd at awesome action. Snuggling with your sweetheart while sharing an outrageously priced soda.

It all sounds great—and totally predictable.

Why not mix it up? Surprise your spouse with tickets for a sporting event neither of you has seen live—a professional hockey game, bull riding, or a monster truck rally. If possible, choose a sport you and your spouse know nothing about, because half the fun involves diving headlong into something new and learning as you go.

Before leaving for the event, gather background on both the sport and the competitors. Surf the Internet or visit the library together, scanning articles and searching online to answer questions like:

- What are the team's or individual's stats?
- What makes their primary coach, manager, or trainer unique?
- Who are the star players?
- Who's out and who's replacing them?
- Why is winning this particular matchup important?

At the event, you can also enjoy watching the quirky, die-hard fans and how they conduct themselves. Look for painted faces and shaved heads! Don't forget to stash some extra money for overpriced souvenirs and $8 hot dogs.

DATE 7
designing spouses

Flip through any cable or satellite lineup and you're sure to find a variety of shows (and even entire networks) devoted to the American dream of owning and decorating your own place. If your home improvement urges have helped these programs become hits, you'll enjoy a Designing Spouses Date.

Start by taking an objective tour of your own apartment or house. Many homes become a comfortable hodgepodge of items we pick up along the way. So think fresh. What theme would you like to see emerge in a room or throughout your home? What area could benefit from a little touch up or minor repair? What project can you do together to add some flair to your living space?

Jump-start your imagination by visiting model homes or going on a parade of homes tour. Take your time walking through and noting features and decorations you like. Listen closely to each other, picking up on likes, dislikes, and areas where your tastes overlap.

Take along a notepad and a measuring tape so you can write down details and dimensions for potential honey-do-together projects. Take photos of features you might like to re-create at home.

Once you've got a good idea of what you might like to revamp, head to a bookstore or library, settle together in a quiet nook, and page through decorating magazines and books. Write ideas on your notepad, and buy or check out resources you can use for your project. At home, power up your laptop and explore home improvement Web sites like these:

• Do It Yourself (www.doityourself.com)

• Syndicated newspaper columnist Tim Carter's "Ask the Builder" site (www.askthe builder.com)

• Better Homes and Gardens (www.bhg.com)

• Dream Home Source, featuring thousands of home plans (www.dreamhomesource.com)

Even if your budget is limited, schedule a follow-up date to roll up your sleeves and tackle an easy project together.

DATE 8
sentimental journey

Some couples experience love at first sight while others have an initial spark that grows over time. Either way, everyone enjoys reminiscing about how they met and what attracted them to each other. Depending on your mood, you might want to find a secluded spot where just the two of you can share intimate memories. Or if you feel like celebrating your love with a lot of friends, throw a party with your favorite married couples. Give everyone a chance to talk about their dating days.

As you revisit the past, be sure to include stops at these key romantic moments in your premarriage relationship:

• *The day you met:* where you were, who you were with, what you were doing, what caught your eye about your future spouse

• *Your first date:* where you went, what you did, how you knew you wanted a second date

• *Your first kiss:* where you were, who initiated it, how you each felt

• *The challenges:* obstacles you faced when dating, how you overcame them, what made you stick together

• *The proposal:* how you knew your spouse was "the one," where the proposal was made, how it was presented, how your spouse responded

While this reminiscing makes for a fine evening, consider creating a keepsake to take away with you. Some ideas:

• Film a five-minute "The First Time I Saw Your Mom" video for the kids.

• Gather photos and mementos and create a "Date Nights" scrapbook.

• Use free space provided by your Internet company to design a simple Web site devoted to "The Story of Us."

- Upload a YouTube video (www.youtube.com) using a Web cam to talk or sing about your mate.
- Write a poem about how you felt about each other when you met and what you still love about each other now.
- Burn songs onto a CD for your spouse, choosing tunes that hold sweet memories for each of you.
- Buy the DVD of a movie you saw when dating, and watch it together.
- "Roast" your spouse, inviting longtime friends over to share funny and poignant incidents they remember from your dating days.
- Visit the sites of your first date, first kiss, the proposal, and so forth. Ask passersby to take photos of you.

DATE 9
back to nature

Nothing soothes the soul like lying back in a sunshiny meadow, gazing at bubbling clouds, then turning over, your face inches above the grass, and studying the amazing miniature world bustling below. Getting *this* relaxed, and this close to nature, is even more enjoyable with your spouse at your side.

Everyone knows we live in a fast-paced world, pulled in all directions by projects, appointments, and responsibilities. Ironically, the best time to take a nature break is when things are at their craziest. So close up your briefcase, turn off the cell phone, cash in some comp time, and escape to the great outdoors.

Do an online search to pinpoint nature centers and parks within a 50-mile radius. If your community has a tourist information center, stop in and pick up brochures. A quick phone call to your local parks and recreation department might reveal some in-town oases you haven't discovered yet.

Pick a promising place, pack a picnic lunch, and then take back roads to your destination. Drive with the windows down and cool herbal drinks in your cup holders. Agree to bypass discussions about work, money, family squabbles, or anything else that might cast a cloud on your perfect day.

You might visit a nature center offering free events like craft classes, nature presentations, and animal exhibits. Or you might prefer a more private, self-guided tour at a botanical garden, munching natural snacks as you stroll together under the trees.

On the way home, find a greenhouse and purchase two matching or complementary plants you can nestle side by side in your own garden or decorative pot. Every time you care for your plants, make a mental note to cultivate your marriage by sharing an affectionate hug or kiss with your spouse.

DATE 10
take time out

Tick, tock—we're slaves to the clock. And many romantic impulses have been squelched simply because there aren't enough hours in the day.

Put yourselves in a timeout! The key to success is removing all distractions and turning off anything that clamors for your attention (except your spouse, of course). Set aside a Saturday and begin unplugging your lives. If you have children, arrange to have them stay with friends or family for most of the weekend. Drop off the kids Friday night and don't pick them up until Sunday morning so you have at least one complete day without interruptions.

Do your best to be inaccessible to the outside world. Disable the doorbell and unplug the house phones; log off the computer and turn off the cell phones. If you *must* have a way for a child-care provider to call you, keep one phone live but on silent mode. Check for emergency calls only—no text messaging, checking e-mail, or yakking with friends about the great time you're having!

For your timeout, think of the clock as your enemy, and get rid of it. Put away watches, unplug wall clocks, and cover digital displays. Let Saturday morning arrive whenever your internal clock wakes you.

Hungry? Throw something together in the kitchen or head to a favorite restaurant. If you slept too late and missed the breakfast buffet that ended at 10 sharp, just order some lunch! Focus on how great it feels to be so rested.

As you savor your meal, decide what you want to do next. Go to a game? Swing at the park? Take in an early matinee? Choose an activity and enjoy it fully, living in the moment. When you're both ready for something else, move on. Don't plan your day—let it unfold naturally. Who knows where you'll be or what you'll be doing six hours from now. You'll find out when you get there!

As you play through the day, let the pressure of schedules and obligations fall away as you create memorable moments with your best friend.

5 GETAWAY IDEAS

Perhaps nothing reignites a married couple's romance like a weekend away! Urge couples in your church to plan longer getaways once or twice a year—farming out the kids to Grandma and Grandpa or trading child-care-duty weekends with another couple. The following ideas offer a few fun and creative ways for couples to escape.

GETAWAY 1
initialize your love

Plan a special getaway where each of the major aspects of your trip—activities, food, and destinations—all tie to your spouse's initials. For example, if your husband's name is *D*avid, you might fly *D*elta to *D*enver, rent a *D*odge *D*akota then *d*rive to *D*urango for some *d*ownhill skiing. Or you might take *H*eather to a *H*ilton, book the *h*oneymoon suite, do some *h*ang gliding, spend part of each day in the *h*ot tub, and place *H*ershey's Kisses on her pillow at night.

Need help matching ideas with your spouse's initials?

• Visit www.hotels.com and click "Destinations" and "Interests" for an alphabetical list of romantic getaway spots.

• Visit the national Web site for your favorite car company, like Toyota (www.toyota.com), for an alphabetical list of automobiles and trucks.

Before your trip, fill a small bag with slips of paper with activity ideas written on them. Link each proposed activity to your spouse's initial, like playing miniature *g*olf with *G*ary. Over the course of your getaway, occasionally draw three slips of paper, and choose one activity you both want to participate in.

To reinforce the idea that you treasure your spouse, surprise him or her with a bouquet of cut flowers all in one color, except for a single stem of a different color that really stands out. Choose a variety that starts with the initial, like *r*oses for *R*andy or *l*ilies for *L*isa. For an alphabetical list of flower names, along with beautiful photographs of each bloom, visit www.800florals.com. If your spouse is allergic to flowers, make the surprise a bucket of mini candy bars that start with his or her initial, such as *P*eppermint *P*atties for *P*am or *B*utterfingers for *B*rian.

GETAWAY 2
all or nothing

Would you like to go on a memorable getaway you don't have to plan—you just get to show up when it's time to go? Then again, maybe you're the type who prefers to plan the getaway from start to finish, tailoring a time away that will make you and your spouse smile every time you think of it for years afterward.

Here's a way to do both. First, grab your planners and block out time for two getaways—scheduled a month, a season, or a year apart. Each of you plans one of the excursions from beginning to end while your spouse relaxes. When it's your turn to plan, you choose the place, the transportation, the accommodations, the child care, the works. You have free rein, with these three requirements:

• You each have the same amount of money to spend on your getaway.

• You focus the getaway totally on your spouse, tailored to his or her personality and preferences.

• You throw yourself enthusiastically into the effort, with the goal of making this the getaway of your wife's or husband's dreams.

Some additional thoughts:

Budget. Focus on creativity with money. When you discuss the budget, plan an amount that you can stash away without straining your finances. You don't want to worry about the mortgage while you're on your adventure.

Inspiration. To help spark ideas regarding where to go and what to do once you get there, take an inventory of your spouse's talents, interests, and passions. Think about the times that sparked joy for your spouse: action or serenity? Steak or hot dogs? Mountains or beaches? Flower beds or truck beds?

If you get stuck trying to come up with ideas alone, talk to your spouse's friends. Or directly ask your spouse for a list of his or her Top Ten dream getaways.

Motivation. Do unto your mate as you'd have him or her do unto you. Think of how much you'll enjoy pampering your spouse and how much he or she will love taking care of you.

GETAWAY 3
and away we go!

For an interesting romantic getaway, drive thoughts about normal modes of travel from your mind. Instead, come up with some imaginative and—if you're game—adrenaline-packed methods to get from Point A to Point B.

You might choose a different mode of travel each day of your trip. Depending on where you're visiting, you might consider:

- Booking a limo to arrive at a candlelit dinner
- Scooting around the countryside on his and hers mopeds
- Going sightseeing via trolley car
- Using a pocketful of bus tokens to visit hot spots around the city
- Buying a same-day, round-trip train ticket to a nearby town
- Snowmobiling across a frozen field
- Rollerblading through a park or down a seaside boardwalk
- Renting an RV and going camping for the night
- Sailing in a hot air balloon
- Cruising in an antique classic car
- Pedaling down a slope on a mountain bike
- Canoeing down a gentle stream
- Rafting through white-water rapids
- Bouncing along on a wintry hayride, munching s'mores
- Getting a bird's-eye view from a chartered plane or helicopter
- Riding horseback across the prairie
- Hiking up and rappelling down a mountainside
- Jet skiing across a lake
- Scuba diving under the sea

If you're traveling a long distance, you can make arrangements through your travel agent or a hotel concierge. Or once you arrive, talk to locals to find out how to obtain everything you need to travel in style during your getaway.

GETAWAY 4
come fly with me

If you love the idea of taking a trip abroad but lack the time or money to travel to another country, consider this alternative. Pack your bags as though you're heading for the friendly skies, and take a taxi to the airport. But instead of picking up a boarding pass, check into an airport hotel for a few days.

A couple of tips for booking your mini getaway:

• Make sure your room has access to a high-speed Internet connection, a CD player, and a TV with a DVD player. Bring your laptop with you; if you don't have a laptop, borrow one from a friend.

• Ask the reservation clerk for a room as high in the hotel as possible, facing the runways. If it's available, the top floor is perfect.

Several days before your getaway, compile a gift basket for your spouse containing cultural music CDs, a travel guide, an English/foreign language translation book, and native fruits and snacks. Include an ink pad and stamp, along with two handmade "passports" wrapped in a map. Have the gift basket delivered to your hotel room to surprise your spouse when you check in.

During your stay, order in ethnic food reminiscent of the country you'd like to visit (such as Italian, Japanese, or French cuisine). Or bring a picnic basket stocked with these items instead. While a CD plays softly in the background, stand at the hotel window or on the balcony to watch planes take off. Imagine that you're flying to an exotic destination together.

Flip through the travel guide, and watch travel DVDs checked out from the library. Power up the laptop, and virtually travel to nearly anywhere you want to be. Use your favorite search engine to find locations around the globe. You can view photos and streaming video while soaking in geographical and cultural details, or discover live Web cams that allow you to view what's happening in foreign cities. Visit www.weatherimages.org/weathercams to find links to hundreds of live cams overseas, as well as many throughout the United States.

To further connect you on your flight of fantasy, look up passionate phrases in your translation guide, and whisper them to each other. Pull out the passports and stamp them for each other when you pass romantic checkpoints.

GETAWAY 5
five of hearts

Celebrate five-year anniversaries (five years, 10 years, 15 years, and so on) to honor the commitment you made to each other on your wedding day. If your employer offers direct deposit, deduct a preset amount from each check, and tuck it away in an anniversary account. This little nest egg can fund your five-year milestone getaways.

Brainstorm what to do during your time away, linking the activities to multiples of five. For example:

• Book a vacation at a five-star resort; or take a backroads trip, staying at hotels that cost less than $50 a night.

• Visit five cities within a 500-mile radius in five days. Or if you stay at one hotel or resort for your getaway, choose a different direction each morning—north, south, east, or west—then drive as many miles in that direction as years you've been married (such as driving 25 miles if you've been married 25 years). Sightsee along the way, and then get out of the car to explore the spot where you eventually end up. Be sure to head a different direction each day.

• Order a five-course meal, or enjoy a two-person progressive dinner, visiting five restaurants in one night.

• Give each other five gifts that cost under $5 each.

• Pamper your 10 fingers and toes—get manicures and pedicures.

• Write a 15-line silly or romantic poem, and present it to your spouse with a bouquet of 15 kinds of flowers.

• Cuddle at 5 a.m. and 5 p.m.

• If you're celebrating your fifth anniversary, kiss five times for five seconds each; for your 10th anniversary, kiss 10 times for 10 seconds each, and so on.

• Describe in vivid detail how your spouse affects each of your five senses.

Renew your wedding vows every five years—just the two of you. These sacred promises will take on more meaning as time passes and as you work and love your way through life's joys and challenges.

5 SPIRITUAL RETREAT IDEAS

While there's certainly nothing wrong with fun and romance, married couples in your church might want to add a little more meaning to their getaway times, too. Provide couples with the following retreat ideas to help them renew their spiritual relationship with each other and with God.

RETREAT 1
garden of eden

The relationship of the first couple began in the Garden of Eden, a place of beauty and innocence where they found oneness with each other and harmony with the world around them. But they lost it all because they lost their trust in God, desiring even more than the paradise they'd been given.

You might look back at the beginning of your relationship and remember a time that seemed like paradise. Use this retreat to reconnect with this simpler time, rediscovering joys that can enrich your present relationship.

At your retreat, read the story of Adam and Eve in the Garden of Eden (Genesis 2:4-25), and talk about the following questions with your spouse:

• Describe a time, before we met, when you felt most alone. How did getting together as a couple help you feel less alone?

• What experiences together remind you of the oneness expressed in Genesis 2:24?

• How successful have you been at leaving your father and mother (2:24) to be with your spouse? Was this process easy or difficult for you? Explain. (Be sure to answer these questions for yourself, not your spouse!)

• What feelings do you recall about the time you first stood naked in front of each other?

• In what ways has shame crept into your relationship? What can you work on together to eliminate this sense of shame? How does God factor in?

Also, during the course of your retreat, share the following experiences:

• Talk about the home and neighborhood where you lived when you first got married. Share memories with each other as they come to mind.

• Bring CDs of the music you enjoyed during the early years of your relationship and marriage. Share memories that come to mind as you listen.

• Play on a children's playground together for at least a half hour. (Don't hog the teeter-totter if other children want it!) Then sit on a park bench or blanket, and talk about how you can bring the joys of childhood into your marriage.

• Spend an hour in silence exploring a garden or a similar area of natural and unspoiled beauty. Choose one part of the garden that reminds you of the best aspects of your early relationship. After the hour is up, share what you chose. Then talk about how your relationship has grown since those early years. What from those early years would you like to restore in your marriage now? How could you do that?

• Spend time at the end of your retreat praying together. Thank God for your spouse and your marriage. List other blessings you enjoy in your marriage, and ask God to remind you to remember your blessings when you return home.

RETREAT 2
mutual respect

The well-known Aretha Franklin song belts it out: "R-E-S-P-E-C-T! Find out what it means to me." One of the most important goals in marriage is learning to respect each other—and learning how to express that respect.

For this retreat, choose a locale where you can disconnect from the roles you typically play during the week. Don't bring work, cell phones, children, or any distractions that might prevent you from taking a fresh look at your spouse.

At your retreat, read the story of Ruth and Boaz (Ruth 2:1–3:11) and talk about the following questions:

• Think back to when you first met. In light of Ruth 2:5-7, who did you talk with in order to find out more about the person who became your spouse? What did you hear that piqued your interest?

• Talk about the respect Boaz had for Ruth in each of these areas: her work ethic (2:7); her devotion to her mother-in-law, Naomi (2:11); and her actions related to traditional rules of propriety (3:6-11). As the husband, talk about the respect you have for your wife when it comes to her work ethic, her feelings about her mother-in-law, and her actions in daily life.

• Talk about the respect Ruth had for Boaz in each of these areas: his generosity in sharing his abundance (2:8-9), his acceptance of her as a foreigner (2:10), and his protection of her from those who might molest her (2:22). As the wife, talk about the respect you have for your husband when it comes to his generosity, his acceptance of you, and his protection of you.

• During the early years of your relationship, what actions and attitudes prompted you to respect your spouse?

• Recently, what actions and attitudes have prompted you to increase your respect for your spouse?

Also, during the course of your retreat, share the following experiences:

• Listen to songs that focus on respect (Aretha Franklin's "Respect" or Tina Turner's "Show Some Respect" or "Better Be Good to Me"). Even if you don't love these music styles, talk about what the words of the songs mean to you and how they relate to your needs for respect.

• Take five minutes each to tell your spouse what makes you feel good about yourself. After each spouse shares, the partner should give a one-minute summary of what he or she heard.

• Plan an activity during the retreat that your spouse does well, but you don't: cooking, tennis, golf, chess, sewing, or writing. At the end of the retreat, share with your spouse how you appreciate his or her skill in that area.

• Spend time at the end of your retreat praying together. Thank God for your spouse and your marriage. More specifically, thank him for the skills, attitudes, and actions that lead you to respect all that your spouse brings to your marriage. Ask God to frequently remind you to thank your spouse for using those qualities after you return home.

RETREAT 3
dreams and pain

Most of us want a spouse who listens and supports us when we share our dreams—and a spouse who shares our pain and provides comfort if our dreams fail. Often, we can only share these highest peaks and deepest valleys within marriage—the most intimate relationship that God gives us as men and women.

During this retreat, consider the story of Elkanah and Hannah. This husband and wife were the parents of Samuel, one of the Old Testament's greatest prophets. But at first, Hannah couldn't conceive children. In Old Testament times, women were valued for having children, especially sons. Read 1 Samuel 1:1-18, and then talk about the following questions:

• What did Elkanah try to communicate to Hannah through the "double portion" of food? Does his message get through to her? Why or why not?

• Does Elkanah understand why Hannah so desperately wants to have a son? Are his actions toward her supportive or not?

• If you were Elkanah, what would you say to Hannah at this point in their married life? What would you do to show that you care?

• What would you do differently if you were Hannah? How would you feel toward Elkanah?

• Can you recall a time when a frustrated dream or desire caused you the kind of pain Hannah experiences in this story?

• What do you need from your spouse in relation to your dreams?

Also, during the course of your retreat, share the following experiences:

• Watch a movie that portrays someone going after his or her dream and someone who supported that goal. Consider *Cinderella Man, Akeelah and the Bee, Freedom Writers,* or *Dreamgirls.* After the movie, talk about what it means to support someone's dream and how the movie portrayed that kind of support.

• Spend a half hour apart from each other. Write a description of what you want your life to be like in five years. What do you want to accomplish? Where do you want to live? What do you want your family to be like? Where do you want to be spiritually? Then spend time sharing with your spouse what you've written. Talk about what you can do to make your spouse's dream come true. Discuss how your dreams coincide and differ—how can you merge your dreams?

• Spend time at the end of your retreat praying together. Thank God for your spouse and your marriage. Pray that God will give you both dreams that fall squarely into his will for your spouse, for your marriage, and for your family. Ask God to show you clear and specific ways you can support your spouse's dream.

> ## marriage ministry retreats
>
> If your church holds a marriage ministry weekend, you can also use these ideas during couples' breakout times during the retreat. See the "Marriage Ministry Retreat Schedule" on page 220.

RETREAT 4
your own song

When was the last time you creatively expressed your feelings toward your beloved? This retreat focuses on poems and other artistic expressions that give voice to how you feel about each other as husband and wife. Try to find an area where you can see and appreciate the beauty of creation.

The Song of Songs in the Old Testament provides God's affirmation of marriage and the sanctity of love. Read these passages aloud from the Song of Songs in this order: wife, 2:1-7; husband, 4:1-15; wife, 5:9-16; and husband, 7:1-9. Then talk about the following questions:

• How do you react to the poetic expressions of love in these passages? (It's OK to react in different ways; some people feel heartfelt inspiration while others laugh at the sometimes archaic images.)

• How do these two lovers express their physical attraction to each other? How would you describe the connection between their physical attraction and their spiritual attraction?

• Which of your spouse's physical attributes do you find most attractive?

• Do you feel physically attractive? How important is that to you? Explain.

• The man says of his love, "You are altogether beautiful, my darling, beautiful in every way" (4:7). Describe various ways people can be beautiful. In what ways do you find your spouse "beautiful"?

• The man calls his bride "my treasure," and the literal Hebrew for that phrase is "my sister." The woman calls her husband "my friend" (5:16). Do you think of your spouse as a "brother or sister" or a "friend"?

• What does your marriage need to rekindle the kind of passion expressed in the Song of Songs?

Also, during the course of your retreat, share the following experiences:

• Spend an hour away from your spouse, silently exploring God's creation around you. Rejoin your spouse and share something you observed in nature that reminded you of a beautiful quality your spouse possesses.

• Play songs that seem like a modern-day "Song of Songs," such as Joe Cocker's version of "You Are So Beautiful."

• Write down what you love or find attractive about your spouse. If you want, expand on what you mentioned earlier when talking about Song of Songs or when exploring God's creation. Share what you write with your spouse.

• Spend time at the end of your retreat praying together. Thank God for your spouse and your marriage. Pray that God will remind you to observe, appreciate, and express the beautiful qualities you see in each other.

RETREAT 5
journey with joseph and mary

From time to time, it's important to examine your life together as a couple. This can help you see where you've been in your marriage and gain a clearer picture of where you need and want to go as you move forward in life. Look together at Luke 1:26-38 and Matthew 1:18-25. As you read, consider the journey of Mary and Joseph, from the time they were betrothed to the incident of losing Jesus in the Temple, then talk about the following:

• What factors made this unusual pregnancy difficult on Mary? What made the situation difficult for Joseph?

• In your own marriage relationship, what situations taxed your ability to trust each other?

• Can you recall a time as a couple when you experienced suspicion or public disgrace, similar to what Joseph and Mary likely went through with this pregnancy?

• When have you sensed God touching or using you in a mighty way?

Now read Matthew 2:1-18, and talk about the following:

• As you look at the places you've moved during the course of your relationship, how has God used each move to further his plan for you?

Finally, read Luke 2:41-52, and talk about the following:

• If you had been Joseph and Mary in this situation, how would you have handled it as a couple?

• Looking back over your experiences as a couple, what have you "stored (or treasured) in your heart"?

Also, during the course of your retreat, share the following experiences:

• Take a hike together. When you come to a fork in the path, stop and talk about a "fork in the path" you've experienced in your marriage relationship. How did decisions you made at that time affect where you are now? Did you depend on God to make your decision? Explain to each other. Along the path, look for items that speak of something you "treasure in your heart" about the journey you've taken together in marriage.

• Watch videos that follow a couple over the course of a relationship, such as *When Harry Met Sally* or *The Notebook*. Spend some time talking about how your journey together compares to the story you watched.

• Spend time at the end of your retreat praying together. Thank God for your spouse and your marriage. Pray that God will always help you see exactly how he guides your marriage relationship even when you don't understand his timing or direction.

twenty ideas
FOR GROWING
TOGETHER
SPIRITUALLY

Most of the married couples who call your church home want to grow spiritually—and they want to see their marriages grow spiritually. In fact, God places this yearning in their hearts! Deep down, these Christian couples know that Ecclesiastes 4:12 rings true: "A person standing alone can be attacked and defeated, but two can stand back-to-back and conquer. Three are even better, for a triple-braided cord is not easily broken." Of course, the two "back-to-back" represents the married couple, and the third strand in the marriage cord is God.

Again, the following ideas are written directly to couples, so you don't need to limit them to an established marriage ministry program. You can share these ideas in a small group, Sunday school class, or during a sermon on marriage. Or you can reprint them in your church newsletter. However you use them, you'll be helping married couples make sure God remains woven into the "triple-braided cord" of their marriage relationship.

5 PRAYER IDEAS

How would your church change if every married couple in your congregation agreed to pray together? Pass on these ideas to help couples begin or strengthen their prayer times together. In addition, you can adapt the ideas for use during prayer times in small groups, Sunday school classes, and other programs that bring together married couples.

IDEA 1
powerful words

God invites us to pray for one another. The Apostle James pointed out, "The earnest prayer of a righteous person has great power and produces wonderful results" (James 5:16).

Explore this "great power" together as a couple by praying regularly for the needs of others, earnestly holding them up before God. Open yourselves to see the "wonderful results" God will work in your life and in the lives of others.

• Pray for family members, friends, co-workers, and fellow church members. Name their specific needs. Then send them a note telling them that as a couple, you've been thinking of them and remembering them in prayer.

• Ask your pastor for a list of people who are hospitalized, confined to home, and anyone else who needs prayer. As a couple, pray for these individuals by name and follow up with visits. If you're comfortable, pray with them in person, and leave behind a card or another small reminder to assure them that they'll remain in your thoughts and prayers.

• Pray for the needs of your community, the nation, and beyond. If a news story touches your heart, take it to the Lord in prayer. Discuss it with your spouse. Ask, "Why is this report touching us? What does the Lord want us to do about this?" God will use your prayers to prompt ideas and actions that accomplish marvelous things for him!

As you experience the awesome power of prayer together, keep a journal of God's work through and with your prayers to encourage and remind you of the "wonderful results" you see.

IDEA 2
the prayer connection

For most couples, the luxury of daily prayer time together is nothing short of a fantasy. However, praying only during crisis situations deprives you of a gift God wants to give you—his comfort, care, and healing. No matter how hectic your schedules, you can use this unique way to connect with each other in prayer:

• Reserve a space on your master bathroom mirror, dresser, or bedroom wall for prayer notes. Keep a notepad and pencil there. Each evening, jot down your prayer requests for the next day. For example: "Big presentation tomorrow! Jeff." "Doctor's appointment in the morning. Jen."

• Before leaving for work or other activities of the day, grab the prayer requests left by your spouse. During the day, pray for one another with short, spontaneous prayers, such as, "Lord, please give Jeff the power he needs to wow 'em!" "Lord, thank you for our health—calm Jen during her appointment today, and remind her that you care for us." A simple private pause to speak of your spouse's needs is all the Lord needs to hear the yearnings of your heart.

• At the end of the day, as you get ready for bed, spend five minutes together with the prayer notes. Talk about how your day went, give God praise for answered prayers, and ask for his help on issues that might still be troubling either of you. Give him praise for all the blessings he provides.

IDEA 3
car prayers

When you pray together as a couple, you see each other's faith and desires. Consistent prayer helps to forge a spiritual bond as you praise God, petition him, and wait in expectation for his answers.

Why not pray together while riding in the car, away from the distractions of home? You talk to each other in the car. Why not talk to God? Whether you're on your way to church, to work, to shop for groceries, or to go out to eat together, use the time to draw your attention to God.

You can even designate what to pray about during car prayers. You might dedicate the time to praying for specific family members going through trying times, or for family issues like finances or house repairs that need to be done.

Of course, the driver needs to pray with open eyes and focus on driving as well. The passenger can keep a record of prayers. At the end of two or three months, schedule a time to review your prayer list, such as during a special breakfast out on a Saturday morning. Celebrate answers as you see God's faithfulness in both big and small things. Continue to pray for items that God hasn't revealed answers about yet, and add new items that need your support.

IDEA 4
your pastor and church

Is anyone praying for your pastor and the people at your church services? If so, join them. If not, take on that responsibility as a couple.

Contact the church office to let the staff know you want to pray before scheduled church services and to ask if a quiet room is available. Arrive at least 20 minutes before the service begins, head to the designated room, and pray for your pastor and those attending the service. Pray for the worship time, offering, and sermon. Invite other couples to join you, or enlist couples to pray during other regular services and events at your church. Imagine the effect on your church's ministry if at least one couple prayed every time the doors are open!

Some other suggestions for prayer during this time:
- Pray for health and safety for your pastor and his family.
- Pray for God to speak through your pastor.
- Pray that people in the congregation will receive encouragement, direction, or solutions to problems.
- Pray for the time to be free of distractions.
- Pray for visitors to find their way to the service.
- Pray that people who don't know Jesus will accept him as their Savior.
- Pray for other pastors, leaders, and programs in your church, such as children's teachers and classes.

If the church is dealing with a building program or adding a new outreach to the community, pray for that as well. Pray for needs as specifically as possible. If you know the amount of money the church needs to raise for a new building, pray for those funds to come in. If your church is thinking about opening a child-care center, pray for wisdom for church leaders and the congregation.

Through this behind-the-scenes ministry, you can minister to your pastor and church. As a bonus, you'll bond and grow spiritually as a couple while you pray for others.

IDEA 5
elected officials

The elected officials who serve at national, state, and local levels make policies that affect families, businesses, education, and even how you practice your Christian faith. As a couple, pray for these officials on a regular basis—whether or not you agree with their politics or conduct.

If you don't know who your elected officials are, check your voter registration document for district numbers and offices. Or call the election office and ask for the names and offices for the people representing your area. Check your county election office Web site for information. In addition, many local newspapers list elected officials from local to national levels.

If you know any of your elected representatives, tell them that you'd like to pray for specific issues or problems. Provide your contact information. Assure them that their requests will remain confidential (and keep them that way).

Write the names on a prayer calendar so you can pray for all leaders on a regular basis. As you pray, be sensitive to the Holy Spirit's leading about how to pray. Remember their families, as well. Serving in public office requires a sacrifice of time and, for some, of finances. Families also face scrutiny, especially when an elected official becomes a media target.

Pray during election cycles, too. Those elected will enact laws that can last for generations. Pray for voters to receive clear and honest information about candidates. Pray for the candidates as they campaign.

Your prayers make a difference in leaders' lives and the nation—and ultimately touch your marriage and family through the laws and policies you'll need to follow.

5 DEVOTION IDEAS

Just as couples praying could change the life of your church, think about the ways your church would be healthier if every married couple in your congregation strengthened their devotional life together. Provide the following ideas to couples in your church. Instead of thinking of these as quick devotions, encourage couples to take their time working through each of these. View them as a way to slow down so couples can establish or grow a devotional lifestyle, rather than quick (and shallow) devotions to do on the run.

IDEA 1
the interdependence of marriage

Scripture declares that men and women were created to be interdependent. In marriage, couples come to rely on this interdependence.

To begin, one of you can read 1 Corinthians 11:11-12, and then the other can read the following thoughts about this passage:

• This passage brings a logical conclusion to two other passages: Galatians 3:28 says,

"There is no longer Jew or Gentile, slave or free, male and female. For you are all one in Christ Jesus." In 1 Corinthians 12 we read that in Christ, we're like a body where all parts are needed equally: "The eye can never say to the hand, 'I don't need you.' The head can't say to the feet, 'I don't need you.' " (1 Corinthians 12:21). Christ sees equal value in each of us, and each of us has a unique role to fill in the body of Christ.

• The Apostle Paul wrote 1 Corinthians 11:11-12 at a time when women were thought of as inferior to men, Gentiles, and even slaves. So Paul's statements were revolutionary. The apostle stepped beyond the values of his time and culture to show how Christ leads us in a new, interdependent direction.

Talk with your spouse about these questions:

• What are three ways you feel you need your spouse right now?

• What helps *you* to feel needed by your spouse?

Do the following activities—just play with them if you're uncomfortable—to focus on the truth of your interdependence:

• Sit on the floor, back to back, locking your arms together with each other at the elbows. Bend your knees, pull up your feet directly in front of you, and push against each other's back to stand up. Talk about how this exercise requires you to depend on each other. Then spend some time talking about how you help each other "stand up" in emotional and spiritual ways.

• Keep a diary during the coming week, recording the ways you depend on your spouse during those days. What actions does your spouse take to support you? Which ones do you find most important to you? At the end of the week, share with your spouse what you've written.

IDEA 2
the fruit of the spirit

Galatians 5:16-26 explores the conflict that all Christians experience—the battle between the Spirit and the flesh. The flesh—our human nature—naturally wants to sin. Our spiritual side—the Holy Spirit living within us—wants to follow God. Only when we choose to follow and abide in Christ can we experience the fruit of the Spirit—virtues that make us more like him.

Begin your devotion by reading Galatians 5:16-26, and look for the contrast between flesh and Spirit. Then spend time studying the words that represent the

---

fruit of the spirit

• Love:

• Joy:

• Peace:

• Patience:

• Kindness:

• Goodness:

• Faithfulness:

• Gentleness:

• Self-control:

---

fruit of the Spirit. Look up each word in a concordance and read the verses listed, writing down references that refer to the fruit. You also can jot down a few words that help you define or remember each quality.

For example, what you write down for "love" might look like this:

• Love: As Christians, our love for each other should be real. All we do for each other can be summed up in the word *love*. Proverbs 17:17; Romans 12:9

Over the next several days or weeks, watch for ways your spouse exhibits these qualities, and talk to each other when you see fruit in his or her life. For example, you might describe your spouse showing *patience* to a slow salesclerk, or showing a surprising amount of *gentleness* in dealing with a rebellious teenager. You might be surprised when the Holy Spirit bears the fruit, because it takes no effort on your part. However, you do need to follow his prompting rather than your flesh.

When you finish your word study of the fruit of the Spirit, study Colossians 3:5-17. Again, this passage explores the flesh and the Spirit, referring to them as the old nature and the new nature. As you study this passage, list fruit of the Spirit mentioned or implied.

End your devotion by reading John 15:1-8. You can't bear spiritual fruit on your own. You must be attached to the vine, Jesus.

IDEA 3
character of god

Did you know that Jesus "expresses the very character of God" (Hebrews 1:3)? In other words, the qualities we see in Jesus belong to the Father. Jesus himself said that "he does only what he sees the Father doing" (John 5:19), so his actions mirror God's actions. Actions reflect character. When you study the life of Jesus, you get to know God better.

Don't hurry through this devotion. OK, so you can't, because you'll be reading the four gospels. However, instead of thinking about that huge task, break down the reading into meal-sized portions of several chapters a day. The payoff: Studying about Jesus will help you grow in him and know God in a deeper way, leading you to love and trust him more.

You need a pencil and paper (or a computer and word processing program, if that's easier) and your Bibles. If possible, use more than one translation to provide a fuller understanding to the passages you read. If your Bibles have study helps or footnotes, read those as you go through this study.

Begin your devotion by reading in Matthew. When you come to a passage that highlights a character trait of Jesus, write down the trait, who Jesus demonstrated the quality toward, and the verse(s). Look for traits that Jesus showed through his words or his actions.

For example:

• Compassion on the crowd: Matthew 14:13-14

• Patience with Peter: Matthew 14:28-32

• Love for children: Mark 10:13-16

After you've read your way through the gospels, look for instances in the Old Testament where God displayed the same traits. Often, you'll find these in Bible stories you learned as a child. For example, read the story of the Hebrew children in Exodus. God showed *compassion* on them by freeing them from slavery. He showed *patience* when he didn't destroy them for their endless complaining, and he showed *love* for his people by providing for their needs in the wilderness. You might also find other character traits in the story. Read at least four other Old Testament accounts, such as Creation or Noah and the ark, and look for God displaying the qualities you listed from Jesus' life.

Once you've finished your Old Testament accounts, spend time going through the traits again. Talk with your spouse about the times God displayed those traits in your life and in your marriage.

IDEA 4
the love chapter

Perhaps the most popular topic of all times for songs and movies is love. Yet most of us struggle to define love. Greek, the language that writers of the New Testament used, has three words for love: *eros,* sexual love; *philia,* "brotherly love"; and *agape,* the self-giving love of God. Yet even with these distinctions, as part of a letter to the Christians in Corinth, the Apostle Paul wrote extensively to better define the meaning of love.

Before you look at the passage, begin your devotional time by listening to a few current songs from your own collection that deal with the subject of love. After listening to each one, discuss how the singer seems to define love.

Now read 1 Corinthians 13, the "love chapter," and talk about the following questions:

• What does Paul say about the importance of love?

• How is Paul's description of love similar to or different from the way the love songs you listened to define love?

• What parts of Paul's definition of love are the hardest to live up to?

• What parts are most important to us in our marriage?

• What role does God play to help us live out the ideals of this chapter?

One spouse should read aloud the following thoughts on this passage:

• This chapter is part of a greater discussion Paul was having about the relative importance of various gifts. Some in the church at Corinth thought the greatest gift was the gift of tongues. Others thought the greatest gift was the gift of supernatural knowledge. Paul, however, stressed that the greatest gift of all is one we all have access to—the gift of love.

• Long ago, someone noted that every time you come across the phrase "love is…" in this chapter, you can substitute the phrase "Christ is…" and have the words ring equally true. Christ ultimately defines what love is for us. He does this by reflecting a God who is love.

Make a commitment to God and your spouse to work on the quality of love this week. Focus on areas where you've felt weak in the past. For example, perhaps you've had a hard time being patient with your spouse. Or maybe you've insisted on your own way in your marriage relationship. No suggesting what your spouse needs to work on! Pray each day for God's strength and direction in this area. At the end of the week, discuss with each other how you did.

IDEA 5
devotions with emotions

Want to add more emotion to your devotions? Explore the book of Psalms. This book is a collection of prayers, poems, and praises. Each one throbs with human passion. You'll find fear, hurt, jealousy, anger, and betrayal. You'll utter soaring words of repentance and confession, and you'll hear all-too-human thoughts of retaliation and vengeance. You'll speak ancient hymns of love, forgiveness, aspiration, and peace. Why all this drama? Because the Psalms, written by real people with real emotions, reflect not how things *should* be, but how they *are*.

Each week, select a psalm for your devotional time together. Read the psalm aloud as one voice, or antiphonally, with each of you reading alternate verses. Then go back to the beginning of the psalm, and take turns putting it into your own words. Name specific emotions and experiences the psalmist's words bring to mind. Apply the timeless wisdom of Psalms to your daily life. You might want to keep a journal of your responses and actions.

The following list of psalms offers you a range of topics for reading, worship, and discussion. Use the questions to get your conversation started:

• **Psalm 1.** What do you see married friends and co-workers doing that you want to avoid in your own marriage? Why is that important to you?

• **Psalm 13.** How can you support each other in times of fear or stress?

• **Psalm 23.** What can you do for each other in times of sadness or loss?

• **Psalm 30.** How have difficulties and challenges you've faced together strengthened your love for each other?

• **Psalm 32.** Are you comfortable asking each other for forgiveness? Why or why not?

• **Psalm 40.** When has the Lord helped you in the past? Do you think he's willing to help you now?

• **Psalm 51.** What role does confession play in your marriage?

• **Psalm 62.** What or who do you put your trust in? Give examples.

• **Psalm 90.** What do you fear most in your marriage? How do you think God responds to your fears?

• **Psalm 120.** What kinds of struggles challenge your marriage?

• **Psalm 133.** How do you resolve arguments? Does this psalm offer an effective and productive way? Why or why not?

• **Psalm 150.** What are you most thankful for in your marriage?

5 SPIRITUAL DISCIPLINE IDEAS

Now, imagine the changes your church would experience if married couples regularly practiced spiritual disciplines in order to fill their minds with the things of God! Share these ideas with the couples in your church as part of a sermon, during a couples' small group, or in a young-married Sunday school class. Or you can adapt them to use at a marriage ministry retreat.

IDEA 1
journaling to grow

Journaling provides a great way to record your spiritual growth. This discipline is between you and God. You write in a quiet place, during a time dedicated to being alone with him.

As a couple, you can practice this discipline by journaling separately each day, but spending a Saturday morning breakfast time or a Sunday afternoon at a quiet coffee shop to share some of your journal entries with each other.

If either of you feels anxious about committing to write every day, simply write a statement such as "I don't know what to write" over and over until something else comes to mind. Or you can journal on a few set topics such as problems, blessings, or prayer requests.

These ideas can help you get started:

• Commit to write for 10 minutes each day. Many people prefer to write in the morning soon after getting up, before the busy day begins.

• Schedule this time to be a part of your individual Bible study when you're likely to be in tune with all that God wants to teach you. However, if you struggle to journal during a study time, simply try writing at a separate time.

• Set a timer and write for the entire 10 minutes.

• After a month—before sharing journal entries with your spouse—read over what you've written. Highlight portions that stand out to you.

To mark the beginning of this spiritual discipline, shop together for journals. Most bookstores sell journals. Each of you should choose a journal that appeals to you personally.

Don't pressure each other to share everything. Journals are a way to practice communicating with God. Neither of you should sense your spouse looking over your shoulder when you write. At the same time, enjoy entries that your spouse willingly shares with you. As time passes, you might decide to share more intimate details. But again, don't feel pressured to share something you want to keep between you and God.

You might discover that God is speaking to you about the same issue. Ask each other what God might be leading you to do. For example, if you both journal about finances and share that concern when you get together, talk about how God wants to change the way you deal with money. Perhaps God is prompting you to cut down on debt or increase your giving. Whatever issues you share, spend time praying together, and commit to obeying God together.

IDEA 2
taking in the word

You get to know your spouse better when you spend uninterrupted time together, and you'll get to know God better when you spend time with him and his Word. Dedicating a segment of your day to take in Scripture and spend time in prayer provides focused attention on God. In addition, you'll be more in tune to hearing about God's love for you and others.

As a couple, commit to a daily time together in God's Word. Mornings allow you to focus on studying before you become entangled with the day's demands. However, if you're a night owl, evenings work fine. You might start with just 20 minutes, but be faithful to keep your engagement. If you miss a day, don't berate yourself or each other. Just get back on track the next day.

You don't even need to use the same approach for your studies. One of you might want to study a book of the Bible, while the other might decide to study a particular topic, such as prayer or faith. One of you might want music playing, while the other wants absolute silence. Your places to study might differ, too. Design your individual times to fit your personalities.

Schedule one day each week to talk about your times of Bible intake. Some questions to ask each other:

• What's something new you've learned?

• How have you applied it?

- What did this teach you about God? about yourself?
- Is God showing us both the same thing during our studies?

As you talk about your study times, you'll learn from each other. You don't need to share every detail, but be prepared to relate a highlight or two when you chat each week. This will strengthen your relationship with God and with each other. God knows each of you intimately because he created you, but you need to be disciplined to know him more. Daily Bible study and prayer will help you reach that goal.

IDEA 3
the silent treatment

Most of us know what it's like to get "the silent treatment" from our spouse. It's generally anything but uplifting! However, silence has been an important spiritual discipline since the time of the earliest monks.

You can practice this discipline as a couple, spending time in silence together. Choose one evening a week, and from 7 p.m. to 10 p.m., vow to say nothing and minimize noise. No TV. Turn off phones or send calls to voice mail. Don't read any news, current events, or entertainment materials. If you want to read, choose devotional books or other material that challenges you to grow. You might want to read what writers like Henri Nouwen, Dallas Willard, Richard Foster, or Thomas Merton have written about silence.

Before your evening of silence begins, post the following Scriptures on your walls, refrigerator door, and other places around your home:

- "Be still, and know that I am God! I will be honored by every nation. I will be honored throughout the world" (Psalm 46:19).
- "I have calmed and quieted myself, like a weaned child who no longer cries for its mother's milk. Yes, like a weaned child is my soul within me" (Psalm 131:2).
- "Better to have one handful with quietness than two handfuls with hard work and chasing the wind" (Ecclesiastes 4:6).
- "Be silent before the Lord, all humanity, for he is springing into action from his holy dwelling" (Zechariah 2:13).

Every time you come across one of the verses, read it anew, and pray for God's message to you in the quiet. Whenever you encounter your spouse, communicate to each other nonverbally. Use some of your time to journal. Write about the thoughts going through your mind, the nonverbal messages you received from your spouse, and any messages you sense from God.

At the end of the time, debrief the experience with each other by talking about the following:

- What messages did you receive from each other? How did the received messages compare to the messages each person meant to give?
- What messages did you sense from God during this time?
- How did the time of silence affect your spirit?
- Which of the verses you posted spoke the most to you during this time? What thoughts did they prompt?

Close with a time of prayer. Spend some time when you both pray in silence, and then pray for each other.

IDEA 4
stewards of our resources

One of the toughest issues married couples face is in the area of finances. Surprisingly, stewardship of money and material resources often serves as a picture of our spiritual health. If you think about that statement, you'll realize its truth. So spend some time together considering how the spiritual discipline of stewardship both strengthens and expresses spiritual health.

You'll need to set aside at least an hour at home to work through the following steps. Choose a quiet time when your children are napping, occupied, or out of the house—depending on their ages. A Sunday afternoon might be the ideal time for you.

Begin by reading Matthew 6:19-21, and talk about these questions:

• What does this passage say about depending on material things for satisfaction in life?

• Besides the ways mentioned in this passage, what else can cause us to lose material things?

• Do you find Jesus' argument about the temporary nature of earthly treasures convincing? Why or why not?

• As a couple, what do you "own" in terms of time, talent, and money? Which of these items represent "treasures here on earth"? Which represent "treasures in heaven"? Evaluate that balance—does anything need to change?

Now, get out your record of bank transactions for the last month, including checks you've written, items purchased by debit card, and any credit card statements or other debts. Talk about the following questions:

• If a neutral party examined your financial records, what would they conclude about where your treasure truly is?

• What items do you find that truly represent investments in eternity?

• What adjustments do you need to make in your spending to more adequately reflect eternal values?

Finally, spend time working on a "stewardship plan." Approach this as you would if you met with a financial advisor to create a financial plan. Decide together on a goal for how much money you want to give to the church and to ministries that serve people's needs. (If you need scriptural guidance, look together at Malachi 3:8-10.) Also set goals for how much time you want to give to ministries that express your faith.

To close, spend time praying over your financial records, and ask God to help you support each other and follow your stewardship plan.

IDEA 5
solidarity with others

Some Christians regularly practice the traditional discipline of fasting. Most people think of fasting from food—temporarily starving their physical bodies to focus attention more closely on God. This idea for growing spiritually gives fasting a bit of a twist.

First, designate a day when both of you will go without one meal—preferably a meal you usually eat together. Instead of eating, spend the time preparing for the fast-breaking meal that you'll share with another couple. Of course, you'll need to extend an invitation for the couple to join you well before the day of your fast. But the idea is to minister to others through a necessary and daily activity—eating—while growing together spiritually through the fast.

Search out a couple that is struggling financially or spiritually. The meal you share will be a time to encourage these friends. During your fast, take your attention off your own needs, and focus your prayers on this other couple.

While you prepare the meal, stop and pray together for other related needs, as well. Pray for people who can't afford groceries, for senior adults who don't have money for three meals a day, and for children around the world who suffer from malnutrition. Continue to pray for the couple who'll be joining you. And ask God to strengthen your own relationship, acknowledging that you're truly sustained by God and not by the food you eat.

5 SERVICE IDEAS

Another way couples in your church can grow spiritually is by taking action—"getting their hands a bit dirty" while they serve others. Of course, serving others has a hidden benefit that many people overlook. Yes, couples will be helping the people they serve. But God can use these acts of service to help couples break their focus from their own problems and difficulties. Along the way, you'll be amazed as you watch God shape their hearts into Christ-like character.

IDEA 1
the world at home

Each year, more than a half million students from other countries study in the United States. Sadly, according to estimates of campus pastors who work with internationals, fewer than 50 percent of these "best and brightest" from other countries ever spend time inside an American home. Many current world leaders studied in the United States but left with negative ideas about both the United States and the Christian faith. But as a committed Christian couple, you have the opportunity to shape the attitudes and perhaps even the eternities of the next wave of world leaders.

If you live in or near a university community, get involved with an international student ministry. Simply contact the local representative of one of the dedicated international ministries, such as International Students, Inc. (www.isionline.org) or International Student Ministry (www.intervarsity.org/ism). If those organizations don't serve the campus near you, almost any campus ministry leader in your area will know how you can get involved with international students and put you in touch with someone who'll use your service in this way.

> To help you determine your skills and gifts and decide where you might best serve together as a couple, see the "Serving Survey" on page 221.

Of course, the main way you can make a difference in the lives of international students is by opening up your home and life to them. While some American students might be prone to short conversations that focus on surface issues, often international students desire long conversations that go deep. Many want to know everything about life in the U.S. and especially how Christianity fits in. As you share with these students about your courtship, wedding, and married life together, you'll both reflect and look ahead, strengthening your own ties. At the same time, your story will be fascinating to your new friends!

When you get to know some international students, offer to provide rides to large discount chain stores. Help students navigate the shopping process. As a couple, you'll not only experience the joy of serving together, you'll have many topics for conversation with each other as you recount times with your international friends and as you plan to meet other needs you become aware of.

By sharing your life with these "strangers," you'll become more aware than ever of who you are individually and as a couple. And in your service, you'll become more committed than ever to one another and to Christ.

IDEA 2
janitor's day off

Church janitors work very long hours, often logging a lot of evening and weekend overtime. They work hard and many times, their efforts go unrecognized. If you and your spouse enjoy cleaning or have a "handy streak"—and you work together well on home maintenance and improvements around your home—then give your church janitor a day off.

Talk to the person who supervises the janitor at your church, and ask what day would be best for you to take over. Get a list of daily janitorial duties, and note where all the supplies are kept. Ask if you can tackle any special painting, cleaning, room setup, or other special jobs the custodian and other staff haven't been able to get to. Don't forget to do the janitor's regular duties as well, such as emptying trash cans and checking bathrooms for toilet paper and paper towels.

By the way, if you want to take on a lot of special cleaning or improvement projects around the church, enlist other couples to help you out.

While you might want to surprise the janitor about a day off, give advance notice so he or she can plan activities for the day and make notes to help you and your spouse to make it through the day.

IDEA 3
computer skills for seniors

While personal computers are wonderful, many senior adults don't enjoy the benefits most of us take for granted. To them, the jargon sounds like a foreign language, and the computers themselves look too complicated to touch. Of course, many seniors lead active and enthusiastic lives, and they certainly have the intelligence to use a computer. They just need patient instruction and encouragement. You and your spouse might be the ones to introduce the senior adults in your church to the world of cyberspace.

If you're even somewhat computer literate, you can put together a basic computer skills class dedicated to senior adults. Meet with the person in charge of adult classes at your church to see if leading this class is possible.

Some questions to consider:

• What senior adults in our church will want or need this class?

• Are computers available for the class? If not, are there people in the church who can buy or loan computers for the class?

• How long should the class be, both in hours and days?

Determine what strong points each of you have. Word processing? Researching on the Internet? Using e-mail? Divide the teaching tasks. Both of you can also be available to help individuals in the class.

You might want to limit the number of students in your class to six or fewer—just so you can give help promptly. If more people want to attend, you can recruit other couples to help. Or ask your youth pastor about teenagers who might enjoy working with older people. If you recruit helpers, they can each provide guidance to one or two seniors while you teach the class.

IDEA 4
assisted living bible study

Life changes a lot when people move to an assisted living residence. Many lived in their own homes for decades, and now they find themselves in smaller quarters, sharing space with others, and without many responsibilities. All these factors can be positive for people who need this kind of help. Most facilities offer a variety of activities for residents to choose from. As a couple, you can volunteer to strengthen the residents' spiritual lives by holding a weekly Bible study, offering fellowship and teaching from God's Word.

Sometimes people in these facilities are unable to attend church services. An on-site Bible study provides a comfortable and easy way for them to continue being fed spiritually. Further, some residents might have very few visitors. Your service can become something they'll look forward to and depend on.

Your pastor or another church leader might already know of a facility looking for this kind of ministry. Before you contact the facility manager, consider the following questions:

• What topics or books of the Bible would you study, or would you use a published Bible study?

• What days or evenings of the week are you available? What times are you available? An hour is a good time frame. The residence might already have a schedule of activities. The manager can tell you what times are available and appropriate.

• What format will you follow? Will you include a worship or prayer time?

• Can you dedicate 10 to 12 weeks to this? Or more?

• Will you and your spouse share teaching responsibilities?

• Can you furnish Bibles to people who don't have them?

Keep in mind that some residents might be more alert and able to track the study better than others. Check for understanding as you teach. You can ask questions and observe their facial expressions and attention. As you spend time with the people who attend, you'll get to know them better.

As you and your spouse serve together in this way, you'll grow closer to each other, and you'll grow spiritually as well. And don't be surprised if the people you meet at the facility end up ministering to you in ways you'd never expect.

IDEA 5
are we there yet?

What about a short-term mission trip as a couple? This act of service will help you and your spouse become more like Jesus and more unified in Christ.

Of course, mission trips aren't easy. They usually involve a group of nervous people traveling far outside their comfort zones to bless people in another culture. However, you'll certainly be transformed by both the people you serve and how you serve them.

If you undertake a mission trip as a married couple, you face a lot of work ahead. Yet, as you research the needs of the place you'll serve, make travel arrangements, perhaps work with a team of fellow short-termers, and actually take the trip, you'll create a life-changing experience for yourselves and the people you serve. For example, imagine the ways that putting together a mission trip will provide opportunities for you—as a couple—to talk more, pray together, and increasingly lean on God together—starting before you ever board the plane!

What about your children? They're actually very portable, and introducing them to serving others in other places is a wonderful legacy to plant within them. As you plan ways that you'll serve when you arrive at your destination, be sure to come up with ways your children can serve, too. This shows them that they matter and can do things to honor God.

But aren't such trips expensive? They can be. However, think of the expenses as a chance to talk about your financial priorities as a couple. Maybe you need to decide the best way to spend your "vacation resources." Each step of planning a mission trip forces you to clarify your values as a couple. Don't be surprised if the trip changes your heart to the extent that you'll want to create similar experiences when you return home. You might also look for new ways to serve "back home"—even being drawn to "foreigners" in your own community.

Mission trips will stretch nearly every aspect of your faith and marriage. When you get beyond the confines of your "normal" life and live for a week or two as full-time agents for God, you'll have a hard time going back to being complacent. When a couple shares a passion to change the world, watch out!

section **three**

twenty-five ideas
FOR MARRIAGE-BUILDING

In some marriages, one spouse suffers from low self-esteem. In other marriages, the husband or wife might not feel supported when it comes to career, dreams, or the tasks of keeping a household running. Some spouses might be bugged by the little things their partner does, or feel that their spouse has a selfish streak. And you can be certain that nearly every married couple faces pressures and trials that they don't feel equipped to handle.

You can use the following ideas to help the couples in your church face all of these situations, even using their circumstances to build their marriage relationship in practical ways.

5 IDEAS FOR BUILDING SELF-ESTEEM

Most couples go through times when one spouse or the other lacks self-confidence. This might happen during tough financial times, after the loss of a job, when facing health problems, or while dealing with a troubled teenager. Pass along these ideas to the couples in your church to try when they see their spouse feeling low.

IDEA 1
"celebrate my mate" book

One of the best ways you can encourage your spouse is by giving others the opportunity to celebrate what he or she means in their lives. A great way to do this is by compiling a "Celebrate [spouse's name] Book!"

Invite people who know and appreciate your spouse to write notes or letters telling why your spouse is important to them. You might tie this in with a birthday or a work anniversary or at some unexpected time.

First, make a list of people who might like to participate. List relatives, people at work, friends at church, and people who know your spouse through other activities or organizations. Draft a note or e-mail explaining the book you're compiling. Ask people to write a quick paragraph expressing their appreciation for your spouse. Encourage them to write about a strong character quality, or about a specific time when your spouse ministered to or helped them.

Set a deadline when people should respond. Encourage them to send a photo of themselves—especially photos of them with your spouse. Ask people to note if they want the photos returned.

As letters, notes, e-mails, and photos start coming in, compile them in a large scrapbook or photo album. Present the book when your spouse is having a tough day, or present the book at a party for your spouse.

IDEA 2
blast to the past

Part of who we are today includes people and places of the past. So show your spouse that you appreciate and enjoy everything about him or her by journeying to the past—visiting places important in his or her life.

Set up day trips or a vacation journey so your spouse can show you important places from earlier in life: childhood homes, old neighborhoods, elementary and high schools, colleges, parks or recreation areas, grandparents' and other relatives' homes, favorite stores or restaurants, and churches. Go down all the memory lanes you can think of. During your tours, ask your spouse about memories of special events and people from these places.

If you're really industrious, make notes of names and try to track down some of these people (get help from local relatives, if possible), and hold a surprise party for your spouse. If that's not possible, encourage your spouse to set up lunch, dinner, or coffee get-togethers with some people from the past. Go along and enjoy hearing stories about your mate's life before you came along.

You can also keep an Internet eye on your spouse's high school and college reunions. As you blast into your spouse's past, you'll both have fun—and you'll better understand what made your mate the great person you know now!

IDEA 3
a month of blessings

How do you love your spouse? Count the ways with a "Month of Blessings." Write a special note to your mate each day of the month, telling all the different things you love or respect about him or her.

Vary how you communicate each day. Mix it up with e-mails, e-cards, notes under the pillow, and printed greeting cards. You can also write a note on a mirror, stick one on the steering wheel of the car, or change the screensaver message on your spouse's computer. Your only limit is your imagination.

Also, use variety in what you say about your mate. Think about the ways you love your spouse, both big and small. Praise character traits (like honesty or kindness), abilities (the ability to make people feel at home or the gift of paying the bills so promptly), specific actions (patiently helping a child with homework, fixing the sink, keeping the house clean), and physical traits (gorgeous eyes, sexy smile, hot body, gentle hands), for starters. Go into details—not just a quick "Love your smile, babe." Be lavish and loving with your admiration and praise. Have fun with it—but not in a negative, teasing way.

After a month, your spouse will feel pretty good about himself or herself—and see what a blessing you are. You'll be closer. You might even spark some life into a tired relationship, as you make your spouse feel loved and remind yourself why you married this person!

IDEA 4
renewed promises

How many years ago did you and your spouse say your wedding vows? Do you remember what went through your mind on your wedding day?

As you think of your vows and some of the ideals and expectations you had when you first got married, you might think, "If only I'd known..." Yet even with all the changes and unexpected encounters of life, why not show your spouse you'd do it all again by renewing and rewriting your vows?

You can do this privately, just between the two of you. Or throw an anniversary party for family and close friends. Or hold a marriage renewal ceremony at your church or a local chapel and invite everyone you know! Be as serious or as fun as you'd like.

Rewrite your vows to reflect where you are in life now. Write about the storms and challenges you've been through and how your love has endured and grown through those times. And mention how you'll continue to support each other in coming years through future trials and joys.

The goal is reflecting together on where you've come from, as well as how you plan to stick together—loving each other—through whatever the future holds.

IDEA 5
look how far you've come!

Honor your spouse on a birthday or another special day by creating and displaying a history of his or her life. Don't forget to celebrate where your spouse is today. You can create a slide show or video presentation, a shadow box for your spouse's office, or a "wall of fame" in your home.

Whatever media you choose, use plenty of photos of your spouse through the years. Dig out pictures from childhood, young adult years, and years of marriage and parenthood. Find songs, memorabilia, and other items to represent the various stages of your spouse's life. For example, if you create a video, record images of the home, school, and hangouts where your spouse grew up. In the background, play favorite or popular songs from those eras. Move into work years by filming places of employment.

As you can, get people from your spouse's life to give commentary—interview past and present co-workers expressing appreciation about your spouse's work ethic, someone who worked with your spouse in a ministry at church commending his or her service, and parents remembering a specific time when they realized your spouse had become an adult.

If you put together a shadow box or a wall of fame, include items like grade-school spelling bee trophies, high school athletic letters, and other accomplishments. If you have children, they can participate, perhaps writing a note of love and appreciation to their parent or recording a special message.

Present your creation at a special occasion, such as a birthday or anniversary. Or give the gift as an "everyday award."

5 IDEAS FOR DEVELOPING PURPOSE AND UNITY

"Always be humble and gentle. Be patient with each other, making allowance for each other's faults because of your love. Make every effort to keep yourselves united in the Spirit, binding yourselves together with peace" (Ephesians 4:2-3). Although the apostle Paul wrote these words about unity in the church, they apply equally to marriage. Encourage couples in your congregation to use the following ideas to build purpose and unity in their relationship.

IDEA 1
intergenerational marriage interviews

Do you have role models of couples who have healthy marriages? In past generations, extended families often lived near each other. This gave couples who were facing troubles parents, grandparents, aunts, and uncles to turn to for guidance. Even if you live far from extended family members, you can seek out wisdom from couples who have been married a long time.

With your spouse, brainstorm a list of married couples you might interview. Divide your list into at least two columns: couples who've been married about 10 years longer than you have, and those who've been married about 20 years longer. You can extend your list to longer marriages if you'd like.

Now generate a list of interview questions that both you and your spouse want to explore with these couples. Choose questions that touch on critical areas in your marriage. Possible interview questions might include:

- Do you have any rules for healthy fighting in your marriage?
- What advice can you give for managing a budget?
- What's the most important lesson you've learned in your marriage?
- How did you come to an agreement on how to discipline your children?

Next, choose a setting for your conversation. Maybe you can meet the other couple for coffee somewhere, or invite them over for a home-cooked meal.

Call through your "prospect list" of couples, and explain that you'd like to go on a double date. Share your list of questions with the couple, and explain that you'd just like to talk about how their marriage has "gone the distance." When you meet the couple, ask them to give examples and tell stories about their lives—this will make the time less like delivering a lecture for them and make the ideas they share more memorable for you.

After you meet with a couple, find a quiet hour to spend with your spouse to debrief the experience. Talk about the following questions together:

- Did any of their responses surprise you? Why?
- What was your favorite story they told? Why?
- Did they offer advice that you think we should *not* build into our marriage? Explain your response.
- What was the best piece of advice you took away from the evening?
- What steps can we do to build this into our marriage?

Don't forget to write a note thanking the other couple for investing in your marriage. And hang on to your interview questions and prospect list. Repeat this date night every three or four months with another couple. You'll make new friendships while strengthening your marriage.

IDEA 2
his strengths, her strengths

Opposites attract. While scientists can explain this rule of physics with electricity and magnets, who knows for sure why it's true with marriage? During courtship, you become enamored with your partner's strengths. But over the years of life and relational pressures, you can forget about those strengths. Worse, you might reinterpret your spouse's strengths as liabilities. For example, during your dating years, you might admire your spouse for being a resolved leader. But in marriage, you see that as being stubborn. To remind yourself and your spouse about the good you see in each other, try this 30-minute exercise.

1. Collect two pieces of poster board, two glue sticks, a stack of old magazines and newspapers, and some markers.

2. Work independently to make a collage of your spouse's strengths. Look through the magazines and newspapers to find images that represent strengths of your spouse. For example, if you think your partner is compassionate, then find and clip a picture of a nurse caring for a patient. Find at least 10 images that represent 10 of your partner's positive character traits.

3. Glue the pictures on the poster board, and use the markers to label each image with the character traits you admire about your spouse.

4. Come together and take turns sharing what you admire about your spouse. Alternate going through the 10 items for each other one at a time. Point out ways you think your spouse's strengths might cover one of your weaknesses. For example, if your spouse is better with finances than you are, then thank him or her for managing the checkbook.

After you've affirmed each other, find a place to hang your affirmation posters—maybe above a bedroom mirror or on the back of your bedroom door. Choose places the two of you will look each day to constantly remind you why you're crazy about each other.

IDEA 3
side-by-side service

Marriage provides a great opportunity to serve God with your spouse, but it's easy to surrender this opportunity to competing tasks and values. Why not make your marriage a vehicle where—as two growing Christians—you and your spouse serve each other as you also serve the church and community?

Here are some ideas about where to serve with your spouse:

• Volunteer together at a local soup kitchen, or volunteer to sort clothing at a thrift shop where sales benefit individuals and families affected by poverty.

• Look for a volunteer opportunity at your church. You might offer to clean and vacuum a wing of the church, join the hospitality team, or offer to become preschool Sunday school teachers together.

For other ideas on how you and your spouse can grow by serving together, see "5 Service Ideas" on page 42.

• Volunteer with a local "Big Brothers Big Sisters" organization in your community, and become a mentor for a child. This is a long-term commitment, so be deliberate as you make this decision.

• Call a volunteer coordinator at a nonprofit that represents a cause the two of you feel deeply about. Describe your availability and talents so the coordinator can identify possible placement opportunities for you.

As you prepare to work together on one of these ministry opportunities, talk though the emotions you're experiencing. Are you nervous or excited? Pray together and ask God to strengthen your marriage as you serve him together.

Find times during your volunteer service to talk about these questions:

• What are we learning about each other as we serve together?

• What are we learning about our marriage as we serve together?

• Do you think this is the right area of service for us long-term? Why or why not?

• Take time to take inventory of each of your strengths and weaknesses. Brainstorm what other opportunities exist. Even better, dream about opportunities the two of you could create to serve others together!

IDEA 4
common chores

Like most couples, you and your spouse probably divide household "to-do" lists between you. Then you each head off to attack your own list. Of course, this allows you to accomplish more in a short amount of time, and it ensures that neither of you feels dumped on. However, this approach has a weakness: As each of you works parallel with the other, you're not spending any time together.

So try this idea for a change. Take a few minutes and look at your chore lists and calendars together. Decide on a few chores or tasks you'll do together this week. And decide what you can do to turn those chores into "mini-dates."

Consider these options:

• Plan a grocery shopping trip together. Spread your cookbooks on the dining room table, and agree on what you'll eat during the coming week. Comb the newspaper for money-saving coupons. If you have time, stop by your favorite coffee or ice cream shop on the way to the store.

• Have a laundry-folding party. Wash and dry several loads of clothes, then fold and put them away together. Play music you both enjoy. Turn up the music, sing loudly, and even dance together as you work.

• Plant a flowerbed together. Make a date of purchasing the flowers, mulch, and other supplies together. As you work in the earth together, talk about what it takes to nurture a growing marriage.

• Rake leaves together. When autumn arrives, rake your leaves into a large pile. Before bagging up the leaves, play together by jumping into the leaves or having a leaves fight!

• Cook a romantic meal from scratch together. Work side by side as you chop vegetables and prepare the food. Cooking is a great activity to do together because many recipes require precise timing. So you'll have to organize and cooperate. Enjoy a candlelit meal, and then wash the dishes together.

After finishing a chore together, talk about the following questions:

• How was it awkward doing a chore together that you normally do alone?

• What other chores can we do together? How can we make them fun?

• What are the benefits of choosing to do more housework or yardwork together? What are the potential risks?

IDEA 5
toasting the future

Have you ever wondered what your marriage might look like decades from now? When you celebrate your 50th anniversary, what do you want your friends and children to say about your marriage relationship? Try this romantic activity with your spouse to evaluate the direction your marriage is headed.

Visit a party supply store to buy a few inexpensive wedding anniversary decorations—balloons, party hats, streamers, and a tablecloth. Swing by the bakery to buy a favorite dessert. Purchase some sparkling grape juice or gourmet coffee to enjoy with the baked goodies.

Now clean the house. Nothing detracts more from a romantic evening than constant reminders of life's pressures. Decorate the dining area; turn off home and cell phones. Present the desserts and beverage on your best china and crystal. Play your favorite romantic music softly in the background.

Now, imagine that it's your 50th anniversary party, and it's time for guests to "toast" the happy couple. Take turns offering toasts to your marriage from the perspective of your imagined guests. Imagine what your close friends, grown children, church members, and business associates would say about you. What would you want them to say about how you served each other, how you served God together, how you romanced each other, and how you raised your children? Take turns offering several toasts to your marriage.

End your "anniversary from the future" by enjoying a slow dance together in the living room, or by watching a romantic movie together. Wait until the following day to talk about your experience. Just let the romantic moment stand on its own. In the next day or two, talk about the following questions:

• What was common about our individual dreams for our marriage? What was different? Why?

• What are we doing well now that will help us arrive at the future we'd like to see for our marriage?

• What, if any, immediate corrections do we need to make in how we relate to each other?

• What long-term goals do we need to set to accomplish our highest dreams for our relationship?

Don't be surprised if this activity unearths some conflict. Every relationship drifts and needs some midcourse corrections. Enjoy the time together, and give God thanks that you're both willing to work toward a healthier marriage.

5 IDEAS FOR MEETING EACH OTHER'S NEEDS

The New Testament contains dozens of "one another" statements, such as "love one another," "encourage one another," and "don't grumble against each other." These admonitions guide how Christians should treat each other. While Christian couples should certainly try to abide by all of Scripture's "one anothers," urge them to try these five creative ideas for meeting each other's needs.

IDEA 1
habit rehabilitation

Here's a news flash: You irritate your spouse. Seriously, you have some habits or nuances that grate on your spouse's nerves. Maybe you chew with your mouth open, leave cupboard doors open, or tap rhythms on the table with your fingers. Your irritating trait might not be something you *do*. Perhaps you've got a favorite shirt your spouse hates. Or your mate hates the picture you've hung in the bedroom. Serve your spouse by choosing to change an irritating habit.

Brainstorm a list of two or three bad habits you think your partner would like you to change. Present the list to your partner. Explain that you want to serve him or her by eliminating a bad habit. Ask your spouse to choose the habit that you'll try to change.

Of course, some habits are harder to break than others. Ask your partner to lovingly remind you if you return to old patterns of behavior. But be careful not to make your spouse responsible. Remember, this was your idea.

If you choose to tackle a major addiction, consider joining a support group. Some addictions are symptoms of deeper emotional issues. If you want to succeed, you need the support of others who have faced what you're facing.

After a few weeks, talk about these questions:

• Were you able to give up your bad habit? Why or why not?

• How does loving someone change your feelings about changing a habit?

• When we see habits in each other that irritate us, how can we exercise love and understanding?

IDEA 2
chore-free saturday

Many busy couples spend Saturdays tackling yardwork and household chores that pile up during the week. Mowing the lawn, laundering clothes, mopping floors, and cleaning toilets—it's just that day to get things done. Consider serving your spouse with the gift of a chore-free Saturday.

Start on Saturday morning and ask your spouse to write a list of all the chores and errands he or she planned to do that day. You might get a tense reaction if your spouse suspects you're trying to "assign" your own honey-do list. So—surprise—take the list from your spouse, and tackle those chores that day.

If your spouse lists a chore you don't know how to do, ask for a quick lesson. Is there a specific way to fold towels so they fit on the linen closet shelf, or a particular way to mow the lawn so the mower doesn't leave clippings?

Urge your spouse to spend the next several hours relaxing any way he or she wants to—at the beach or a coffee shop, or just sitting at home reading a book, watching a movie, or enjoying sports on TV.

Get cracking on the chores. Of course, you'll be working double duty completing your own chores and your spouse's. It's not really meeting the other person's needs completely if you let your own duties stack up. As you work, keep a cheerful attitude. You'll drain out all the joy if you sport a sour attitude.

At the end of the day, allow your partner to inspect your work. Is there anything not quite right? Also, end the experience enjoying a meal with your spouse and asking how he or she spent this chore-free Saturday. Express how happy you were to give your spouse this gift of time.

IDEA 3
a night with pals

Give your spouse a special night out with friends. Sure, you need exclusive time as a couple, but it's also healthy for each of you to stay connected with your own friends. You can't meet all of each other's relational needs, so you *both* need time to get out. Arrange for your spouse to score a night out with pals.

Consider these ideas:

• Surprise your spouse by calling a handful of his or her friends. Explain that you want to give your spouse a night out. Suggest a few different dates far enough in advance so the friends can find a common night. Ask your spouse to keep that night free. When that day comes, give your spouse a card with a certificate for a night out on the town. Include gift cards for a restaurant and a movie or a prepaid credit card your spouse can use at most establishments.

• Insist that your spouse attend the next men's or women's retreat on the church calendar. Promise to cover all of the chores, meals, and child care while your spouse is away.

• Kick yourself out of the house, and let your spouse and friends have free reign of the place. Before you go, clean the house from top to bottom, and stock the refrigerator with snacks and drinks. If you have children, take them out for a fun activity to keep your spouse from needing to parent during the evening.

• Tell your spouse to invite his or her friends over. Then take charge of the hospitality throughout the evening. Prepare a home-cooked meal, or serve the drinks and snacks throughout the evening. If you have kids, set them up in a separate part of the house. Instruct them to find *you* if they need anything.

IDEA 4
serving cheat sheet

One frustration in marriage comes when you *assume* to know your spouse's needs. You might assume that your mate is overwhelmed by demands of the house or the office when he or she really needs time with you to discuss a problem.

Become a student of your spouse's needs. Of course, the most accurate and loving way to discover these desires takes place through times of talking. Photocopy the following list of questions, and carve out a quiet hour. Tell your spouse you want to be able to meet his or her needs, so you're going to read a series of sentence starters your spouse needs to finish.

- I feel most appreciated when you…
- The chore I dislike the most is…
- I love it when you…
- One dream I have that I'm not sure I can accomplish is…
- When we're having sex, I am most turned on when you…
- I feel listened to when you…
- My favorite way to spend an evening with you is…
- I feel overwhelmed by our marriage when…
- My favorite dessert is…
- My favorite meal is…
- If I could start any hobby, I'd…
- I'd feel more supported if…
- The small thing you do that I love the most is…
- I don't feel listened to when you…

Make this list your personal cheat sheet for meeting your spouse's needs. Don't try to accomplish every item on the list at once. Keep the list where you'll see it often. Each week, choose an item to work on. Every few months, revisit the list with your spouse. Ask if you can do anything else to serve him or her today.

IDEA 5
calendar coordination

Careers probably keep you apart for most of each weekday. But you can still meet each other's needs. Ask your spouse to give you a detailed schedule of his or her week. Add his or her schedule to your calendar or day. Add times and reminders to take breaks from your schedule and touch base with your spouse. Try these ideas to get started:

- Text message your spouse before a big meeting or appointment to say, "I'm thinking about you!"
- Arrange to have a favorite lunch delivered to the home or office. If possible, deliver the meal yourself, and enjoy it together.
- Schedule a quick phone call during a work break.
- If you know your spouse faces a difficult meeting or appointment, block off a moment to stop and pray as the meeting begins. When you know you won't be a distraction, send a text message to say that you've been praying.
- "Steal" your spouse's car, and take it to get it washed and waxed. Imagine how fun it will

be to return to a sparkling clean car.

• Send brief, playful meeting reminders to your spouse 15 minutes prior to appointments. Some e-mail programs allow you to time when messages are sent.

• Arrange to have flowers or a cookie-gram delivered to your spouse.

• Use your spouse's schedule to ask better questions at the end of the day. Instead of "So, how was your day?" ask "How was your staff meeting?", "How did the kids do at swimming lessons?", or "How did lunch with Bill go?" Because you know more about your spouse's days, you can more easily connect emotionally when you're together again.

• See if you can relieve your spouse's schedule. Offer to take the kids to the dentist or to mow the lawn. Urge your spouse to use the newfound time any way he or she wants to.

10 IDEAS FOR BUSTING STRESS

Pressures in married life can stem from financial issues, communication meltdowns, stresses of career, the inability to find time to spend together, or a host of other trying circumstances. Perhaps what causes the stress is less important than relieving the pressure. Couples can use the following ideas to release some steam. If you have a group or class of couples that meets regularly, assign one idea each week or once a month as homework, and build class time around sharing what the couples learn.

IDEA 1
household hints

If you and your spouse both work, some days probably get pretty crazy. If you want to improve how your household runs, try the following.

• Divvy up jobs. One of you can cook and clean while the other takes responsibility for laundry and grocery shopping. Let your spouse pick what he or she likes to do, or take turns choosing from a chore list. One secret for maintaining a good relationship is to be "slightly more than fair." In other words, always aim to do just a little more than your spouse does. If you're both doing that, you'll both be endlessly grateful for each other.

• Play to your strengths. If one of you is a natural financial planner, make sure that individual pays the bills and balances the checkbook. If one of you is better at seeing "the big picture," put that person in charge of planning a dream vacation or keeping long-term home improvements moving forward.

• Put your kids to work. If you have children, make a list of chores and schedule a family meeting. Kids can choose their favorites so they have some jobs they enjoy, and parents can dole out the rest based on fairness and on the "strengths" of your children. For example, if one of your teenagers is a computer whiz, make her responsible for maintaining the electronic address book, updating software subscriptions, and burning the family's digital photos to CDs.

• Do projects together. Make Saturday house-cleaning day. One of you does the vacuuming, mopping, and putting things away while the other concentrates on laundry, cleaning bathrooms, and dusting. If you have kids, get them involved. They can clean their rooms and tackle the family room. Celebrate when you're finished by going out for an ice cream treat—or just collapsing on the clean furniture and taking naps.

• Do a little each day. Maintaining a tidy house is a great example of using this idea. If newspapers always go in the recycling bin at the end of the day and shoes get put away when one of you walks in the door, you won't have to tackle those tasks after items pile up.

• Get organized. Spend a few days off together to organize closets, cupboards, dressers, the garage, storage areas, etc. If things around your home have a place, you'll both find it easier to make sure things get put away into those places. Plus, it's much less stressful to live without endless clutter.

• Do what works for you. It might be sweet to talk to each other at length while you're both at work. But if it's more efficient to e-mail during the day with information, do that. Except for following biblical guidance, don't let anyone else's expectations dictate how your marriage and household run.

• Be willing to change. After several months of trying any of these ideas, sit down with your spouse to evaluate what's working and what's not. Trade jobs, assign new tasks, hire outside help to do deep cleaning, change calendar systems, or do whatever it takes.

IDEA 2
budgeting buffer

Sometime when you're not paying bills or writing checks—and definitely not around tax time—take time to sit down together to chat about money. You might want to head to a favorite restaurant or coffee shop. Rather than the usual anxieties or complaints, you're going to talk about money in a fun way.

First, each of you should make a list. What would you do if you had a personal expense account each month? Imagine a business executive who has a corporate expense account for travel or dinners. What would you do if you had $100 per month to spend? $1,000? $5,000?

Spend a few minutes talking about your list. Each spouse should then describe what the other seems to value or desire the most. Make this fun and supporting, not critical. You're just imagining.

Now think about your monthly family budget. Among all the bills, rent or mortgage, and other expenses, you probably have some small amount you use for entertainment. If you don't think you have any entertainment money available, make a list of movies, concerts, dining out, sports, and recreation activities that you both participate in during a typical month, and determine what you spend on those activities. Now, determine a monthly amount to set aside for each of you—an amount that won't be a burden on the family budget. Even if you can only come up with a small amount, figure out how to give each of you an equal portion.

Here's your expense account! Each of you can spend this money in your own personal way each month.

You might want to agree to some of the following guidelines:

• Each of you can spend your account on whatever you want.

• Neither of you can ask what the other is using the money for.

• If one of you decides to save your money for a special purchase or just to save, that money doesn't later become part of the family budget. It remains with the individual.

• You can agree to pool money for something you want to do together.

This can provide some needed freedom within your marriage. Money can cause stress in relationships. So this freedom can create a bit of independence, helping you be more committed to dealing with regular expenses together.

IDEA 3
three little words

What words do you say that add stress to your spouse's life? Plan a quiet evening together, over dinner if you want. You need paper and pens for an exercise to help you focus on the words you use on a casual basis each day and to think about how those words affect your spouse.

Write down five words or phrases you most like to hear from your spouse, and five words or phrases that you least like to hear. This isn't the time to complain or rehash old arguments. The point of the exercise is to discover something constructive and helpful.

Make your list clear, using words or phrases that go in quotation marks:
- "I love you."
- "Thank you."
- "I prayed for you."
- "Please."

Now trade lists and read through what your spouse wrote. Don't get defensive, and don't edit. You can ask questions to clarify, but don't debate. Find a place to keep your spouse's list where you can look at it regularly.

Now that you've created your lists, each of you should name a reward that you'd like to receive when you say things your spouse likes to hear and when you avoid the things he or she doesn't like to hear. Perhaps a favorite dessert or a back rub. Over the course of the next week, keep track of how many times you say the good phrases and avoid the bad ones. At the end of the week, show your spouse your tally, and collect your reward. Your spouse can do the same!

At the end of the week, you might think of different phrases you'd like to hear. So create new lists and repeat the exercise. Over time, the lists and rewards won't be needed.

IDEA 4
a free night out

Most of us can use a night out with our spouse, but not everyone can afford babysitting, particularly on a regular basis. So pair up with another couple to take care of one another and give each other a needed break.

Of course, the other couple should have children, too. If the ages of their kids are close to your children's ages, that might work best. The idea's pretty simple: One week you go out while the other couple baby-sits all the children. The next week, the other couple gets their date while you baby-sit.

Obviously, the challenge lies with the couple on child-care duty. So pull from the following ideas to make the night great for the kids as well:
- Door Prizes. Wrap the doors of the house with Christmas wrapping paper and a large bow.
- Future Sculptors. Use a clean sheet of wax paper, and create sculptures out of modeling clay or modeling dough. Keep one or two as souvenirs for when the parents pick up their kids.
- The Louvre. Supply white paper, crayons, and images of famous artwork printed from online. Have the kids create their own versions of well-known pieces of artwork. Put them

inside the frames of pictures hanging around the house.

• Maid to Order. If you're babysitting at the home of the couple on the date, have the kids go around the house and touch it up the way a hotel maid would: Put mints on the pillows, fold the ends of the toilet paper into triangles, and spray scented aerosol in the bathrooms.

• Mischief and Moustaches. Give the kids clear sheets of acetate like those used for overhead projectors (available at office supply stores). Go around the house, cutting out sheets and placing them inside frames over the pictures. Drawing *only* on the acetate, children can draw on moustaches and other funny additions to family photos. Everyone gets a new look, but the pictures can be returned to normal at any time.

• You Are Here. Have the kids use paper and colored pens to draw a map of the house. They can give new names to each room, like "Sleepyland" or "Stinky Swamp" (use your imagination). Encourage them to add rooms they wish their house had, like a dragon coop.

IDEA 5
oh! i remember you!

Too often, when you get the chance to spend time together as a couple, your conversation moves to the kids, the house, or other issues of life. When you do finally look into your spouse's eyes, you realize you haven't really looked at each other in days. Because so many things compete for your attention, you must be intentional about creating time and energy for meaningful conversation.

Get to know each other again. Set aside an occasion just for the two of you. Farm out the kids and go on a picnic, or make a dinner together at home. Or if staying home will distract you, go to a quiet restaurant. Just be sure to choose a place that will allow private conversation.

Look each other in the eyes. Say hello! Then use the following to spur conversation to new depths and significance.

Share with each other:

• Describe how valued you feel at work, and how valued you feel with extended family. How valued do you feel in your marriage?

Ask one another:

• What do I do that makes you feel valued and cherished?
• Do I ever say or do anything that makes you feel devalued?

• Describe to your spouse what it means to you to respect a person.

• What do you respect most about me?
• Which of my actions or words show you that I respect you?
• Do you ever feel that in some way I communicate that I don't respect you?

• Share the activities you most enjoy doing with your spouse.

• What would you like to do together more often that you don't do now?
• How important is it to you that we spend time together?
• How would you like to be included more

(or less) in my activities?

• Do you ever feel isolated or left out of my life? Explain.

• Describe what quality you cherished most about your spouse when you first fell in love. Share what quality you cherish most now.

• When during our marriage have you felt most loved by me?

• Which of my actions or words convey to you that I love you?

• What do I do that leaves you feeling unloved?

• What would you like me to do instead?

• Talk about your comfort and desire to discuss physical intimacy. If this topic is difficult, consider why that's the case.

• How does physical intimacy make you feel emotionally?

• Does our lovemaking make you feel cherished and respected?

• What can I do to help you feel more loved through physical intimacy?

IDEA 6
chef surprise

Kidnap your spouse for lunch! Surprise your partner with an unexpected treat in the middle of the day. Plan a getaway and take your spouse away from it all. If necessary, make arrangements with the boss or co-workers. Ask about any restrictions or guidelines you might need to be aware of. They might have suggestions for making your surprise more fun and successful.

Pick up a meal-to-go, or prepare a picnic basket. Bring along a blanket or umbrellas and eat at the beach, bring camp chairs for a respite beside a creek on a mountain trail, or find a grassy terrace near a fountain or flower gardens. You can even head to an indoor mall and picnic under center-court foliage. Know ahead of time where you'll eat and what's available to save time when lunch hour begins.

To add suspense, ask co-workers to escort your spouse to meet you. Or call from the entrance to request a meeting. Be creative! Consider the unique circumstances of your spouse's workplace, and create a plan to enhance the fun.

If your spouse can't leave work, eat lunch there. Bring along a favorite food. Include candles for ambience. If open flames aren't allowed, bring a vase and a rosebud for an intimate centerpiece. Include dessert to add some flair.

Bring along a humorous book, a play, or poetry, and read to each other. If time permits, take a walk, bowl 10 frames, or play a game of chess. Do something you'd never do on a typical day.

When you return your spouse to the workplace, give a small farewell gift of a chocolate bar or a flower stem as a reminder of your time together. Express how much you enjoyed the break, and make sure your spouse knows you're looking forward to seeing him or her at home at the end of the workday.

IDEA 7
same old family, new family gatherings!

When extended family gathers for holidays, special occasions, or just because that's what you've always done, diverse personalities, conflicts, and other "old baggage" can ruin a good time. Dispel stress by starting new traditions.

Changing locations can take the burden off family members who always plan and host. Propose a new, neutral meeting place for your next family gathering. Do some research ahead of time so you can present your ideas along with benefits and amenities everyone can enjoy. List positives, such as relieving the workload for some family members and the variety of activities available at the proposed location. Provide brochures and information about costs.

If you plan to spend several days and nights together, look for accommodations such as camping sites, lakeside or mountain cabins, time shares, or hotels/motels with group-rate prices. Some church camps offer family lodging, as well as other facilities like YMCA camps. Some locations offer meals, so the task of cooking doesn't fall on anyone in the family. Or divvy up meals so everyone takes a turn to prepare, serve, and clean up.

If you're just meeting for an afternoon, get together in a city park. Or a church might make a great meeting place. Be sure to leave the facility clean and in good order. Even restaurants will accommodate large groups, often providing a special menu and a private room to use.

If you choose a location with outdoor activities, such as swimming, ball playing, boating, or hiking, be sure to include something for everyone. Bring along puzzles and games for quiet activities. Consider spending time each day for shared activities, such as skits, parlor games, chapel, or a talent show.

At the end of the event, ask where people want to meet the next time. Your new setting and structure might inspire all kinds of ideas for future gatherings!

IDEA 8
give me a break

No matter where hard times originate—health issues, financial difficulties, a parenting crisis, relational problems—they all cause stress for even the strongest couples. For the sake of your marriage, take a break when the going gets tough and chronic. Getting away from the strain of the following circumstances, even if only for a short time, can help replenish your energy and restore hope.

• Health issues, such as caring for a chronically ill family member, can be challenging. Work to be united and compassionate to each other when facing these circumstances. Ask for help. Perhaps members of your church can care for your loved one so you can get away as a couple for a short time. Or check with your local hospital for community agencies that might be able to help.

• Financial difficulties can make it tough to escape. So share a diversion that has no cost. Try a hike, take a tour, visit the library for a movie or book, or visit a free museum together. When you're refreshed, take time to examine your situation. Evaluate your needs and explore change. Seek help from experts who specialize in financial planning. Be open to new ideas.

• Parenting crises often lead to relationship difficulties. So take time to show a troubled child that you still love him or her. Maybe a greeting card or note that says you still care and hold on to hope. You can also take your mind off your own struggles by volunteering to help others in tough situations.

In any of these circumstances, spend time talking with your spouse. Express your feelings. Use a phrase like "Today, I feel…" to connect with each other's feelings. Say, "I think it would help me today if I could…" to explore what each other's needs are.

Choose positive activities to do together. Go for a walk, see a play or movie, or go to a concert.

Seek counsel where appropriate. Invite people who've been through similar experiences into your life.

IDEA 9
a time out

Conflict happens. Every couple argues and stresses out. While you can't have a conflict-free marriage, you and your spouse can handle conflicts fairly. Here's one approach:

When conflict happens and communication starts to break down, take a break from each other to cool off and think through the issues.

While apart, write down what you thought the conflict was about and how you felt. Remember, no feelings are invalid. Some phrases to help you express your feelings include: "When we were arguing, I felt ____" or "When you said ____, I felt ____." Don't focus on pointing fingers. Instead, try to open up emotionally to your spouse.

Now list some ways you might have acted inappropriately during the conflict. Did you say something unkind, hurtful, or rude? Write down what you said so you can ask your spouse for forgiveness. Confession might allow you to take the log out of your eye (Matthew 7:3) to see the situation more clearly.

Finally, list some ways to resolve the conflict and how you can avoid battling about the same issues again. For example:

• I need to listen to you more and not read into what you're saying.
• I'll try to be more patient with you.
• I won't say harsh or unkind words to you.

Get back together and talk. Remember, your goal is to resolve the conflict. Take turns so that you both can speak and both actively listen. Share what you wrote while you were cooling down. You might need to "give" a little more to compromise, so humility and cooperation are important. Spend time in prayer together to end your discussion.

IDEA 10
make a 25-hour day

Have you ever wished you had more hours in a day? And wouldn't it be nice to use the bonus time to add enjoyment and fulfillment to your marriage? By looking for what steals your time, you can discover new ways to create usable and valuable periods of time.

• Keep a record or diary for a week to see how you spend each hour of the day. Record when you sleep, exercise, work, travel, attend nonwork meetings, play, do household chores, watch TV and movies, browse online, prepare food, go shopping, and so forth. Just seeing your schedule in print might make it clear where valuable time goes.

• Take your time diary and categorize different uses of time. Divide items by headings, such as required, negotiable, nonessential but enjoyable, unnecessary.

• Look over your schedule. Where do you see wasted time right away? What activities can't be changed? What don't you want to change? What would you like to spend less time on? With your spouse, brainstorm ways to reduce or eliminate things you dislike most or that take more time than you wish. Or just get rid of obvious time-wasters. For example, reduce the time you spend online, playing solitaire, or watching TV. Limit yourself to a half an hour or so for answering e-mails. Spend the saved time interacting with your spouse.

• Make a to-do list. Prioritize the tasks. Work on them together. Include the kids. Break large projects into smaller jobs. Set a timer for 15 to 30 minutes, and work on a task just that long.

• Examine how you approach tasks. Adjust time-eaters so they consume less of your day. For example, sort and throw out the junk mail pile on the counter. Then, the next time you bring in the mail, look at each piece once, throw out junk, take care of anything that will take less than two minutes, and then file remaining items.

• Cook for several meals at once, or share cooking with friends. Or double up recipes to freeze and serve a similar meal again in a few days. On days you don't cook, use the newfound time to do something together.

• Try a new approach to an old chore. For example, if laundry takes all day to get done, head to a laundromat and do it all at once. In about an hour, while you play a game of Scrabble together or take turns reading chapters out loud from a favorite book, your laundry gets done!

• Evaluate your standards. Are you an impeccable housekeeper? a meticulous organizer? What's the cost to your relationship? Consider letting some things go a little longer between cleanings. Allow the house to be a little less perfect. Or if you operate toward the other extreme, clean up the mess and keep it that way to save time hunting for lost items.

section **four**

twenty ideas
FOR FAMILY-
BUILDING

If you want to have a healthy and growing church, you'll probably agree that you need healthy and growing people in your church. What does healthy and growing mean? Among other qualities, you hope to see people maturing spiritually, building strong relationships, and serving others.

So if you want a healthy and growing church, here's an idea—start with making sure you encourage married couples to have healthy and growing families, where family members are maturing spiritually, building strong relationships, and serving others. Share these family-building ideas with the couples in your congregation—and build your healthy and growing church from the family-foundation level on up.

5 RELATIONSHIP-BUILDING IDEAS

How do couples build solid relationships with each other and their children? A key ingredient is spending time together. Suggest these activities to families in your church to create an atmosphere where their relationships can naturally grow stronger. You can simply photocopy these ideas and distribute them to couples in your church or reprint them in your church newsletter. Or reprint one idea each week for a special five-week church bulletin insert series.

IDEA 1
life journey map

This activity can give family members a little insight into each other's personalities and create understanding among family members who struggle to get along. It works especially well with teenagers and young adults, as well as Mom and Dad. You'll need:

- Heavy-duty white construction paper (at least one sheet per person)
- Colored lightweight paper
- Glue and/or tape
- Markers, pens, and pencils
- Stickers
- Scissors
- Old magazines (ask group members to bring these so you have plenty of materials to choose from)

Each family member should use these materials to create maps describing their life stories. The maps can be linear, showing the chronological order of their major life events. Or the maps might be "circular," illustrating what their experiences have taught them in life. The maps can be as detailed as each person feels comfortable. But urge each other to push your comfort limits a bit.

To get creative juices flowing, tell family members to think about people who've had a strong influence in their lives—both good and bad. Encourage them to think through times when they've been confused, times when they've grown, or times when they felt a sense of peace. Read Acts 26 and 2 Corinthians 6:3-13, where the Apostle Paul provides a great example of being vulnerable about his life experiences and lessons.

When the maps are finished, ask each family member to "show and tell." As each person shares, these questions might lead to deeper discussions.

- What points along the way have been major learning points, and what did you learn?
- What's a possible next step in your life?
- What cycles has your life taken so far?
- Where is God in your map?
- What role does God play in your life now?

IDEA 2
game night

Have a family game night—a great way for family members to reconnect and get to know each other better without even realizing it. Request that older children clear their schedules for this one night, and make it fun for younger kids by including some games they'll be good at as well.

Each family member can choose a board game to play. Draw numbers, go in age order, or go by order of birthdays during the year to decide which game to play first, second, third, and so on.

Mom and Dad can intentionally choose games that will dig a bit deeper into what family members are thinking—games that encourage self-expression or games that draw people out of their comfort zones. A few choices:

• Balderdash—a bluffing game that encourages some brain cell use and creativity

• Life—a game that can take awhile to play but also offers opportunity to talk about making choices and where your choices lead you

• Cranium—a game like charades, but with creative methods to make partners or teammates guess, which can draw family members out of their shells

Of course, what's a family game night without some decent junk food? Before you start, order a couple of pizzas, throw some popcorn in the microwave, or set out the chips and dip.

Then, let the games begin!

IDEA 3
make a mosaic

Often, family life is fragmented. Family members head off to work or school each day and struggle to maintain relationships when they're all back under the same roof. So help family members reconnect with this fun activity.

You'll need:

• Solid-colored tiles

• Tile mastic

• A large picture frame (check discount or secondhand stores)

• A large board that fits the frame (perhaps cut from lauan, a lightweight product available at home-improvement stores)

• Grout

• Brushes and trowels

• Hammers

• Old cloths

Most items can be purchased at a home-improvement store. Save money by checking the broken tile bin while you're at the home-improvement store, or try breaking up old ceramic dishes from a garage sale.

Before you start creating your family masterpiece, ask family members to think about areas of their lives: work, school, friends, hobbies, activities, and so on. Then talk about the following:

• What parts of life feel whole?

• What parts of life seem to be in pieces?

• What parts of our family life feel whole?

• What parts of our family life seem to be scattered or in pieces?

Now, take tiles and pieces of tiles or ceramic dishes and make a family mosaic. It can show any or all of the answers to the questions above. Children can each claim part of the board to represent their lives. Parents and older kids can help younger children. Cover the board with tile mastic, then press the pieces of tile into the mastic and allow it all to dry. Then brush the grout between the tiles.

Later, once everything is dry, place the mosaic in the frame. Be sure to display it in a prominent place in your home. It will remind family members that even though you're all individuals, you also are part of a whole—your family.

IDEA 4
road trip

Sometimes half the fun in going somewhere is enjoying the ride. Plan a family day trip. The destination isn't as important as the idea that you're going somewhere together.

First, figure out where you want to go. It could be as simple as driving to a town an hour or two away, grabbing a meal there, and heading home. Or, it could be traveling to a bigger event like a concert or a play. If you're from a bigger city, your family might have fun traveling to a smaller town and enjoying a slower-paced day. Or, if you live in a small town, a trip to a bigger city is always an adventure. For a slightly strange destination, check out www.roadsideamerica.com—"your online guide to offbeat tourist attractions"—to find the giant ball of rubber bands or house of reptiles nearest you.

Don't overlook the time you're together in your car. Urge your kids to leave home MP3 players, portable games, laptop computers, and so on. If the time in the car will take awhile, maybe kids can bring those items but agree to a predetermined amount of time when all devices stay off. Spend the time talking, but make it fun.

• Tell knock-knock jokes or riddles. You can buy an inexpensive joke book for kids, grab the stack of Highlights magazines in your grade-schooler's room, or just take turns making up silly jokes. Even a 4-year-old can tell a joke—it'll be funny even if it doesn't make any sense!

• Play 20 Questions. One person thinks of a famous person, place, or thing, and family members ask a total of 20 "yes" or "no" questions to try to guess who, where, or what it is.

• Tell a progressive story. You start telling a story with two or three sentences, and go clockwise around the car as each person adds a few sentences. You can come up with a completely original story, or retell a classic like "Goldilocks and the Three Bears" or "The Three Little Pigs" in your own creative and humorous way.

• Sing silly songs. Pop in a CD of kids' songs, or relive your youth (and crack up your kids) by leading the singing of classics such as "On Top of Spaghetti" or "John Jacob Jingleheimer Schmidt." Old TV show theme songs are often fun to sing together as well.

You can keep the destination a secret until you get there. Or let family members know ahead of time to get them excited about what you'll be doing.

Regardless of where you end up, your family is certain to bond in the car and at the destination as you journey together.

IDEA 5
in the affirmative

This activity is kind of like a gift exchange, but instead of presents, family members will give each other affirmation.

The first step doesn't even require everyone to be in the same room at the same time.

Simply write the names of each family member on a slip of paper and place all the slips in a bowl or hat. Each person draws one slip—just draw again if you draw your own name.

Set a day and time when your family will get together. Before then, each person must come up with a creative way to affirm the family member drawn. This can be food, an act of service, a skit, a home video, a gift, an experience, or any combination; the only guideline is that it must be a surprise.

On the arranged day, get together as a family and reveal your creative affirmations to each other. In addition to the gift you give, share in words specifically what you like and appreciate about the family member you drew.

If you have time, discuss the following questions together.
- How did it make you feel to give and receive this affirmation?
- What role does affirmation play in family relationships?
- How can we intentionally affirm and encourage each other?

5 FAITH-BUILDING IDEAS

Building a Christian family means taking time to pass along values and faith to children. The following ideas work great for families to do just that at home, and again you can photocopy these to distribute to couples or reprint them in church publications. In addition, you might want to schedule a family faith night at church, set up tables in your auditorium or classrooms, and adapt one or more of these ideas for families to talk about or work on together.

IDEA 1
family faith books

You probably record all kinds of significant events in your family. Baby books to track growth; photo albums to record vacations; and tubs to hold report cards, art projects, and school papers. But what about your family's spiritual journeys? Shouldn't this significant aspect of family life be recorded, too?

Make one (or all) of these books to record your family's faith journey. They can be as simple or complex as you'd like—from an embellished scrapbook to a spiral notebook to blank computer paper folded and stapled together.

• **ABC Scripture Scrapbook.** Make a book of 28 pages. Use the first page as the title page, calling it The [family name] ABC Scripture Book. Or make up another title. The last page in the book can be your family's favorite Bible verse. Put one letter of the alphabet on each of the remaining pages. Then, as a family, choose a verse for each letter. The verses can start with that letter or have a topic beginning with that letter. (For example, "As for me and my household, we will serve the Lord" [NIV] could be used for the letter H for "household.")

On each page, paste family photos, pictures cut from magazines, or family members' drawings to illustrate the verse. Kids will enjoy reading the book together, and they'll learn Bible verses as well.

• **Family Faith Journal.** Find a blank book that can be your family's faith journal. Have Mom and Dad start the book by writing how they became Christians. As each member of the family accepts Christ, record their stories in the book. Record significant spiritual milestones, too, such as church membership, baptism, and mission trips. This book will become a special family legacy.

• **Prayer Book.** Take a simple spiral notebook, and as a family, add decorations to the cover. Include your favorite Bible verse or a Scripture on prayer. At the top of the left-hand pages, write "Prayers" in large letters; at the top of right-hand pages, write "Answers." Record all the things your family prays about and how God answers them. Date each entry. When a family member feels discouraged that God doesn't seem to be answering his or her prayers, go through the book together to be reminded of God's faithfulness.

IDEA 2
a sweet lesson

Use this fun activity to learn how God uses both good and bad situations in our lives to guide us and help us grow.

Gather all the ingredients to make your favorite cookie recipe. As an example, for chocolate chip cookies you'd need flour, white sugar, brown sugar, butter, eggs, vanilla, salt, baking soda, chocolate chips, and nuts or oatmeal if you'd like. Have the recipe on hand, but don't let your family know what you're making yet. If you don't have a favorite recipe, use the one on the back of the chocolate chip package, or search the Internet using the keywords "chocolate chip cookie recipe" for something that looks scrumptious.

Tell your family that you're going to have a taste test. Have everyone taste each of the ingredients one by one. *(Note: Don't actually eat the raw eggs—they're not safe to consume. Instead ask if anyone would want to eat a raw egg and why everyone reacted the way they did to the idea.)* Discuss how each ingredient tastes. What was each person's favorite and least favorite ingredient? Would you want to eat a bowlful of flour, butter, salt, or baking soda? What about a bowl of sugar or chocolate chips? Would you like a dinner consisting of a plate with some of each of these ingredients?

Now bring out the cookie recipe and work together as a family to mix up the individual ingredients into cookie dough. While the first batch of cookies bakes in the oven, say something like:

"Life isn't always easy. Sometimes we go through hard times—like the yucky ingredients we tasted. But when we stay faithful during those hard times, God blesses us with what the Bible calls the fruit of the Spirit: love, joy, peace, patience, kindness, goodness, faithfulness, gentleness, and self-control (Galatians 5:22-23). Those are like the sweet ingredients we tasted. When both the yucky things and the blessings go into the oven together, it's like going through each day of our lives. All those things combined help make us better people."

Continue your discussion while you enjoy warm cookies and milk.

IDEA 3
go and do

A hundred years ago, children grew up with a sense of who they were, what they could do, and what role they played. Farm children gathered eggs, pulled weeds, or fed animals. Town kids lugged wood or coal to help heat. They cooked and cleaned. From a very early age, children knew they mattered.

Few families live on farms anymore, and town kids might occasionally load or unload the dishwasher. So how can kids get a true sense of belonging and a feeling that they matter?

Serve together as a family. This doesn't have to be a huge commitment. Most important is serving *together* as a family. Here are a few ideas:

• Care for the elderly. In our culture, where families live halfway across the country from grandparents and great-grandparents, this can be a new experience. However, it shows your children that people in the church take care of each other. Rake a yard, paint a room or a whole house, or bake and deliver cookies to an elderly individual or couple.

• Bless a missionary. Write letters and collect and send hard-to-get-in-their-country supplies. This personal connection is an excellent way for kids to be a part of world outreach.

• Help other kids. Children's homes have many tasks for hands of all ages. Take your kids to help plant trees or paint a barn or sort canned goods. This teaches servanthood—and offers kids a new perspective on life.

In the kingdom of God, there's no minimum age for serving others. If we want our children to grow up to be God-loving servants, we need to raise them up that way, teaching them to serve others.

IDEA 4
a little one-on-one

Ever wish you had more time to really talk with your family members? One-on-one time? Set up a prescheduled talk time. All you really need is a calendar, a comfortable place to meet, and no distractions.

• Decide how often to meet. If you have a large family, scheduling each individual once a month might be all you can do. Keep in mind that your talks might be five minutes or five hours—it's up to the two of you. Next, put dates on your calendar for each family member so you don't forget.

• Decide where to meet. This can be last minute. Your spouse might like coffee on the back porch or a long walk in the evening. But a child might choose playing catch in the backyard, building a sand castle on the beach, or playing a video game in the living room. It doesn't really make any difference what you do or how long you meet. Just do it together, and keep the window open for talking.

• Try to listen more than you talk. This is true even if you have to bite your tongue. Often the family member who wants to talk isn't looking for advice, just a safe place to say what's bothering him or her. If you are asked for your thoughts, give them honestly. And if the subject is spiritual, avoid being preachy, especially with children who are usually just trying to make sense of their world.

• Urge patience and prayer. Most of us face times when we get impatient about where we are in life. Again, you don't need to be preachy, but the Bible offers some great verses on trusting God each day and throughout our lives. You might look up these verses and talk about them together: Psalm 34:15-18; Philippians 4:6-7; 1 Thessalonians 5:17-18; Hebrews 4:14-16; 1 Peter 5:6-7.

Family members support each other in many ways. But when it comes to sharing feelings, thoughts, and dreams, the opportunities might be fleeting. By scheduling times for everyone to express themselves, families can offer valuable emotional support.

IDEA 5
tech-free weekend

Like most families, you're probably plugged in during all your waking hours. With a click of a button or flip of a phone, technology makes it so easy to connect. Yet somewhere along this futuristic road, has your family lost the ability to connect personally?

If this sounds familiar, help your family step off the technology treadmill and unplug from the world by setting up a tech-free weekend.

• Have a family meeting and talk about the need to stay connected with each other. Propose setting aside some time to reconnect, and then suggest trying a technology-free approach. Don't be surprised if a few family members balk about jumping aboard.

• Choose a date that works for all. If you can't set aside a whole weekend, even several hours can be beneficial.

• Decide as a family what technology means. You might hide everything from the TV to the iPods. Or you might decide to limit times on certain gadgets—such as restricting cell phones, computers, and TV/video for several hours. Or halfway through the day, give everyone a half hour on an "off limits" item.

• Make plans. Don't expect your family to sit in a circle, hold hands, and sing old campfire songs. Use the time to get to know one another again. Plan to have fun! Get out favorite board games, or plan a trip to an amusement park. Whatever you do, be creative, enjoy one another, and listen to each other.

• Focus on faith. Send everyone off to gather these items from their rooms: a belt, a coat, a pair of shoes or boots, a pair of sunglasses, a baseball cap, and a Bible. Now read Ephesians 6:13-17, and as you read, ask family members to put on each item as you read about it. Pause to talk about what each item might mean. Belt: "Putting on the belt of truth"; coat: "The body armor of God's righteousness"; shoes or boots: "The peace that comes from the Good News"; sunglasses: "Hold up the shield of faith to stop the fiery arrows of the devil"; baseball cap: "Put on salvation as your helmet"; Bible: "Take the sword of the Spirit, which is the word of God."

• Plan menus to please everyone's palate. Keep in mind that food and togetherness go hand in hand. Of course, you don't have to exist on cupcakes and pizza because these are someone's favorites. Keep nutrition in mind, but throw in a few treats. After all, this weekend is a celebration of your family.

• Specify meal times, but don't make every meal an obligation. For example: Breakfast and lunch might be "come when you're hungry" meals, to allow sleeping in, reading, or time for private reflections. Then expect everyone for dinner whether you go out or stay in.

• Don't expect miracles. Taking time to live without distractions once won't make communication problems go away. But if you create a fun atmosphere and the goal is to reconnect, you might be pleasantly surprised at the results.

5 DISCIPLINE HELP IDEAS

Most couples will likely admit that one of their biggest parenting challenges is keeping discipline fair and consistent. Here's your chance to help. Pass along these ideas to parents in your congregation. Or use these as discussion starters in a Sunday school class or small group setting. Couples can spend time discussing these ideas and brainstorming solutions with other parents, and they can break into individual couples to talk about how to make the ideas work in their homes.

IDEA 1
a united front

Kids seem to learn at an early age how to pit one parent against another to get what they want. It's important to present a united front and to teach your children not to manipulate you and other authorities in their lives.

Before you and your spouse face this situation, spend some time away from your kids discussing how you'll handle areas where the two of you might disagree. If a question comes up that you haven't thought of, it's OK to step away, discuss the issue in private, and then go back to your children united in your decision.

Often, kids who pit Mom and Dad against each other have seen a difference in your parenting approaches. Perhaps one of you is more the drill-sergeant parent who simply expects obedience "no matter what," while the other is more laid-back, figuring your kids will turn out just fine even if they don't have a lot of boundaries. While these are extreme descriptions, your kids will probably pick up on all kinds of more subtle differences and use them to their advantage.

Here's a sampling of topics you'll want to think about and discuss before your children try to divide and conquer. As your kids grow up, you'll certainly face many others not on this list:

- Appearance: Choices about clothing, hairstyles, piercings, tattoos
- Bedtime: Just in bed or lights out completely?
- Cars: Choices about going with friends and their parents, and about riding with other teenagers when your kids are older
- Church: Should kids be required to attend, or is it a choice?
- Curfews: In the house by a set time; following local laws
- Dating: When to start; age differences with the people they date
- Grades: Rewards for good grades; removal of privileges for bad grades
- Music: What styles are OK to listen to; dealing with parental advisories
- TV: What shows to watch; how much TV and other media is OK

IDEA 2
to buy or not to buy?

Discriminating between wants and needs is a key element to living within a budget, and it is an important skill for adult life. One way you can teach kids in this area is to give them choices about items they want or need.

Start this training at a young age—6 or 7 for most kids. Children this age often have money from gifts, allowance, and chores. While it's never too late, the younger your kids are when you start this process, the better.

Consider these questions with your spouse before talking with your kids:

- What items will they have to buy with their own money? Toys? Candy? Designer jeans?
- Will purchasing those items with their own money always be the rule?

• What items or activities are off limits—not paid for by anyone's money—such as certain kinds of movies or tobacco products?

• Does timing matter—for example, can they buy ice cream before dinner?

A great place to start training in this area is the grocery store. When you get in the checkout line and your kids start begging for candy, you can say, "You can choose to buy that with your own money. Do you have it with you?"

Children learn from what we do as well as what we say. Point out when you make a choice to refrain from buying an item that doesn't fit in the budget. Make decisions as a family: "We can either go to the zoo today or save our money and go to the carnival next month."

Your kids benefit from learning how to weigh the value of possible purchases—a skill they can use into their teen years and adulthood. And as parents, you benefit because this strategy can drastically cut down on your children's begging when they see enticing items to buy.

IDEA 3
media boundaries

For better or worse, our culture often reaches our children most through the media—television, music, movies, the Internet, and print media. As a couple, you'll want to decide what boundaries to set for your kids and then monitor what they see and hear from an early age.

Even cartoons can send messages that parents might not want their children exposed to. Watch several cartoons or children's programs to decide if they line up with your values. Then let your children watch what you believe is appropriate.

As children mature, talk about why you establish boundaries. For example, discuss how both graphic violence and immoral behavior can devalue people. Because God values every life, your family does as well.

Of course, you won't always be able to protect your children from material you don't want them to see. So follow up any actions with a conversation. Again, talk about the value of boundaries, and don't just say, "because I said so"—help children understand your reasoning. Also, remember that your kids are watching you. Your example might be the best way you can teach children to discern what's appropriate for them to watch or listen to. Then they can make good choices when they're at the neighbor kid's house or other times you're not around.

To set boundaries for your children and to help them learn to set their own boundaries when you're not around, try these ideas:

• Set up a media budget. You might use a chart or pennies or Monopoly money. Your kids receive an allotted amount for watching TV and movies, for playing video games, or for surfing on the Internet. They "pay" you when they want to do any of these activities (which lets you know to keep an eye on what they're watching and what Web sites they visit). When the budget is gone, those media stay off until the next budget period. Some technologies such as TV Allowance and WallFly turn off the TV or computer when kids reach their time limit.

• "Co-view" with your kids. Watch TV or movies and surf the Internet with your children so you can discuss what you see and hear. Often, this eliminates temptations to view something they know you probably wouldn't approve of.

• Model media boundaries. Limit your own use of media. Use good judgment about TV shows and movies you watch—especially when your kids are present. Choose alternatives, such as reading, participating in sports, or serving in your church or community.

IDEA 4
live with the consequences

Have you ever heard one of your kids say, "He made me so mad, I just blew up"? Most children naturally play the blame game, but adults often do the same when they behave badly. A valuable lesson you and your spouse can teach your children is to take responsibility for their behavior and face the consequences that result.

Consequences that mirror real life work especially well. For example, you might require your children to pay for anything they break in a fit of anger. If your 6-year-old child slings a bowl of cereal across the room and shatters the bowl, the immediate consequence might be a timeout. But after he calms down, ask what he did. His answer should begin with "I," not anyone else's name. As a consequence for his behavior, ask him to clean up the mess and pay for the bowl. He can pay with money from gifts or allowance or work off the debt by doing extra chores.

Rebellious behavior should also draw the repayment consequence. For example, maybe you've told your kids not to play around your flower garden, but they start wrestling and tumble through your flowers. The consequence would be cleaning out and replacing any mangled flowers. All involved kids should take responsibility for their disobedience and share in both the work and payment.

At the same time, affirm your children when they make good decisions, especially when you observe them weighing behaviors and choosing the appropriate one. Applauding good choices communicates to your kids that you notice when they do things right as well as when they're wrong.

You give your kids a skill for life when you train them to take responsibility for appropriate and inappropriate behavior. Of course, make sure they know you love them regardless of their behavior.

IDEA 5
parenting seminar

Here's a great family-building idea your church can put together for couples. Even the best parents need help from time to time—or even just reassurance that they're on the right track! Host a parenting seminar. Look at the basic demographics of your church, and focus on areas that will serve the most people. For example, you might want to have a new parents' seminar, a parents of preschoolers seminar, or a parenting teens seminar.

Invite a speaker to give talks on topics relevant to the parents attending. Or ask two to three especially gifted parents from your own congregation to speak. You can also have experts in parenting each age group give presentations in different rooms in your church. A panel of parents might close the day with an open-question session. Among the topics you can discuss:

- How to set boundaries with teenagers
- The challenges of single parenting

- Building character in your children
- Maintaining a healthy marriage for the sake of healthy children
- Understanding and developing your children's faith
- Insights into how your child's (or teen's) brain really works
- Parenting with Love and Logic (log onto www.loveandlogic.com)

Your seminar might just be a class that lasts one or two hours. Or you could host an all-day parenting seminar with various different classes. Before and after the seminar, have displays set up to showcase your church's parenting-focused small groups, to offer parenting resources such as books and pamphlets, and to present available services in the community such as child-care providers, private schools, counseling services, and so on.

Provide a pleasant, warm atmosphere with a wide selection of refreshments. Have volunteers greet parents. After the seminar is over, offer short-term small groups on the subjects you've covered. A great small-group series that will help couples explore parenting together in more depth and from a biblical perspective is the HomeBuilders Parenting Series (FamilyLife).

5 IDEAS TO CONNECT WITH YOUR TEENS

Some parents claim to get less sleep during their kids' teenage years than they did when the kids were fussy babies who didn't sleep through the night. Certainly, the teen years can be challenging for parents. Here's your chance to help couples stay connected with their teenagers. Pass along these ideas that teenagers will tolerate—and if they let down their guard, might actually enjoy.

IDEA 1
the happening place

Despite text messaging, PDAs and myspace.com, teens still crave real socialization with real people. They want "face time" with each other and even with caring adults. Why not provide a safe place for teens to hang out at your house?

Remember that teens seem to have ultra-sensitive "bogus detectors." But if your home is a place where parents and teens already talk and play and laugh together, try opening your home to others.

Start by asking your own teens what they like about your home. Is it something that most of their friends experience? Chances are, they'll express that they like the security they feel in your family and stress how most of their friends want but don't have that sense of stability.

So offer some "homeyness" to your kids' friends. Keep in mind that teenagers tend to be rowdy and noisy. They're always hungry. Where teens gather, things are likely to get broken and dirty. Just be prepared.

Here are some other guidelines:

• Have your own teenagers decide when to invite the band, the color guard, the debate squad, or the high school Sunday school class over and what to do when everyone is there. Again, it will definitely need to include food.

• Pray together with your own teens (before friends arrive) that your home can bless the lives of their friends. But also promise that you won't say or do anything to embarrass them.

• Try to steer your teens away from just watching a DVD and to try something more interactive. If they think an activity might be corny (like playing Monopoly), convince them that it's "retro" and therefore cool. Most of their friends will probably be more excited about a cool place to hang out (with food!) than what they do.

• Take time to evaluate after each gathering. Talk with your teens about the friends who showed up and the needs you perceived. Gently remind your teens that the qualities in your home are due to Christ's Lordship there.

• With your spouse, thank God for the opportunity to serve in this way. And get ready for your teens' friends to ask, "When can we come back to your house?"

IDEA 2
family adventures

Marriage and family hold the promise of adventure. The adventure continues all the more as each child comes along. And it doesn't need to end simply because your children have reached their teens. Keep your marriage strong and vibrant by getting intentional about adventure in your family. Ask these four questions to help you do just that:

1. What adventure is on the calendar this week? An "adventure" might be a movie premiere or a free concert in the park. You don't have to spend a lot or do a lot of planning. But you do have to be intentional to get it on the calendar. Keep your ears open or check the activities section in your local paper for ideas.

2. What adventure is on the calendar this month? Plan a bigger adventure for the "first Friday" or the "last Monday" of every month. Maybe it's a trip to the zoo or other local attraction. An easy way to plan a once-a-month adventure is to pretend you're a tourist in your own community. What attractions are nearby? Has your family taken them all in? What can you see and do within, say, a 50-mile radius?

3. What adventure is on the calendar this quarter? Here's where you ratchet it up a notch and get creative. Get tickets to the local theater or ballgame. Or head out on a weekend getaway such as camping or checking into a hotel in the "big city" near you. Other adventures include hunting, fishing, antiquing, or shopping at *the* place to shop that's neither too near nor too far away.

4. What adventure is on the calendar this year? Yes, it's family vacation time. Pull out all the stops—or at least most of them! Remember, your children won't be at home forever. Get out of town and make some memories. Most kids prefer active vacations over time in the car. So stay at a hotel with a water park. Ride burros into the Grand Canyon. Rent a four-wheeler and drive mountain trails. Spend a week on the beach (don't forget to go snorkeling!).

Don't be one of those families who never ventures outside a five-mile radius of home. Keep the promise of adventure alive in your marriage by venturing out around town, across the nation, and even around the world!

IDEA 3
family night boosters

Setting aside one night a week as family night is a recipe for a healthy marriage and family. To prepare a family night feast, you need three ingredients:

Ingredient 1: Food. If you want your kids to hang with the family rather than friends, food can be a huge motivation! For some families it might be homemade pizza, while others say hooray to a bucket of chicken. Still others enjoy the variety of family members taking turns at choosing the meal.

Ingredient 2: Fun. Play games, watch movies, get hooked on a TV show. Play Buzzword ("the lively, addictive, and challenging game that fuzzes your memory and buzzes your brain!") or iMAgiN*iff* ("the funniest game you can imagine!"). Or take the fun outdoors with croquet or "lawn bowling" (see www.BocceBallSets.com). Bottom line: No fun, no kids!

Ingredient 3: Faith. This ingredient is like a seasoning that you and your spouse can stir in subtly but constantly. Start the night with a quick prayer for God's blessing. Of course, give thanks for the food. Do a brief family devotional.

Family nights can also create family traditions. For example, one family decided to eat Chinese takeout picnic-style in the middle of the living room one Valentine's Day. The following year, one of the daughters exclaimed, "It's almost Valentine's Day! I can't wait for our Chinese-food picnic—it's *tradition!*"

One caution: Don't force your family into weekly family nights. Start small—say, every other week or once a month. When you mix all these ingredients together, the kids will naturally come back for more!

IDEA 4
active servants

God's people are to look not only to their own interests, but also to the interests of others (Philippians 2:4). This not only *applies* to families, it's *great* for families!

Just because your kids have entered their teenage years—when activities sometimes consume life and the teenagers themselves become more introspective—don't pull back on serving others. Instead, try these practical ways that your family can reach out to the needy around you:

• Pray regularly. Spend time in prayer during mealtimes or during family devotions. Pray for friends, neighbors, extended family members, and for people around the world. Ask God to meet the needs of the world's afflicted. Ask him to break your heart over people's needs and to give your family wisdom about how to be part of his answer to your prayers.

• Develop a world vision. Many organizations will help you do just that. Log onto www.gospelcom.net and click on "Alliance Ministries." You'll find links to hundreds of ministries that range in size, vision, and purpose. Tap into them to help you raise your own and your family's awareness of the needs that exist nearby and far away.

• Get involved. While every need isn't a personal call, some are. How is God leading your family to take the next step toward involvement? This might be making a contribution as a family or gathering information on short-term missions opportunities for families.

• Get informed. Learn about missions, ministries, and missionaries your church supports. Are there needy families within your own congregation that your family can serve? Every family member can do something, such as yard work, making a meal, or giving a "love offering."

• Raise awareness. Help your congregation learn about local, national, and international needs that they're unaware of. Christmas is an especially difficult time of year for many families. Samaritan's Purse (www.samaritanspurse.com) runs Operation Christmas Child to help people give gift-filled shoe boxes to needy children around the world. Prison Fellowship (www.pfm.org) sponsors Angel Tree to help prisoners' children receive gifts. Both programs make sure the message of salvation accompanies each gift.

One word in the Great Commission stands out: *go* (see Matthew 28:19-20). Your family can help hurting families find hope when you *go* with your prayers, gifts, and even your feet to places near and far away, in Jesus' name. And your own family and marriage will never be stronger!

IDEA 5
working out works wonders

The family that works out together stays together. Who knows if this is true, but it might be worth a shot! Certainly, the teenage years, when your kids are likely very conscious of their changing bodies, offer a great time to get the whole family to the gym or health club together. So how do you get started?

1. Call a family meeting and make working out a family priority. Agree that getting out and active as a family is healthy all around. Make it a plan. Your teenagers might be surprised at your sudden interest in getting out and active. Tell them the truth: You want to build healthy bodies and a strong family, and taking time to work out with one another is an ideal way to accomplish both! Besides, it's fun, it relieves stress, and it provides renewed energy.

2. Determine what you're going to do as a family. Purchase a family membership at a health club or the YMCA to take advantage of a variety of family-friendly options. Your family can take part in an aerobics class or family swim time, play racquetball, or go through the exercise equipment circuit.

Other families find creative ways to get active outdoors. What walking and hiking trails are nearby? If everyone has a bike, set a distance or a special destination to work up to. Or start with a simple family walk or backyard games.

Some families get competitive, such as competing in a local fun race or even a marathon.

As you stay healthy and fit as a family, you may find some benefits you haven't considered. In the midst of working out, you'll find natural opportunities for meaningful conversations, such as helping your children navigate healthy life options and a godly perspective on body image.

In addition, Dad and Mom will find that regular fitness helps build healthy marriages. Don't underestimate what a model this will be to the next generation!

section **five**

ten bible studies
FOR COUPLES

Bible studies provide a great way for couples in your marriage ministry to deepen their faith. This section contains 10 stand-alone Bible studies you can use for small or large groups of couples. And they work well for a group of couples wanting to meet on their own or for a Sunday school class of married couples.

While the studies are largely self-directed and written directly to participants, a leader does need to provide copies of the studies and gather supplies. A leader might also be called on during the study to lead a discussion. So be sure to read the study, gather and set up the supplies, photocopy the study for each participant, and be prepared to lead the group from the front when necessary.

Feel free to adapt these studies to your group's needs. The time limits are just guidelines, for example. If you want to use the suggested times, you'll probably need to encourage people to slow down as they work through the questions, reminding them that the goal is to generate good discussion, not to finish fast. You can also add or delete questions or Scripture passages. Change the prayer times to fit your group. However you use these studies, urge participants to break into smaller groups when the studies direct them to. This allows everyone to participate. Most important, enjoy these Bible studies, and use them to help couples grow closer to God and to help spouses grow closer to one another.

STUDY 1
Communication

Effective communication in marriage involves much more than sharing information. We've all heard the phrase, "It's not what you say, but how you say it." But we need to rewrite that sentiment: "It's both what you say *and* how you say it." And perhaps *not saying something* at all might be appropriate. This study offers principles that will help couples develop healthy and godly communication.

Items Needed
• 1 large piece of red poster board (At the top, write "Things Not to Say to Your Spouse; below the title, use a wide-tipped marker to create a large "do not enter" symbol.)
• 1 large piece of yellow poster board (At the top, write "Things to Say to Your Spouse; below the title, use a wide-tipped marker to create a large smiley face.)
• A felt-tip marker for each participant

Opening (10-15 minutes)
Divide into two groups. Assign one group to the "Things Not to Say to Your Spouse" poster board. Assign the other group to the "Things to Say to Your Spouse" poster board. Give each person a marker. Take five minutes to write as many words or phrases that you can think of in relation to your poster board. You might take these from personal experience, what you hear friends say, or lines in movies and TV shows.

Discuss:
• Identify some attitudes that might be behind these comments.
• How would you react to each of these statements if your spouse said them?

Bible Study (30-45 minutes)
Break into groups of three or four couples each. Read James 1:19-20, and then discuss:
• On a scale of 1-10 (1 least, 10 most), rate the importance of each of these aspects of communication in marriage:

• talking   • • • • • • • • • •
               1 2 3 4 5 6 7 8 9 10

Great Discussions!

Remember to take your time as you work through these questions. Your goal isn't to finish fast, but to generate good discussion.

Here are three ways to make sure your discussion gets down to the depth you'd like:

1. When someone answers a question quickly or simply starts to move the group to the next question too fast, follow up with one of these go-deeper comments or questions:

   • "Please say more about what you mean…"

   • "I've never thought of that before—could you explain more?"

   • "That's the answer we expect—how would you explain that to someone who didn't know the 'expected' answer?"

2. If an answer is surprising or insightful, try the following:

   • To the person who answered, say, "That's an important insight. Talk a little more about what you just said."

   • Open the discussion to the group by asking, "What do others think about what [name] just said?"

3. Some of the questions are more personal than others. Because the questions sometimes focus on private matters of marriage, not everyone will feel comfortable sharing answers. However, as your group grows more comfortable with each other, you can probe deeper with more personal questions, using statements such as:

   • "That seems like the 'right answer' in theory, but does anyone have an example of how that works in real life?"

   • "If that occurred in your marriage or with your spouse, how would it make you feel?"

• listening   • • • • • • • • • •

1 2 3 4 5 6 7 8 9 10

Read 1 Corinthians 13:4-7, and then discuss:

• As you consider this list of qualities describing love, how would you translate each into a principle of communication for couples? (For example: "Patience: Love listens, without interruption, in order to understand.")

• "The Chinese character for hearing includes symbols for the eyes, the heart, and the mind as well as for the ear" (Nicky and Sila Lee, *The Marriage Book*, New York, NY: Alpha Resources, 2000, p. 71). Think about which way of hearing applies to each principle of communication you've identified, and draw a set of eyes, a heart, a person's head, or an ear next to each one.

• Identify several principles of godly communication that are strengths in your marriage.

• Identify several principles of godly communication you'd like to strengthen in your marriage.

Closing (15-20 minutes)

With your spouse, find a quiet spot to compare answers from the last two discussion points in the Bible study section on the previous page. Then discuss the following questions.

- Did you identify the same strengths? If so, talk about how you can keep these areas strong.

- Identify ways you can improve your communication with each other, and discuss an action you can take to accomplish it. Decide that when you start to argue, you and your spouse will thumb wrestle instead. This will help defuse the situation and allow you time to settle down—and laugh together. Then you can calmly discuss the issue.

Come back together as a large group. Spend time voicing prayer requests for each other. Then close in prayer, with members of the group thanking God for one quality they appreciate about their spouse.

A leader can then end the prayer time by verbally summarizing the principles about communication drawn from this lesson, asking God to show couples ways to improve communication with their spouses. When the leader expresses a principle in prayer—for example, "God, please help us to take time to really understand what our spouse wants to communicate to us"—each person can respond, "God, please help me."

STUDY 2
Keep Romance Alive

Is romance just for fairytales and novels? Or is it a necessary part of love? What would marriage look like without romance? This lesson will help you discover God's view of romance and how that affects your marriage.

Items Needed
- 2 large red poster boards cut into large hearts
- Sticky notes
- Felt-tip markers for everyone
- A romantic card (blank inside) for each participant
- A dictionary
- A synonym/antonym dictionary
- A thesaurus

Opening (10-15 minutes)
Divide into two teams (or more if the group is large). On sticky notes, write every romantic book, movie, and song you can think of. Then stick the notes to your team's heart. Now talk about the titles you came up with by answering these questions:
- What are some of the ways Hollywood portrays romance?
- How do these portrayals shape our thinking about romance?
- What makes good romance?
- What's the role of romance in marriage?

Divide the larger group into three smaller groups. Give the first group a dictionary, the second a thesaurus, and the third group a synonym and antonym dictionary. Have them locate the words *romance* and *romantic*, and then read those meanings to the larger group.

Bible Study (30-45 minutes)
Stay in three small groups. Read Genesis 1:27-28a, 31a, and then discuss:
- How does romance seem to fit into God's plan?

Great Discussions!

Remember to take your time as you work through these questions. Your goal isn't to finish fast, but to generate good discussion.

Here are three ways to make sure your discussion gets down to the depth you'd like:

1. When someone answers a question quickly or simply starts to move the group to the next question too fast, follow up with one of these go-deeper comments or questions:
- "Please say more about what you mean…"
- "I've never thought of that before—could you explain more?"
- "That's the answer we expect—how would you explain that to someone who didn't know the 'expected' answer?"

2. If an answer is surprising or insightful, try the following:
- To the person who answered, say, "That's an important insight. Talk a little more about what you just said."
- Open the discussion to the group by asking, "What do others think about what [name] just said?"

3. Some of the questions are more personal than others. Because the questions sometimes focus on private matters of marriage, not everyone will feel comfortable sharing answers. However, as your group grows more comfortable with each other, you can probe deeper with more personal questions, using statements such as:
- "That seems like the 'right answer' in theory, but does anyone have an example of how that works in real life?"
- "If that occurred in your marriage or with your spouse, how would it make you feel?"

Read 1 Corinthians 7:2-5 and Proverbs 5:18-19, and then discuss:

• According to these passages, what advice could you give someone about romance in marriage? How does this differ from romance as portrayed on TV, in movies, and in books?

Read Song of Songs 2:15, and then discuss:
• This whole book is a love story about marriage and God's intimate love for us—using many metaphors and similes from nature. What do the foxes represent? Look again at 1 Corinthians 7:2-5 and Proverbs 5:18-19 and identify what cunning "foxes" do to romance in marriage if not caught.

Read Song of Songs 4:12, 16–5:1, and then discuss:
• What qualities of romance do you see here? In ancient Middle Eastern culture, milk was considered vital and essential. When mentioned in connection with honey, it was a delicacy. How do you think romance is like a delicacy?

• Talk about how these qualities can improve romance for couples.

Closing (15-20 minutes)

Read 1 John 4:10-11, 18. Divide men and women into two separate groups, and give each person a blank greeting card. Brainstorm ideas for implementing romance to improve marriages. Some ideas might involve teamwork, such as trading babysitting for less expensive date nights. When you find an idea you'd like to use, write it inside the greeting card, along with your plan for implementing the idea at home. Find a creative or surprising way to give the card to your spouse, such as placing it under a pillow or taping it to the bathroom mirror.

Break into couples. With your spouse, spend time praying for each other to be the kind of husband or wife who models the romance God desires in your marriage.

STUDY 3
Authentic Connection

When love in marriage is new and fresh, spouses naturally want to connect with each other. But before long, little irritants can erode the closeness, and couples grow apart from each other in ways they never intended. Producing unity in a marriage needs to be intentional. In this study, you'll discover principles to help you make more intimate connections with each other.

Items Needed
• 2 large pieces of poster board cut in half lengthwise. Use a wide-tipped marker to label one end of each strip + (positive) and the other end - (negative).
• 1 piece of plain 8½ x 11 paper cut in half (each 4¼ x 5½). On one piece, use a wide-tipped marker to draw a line with arrows at each end pointing away from each other (like an endless number line). On the other piece, draw two arrows facing each other.

Magnet Activity Explanation

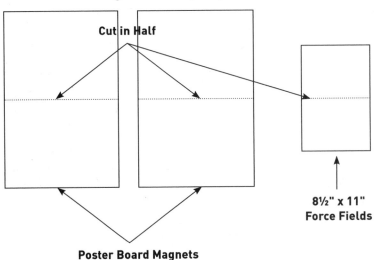

Cut in Half

8½" x 11"
Force Fields

Poster Board Magnets

• A fine-tip marker for each participant
• Clear or masking tape
• Card stock (business-card size with a hole punched in one corner), 1 for each couple
• 1-foot pieces of thick yarn in three colors (1 set per couple, knotted together at one end)

Opening (10-15 minutes)

The long strips of poster board represent magnets, while the smaller pieces of paper with arrows represent the force fields of the magnets. At opposite ends of the room, tape up two opposing "magnets" (with either both + ends or both - ends in the center). Place the "force field" paper between the two "magnets" (think back to your basic junior high science classes—both of these sets of magnets would repel each other).

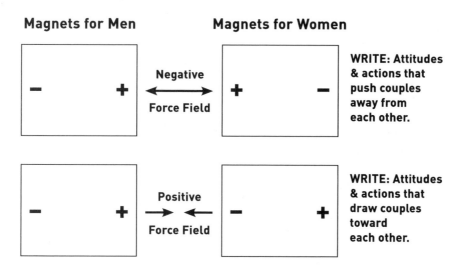

All the men should be at one "magnet" and the women at the other. Take a few minutes, and write as many attitudes and actions as possible that can push marriage partners away from each other to create disengagement or a lack of intimacy. For example, working too much, conflicts about disciplining children, spending too much money on hobbies, and so on.

After three or four minutes, under the opposing magnets, tape up the remaining "magnets" to attract each other (one with the + end in the center and the other with the - end in the center). Place the "force field" paper between them (this time, with the arrows pointing at each other).

Now, take a few minutes and write as many attitudes and actions as possible that can draw a couple toward each other to create intimacy. For example, showing each other affection, laughing together, helping each other with household or parenting responsibilities.

Afterward, discuss each set of "magnets":

• What behavior do you see when a married couple seems to disengage from each other? What behavior do you see when there is intimacy?

• While you listed some attitudes and actions when a couple experiences both intimacy and a lack of intimacy, what additional actions and attitudes would you see over a period of time? Why?

Great Discussions!

Remember to take your time as you work through these questions. Your goal isn't to finish fast, but to generate good discussion.

Here are three ways to make sure your discussion gets down to the depth you'd like:

1. When someone answers a question quickly or simply starts to move the group to the next question too fast, follow up with one of these go-deeper comments or questions:
- "Please say more about what you mean…"
- "I've never thought of that before—could you explain more?"
- "That's the answer we expect—how would you explain that to someone who didn't know the 'expected' answer?"

2. If an answer is surprising or insightful, try the following:
- To the person who answered, say, "That's an important insight. Talk a little more about what you just said."
- Open the discussion to the group by asking, "What do others think about what [name] just said?"

3. Some of the questions are more personal than others. Because the questions sometimes focus on private matters of marriage, not everyone will feel comfortable sharing answers. However, as your group grows more comfortable with each other, you can probe deeper with more personal questions, using statements such as:
- "That seems like the 'right answer' in theory, but does anyone have an example of how that works in real life?"
- "If that occurred in your marriage or with your spouse, how would it make you feel?"

Bible Study (30-45 minutes)

Break into groups of three or four couples each. Read Genesis 2:20–3:10, and then discuss:

• God was very intentional in creating Adam first, creating Eve with a rib from Adam's side, and then bringing her to Adam. What was the significance of God's actions?

• What do you think the phrase "a man leaves his father and mother and is joined to his wife, and the two are united into one" means?

• What does "they were both naked, but they felt no shame" mean to you?

• When have you felt "no shame" in your marriage? Has that changed over the years? If so, how?

• Describe what shame did to Adam and Eve and how that could affect any marriage.

• How do you think you can restore marriage after experiencing shame?

Read Philippians 2:1-4, and then discuss:
• How can we follow Christ's example in order to restore intimacy in our marriage after it has been lost?

• What steps do you see that you need to take to experience greater intimacy with your husband or wife?

Closing (15-20 minutes)

Pass out three different colors of yarn and a business card to each couple. Find a quiet spot to talk with your spouse. Read Ecclesiastes 4:9-12 and discuss:

    • How can this passage help you experience greater intimacy in your marriage?

    • As the passage indicates, the third strand represents God. How do you benefit when God is an intimate third party in your marriage? (See Psalm 127:1.) What actions can you take to make God the third strand in your relationship?

    • On your card, write one action you'll take to create or restore intimacy between you and your spouse, such as spending time praying together before you fall asleep each night or putting your spouse's need for a few minutes of alone time ahead of your own. Place the yarn through the hole of the card, and braid the three strands together before knotting one end. Place the card in a prominent place at home to remind each of you to follow through with your planned action.

    Spend time praying as couples. Ask God to strengthen your relationship with each other. Ask him to give you the courage to always make him the third strand in your marriage relationship.

STUDY 4
Conflict Resolution

"When we get married, we aren't going to fight!" Did you have that expectation? Or have you heard another couple set this lofty goal? In reality, conflict occurs in marriage. So the issue isn't how to not fight, but how to fight right. This lesson digs into the Bible's practical guidance on how to resolve conflict.

Items Needed
• Blindfolds for everyone
• Bandannas or thin dish towels (one per couple), each long enough
to tie two wrists together
• Thin crispy potato chips (2 per couple)
• A red construction paper heart (can get 4 per sheet) for each individual
• Markers or pens for everyone

Opening (10-15 minutes)
All the couples in your group should be seated at tables. Use a bandanna or dishtowel, tie the right wrist of one spouse to the left wrist of the other, palms facing outward, and then blindfold each person. Quietly place just two potato chips on a table in front of the couples. Now, tell each couple that they must work together as quickly as possible to find, pick up, and feed each other a chip without breaking it, using only the backs of their tied hands (palms facing outward). Those using the inside of their tied hands or their free hands will be disqualified. Give couples two or three minutes to complete the task, then have them take off their blindfolds, untie their hands, and sit down. At their tables, have them discuss:
• What went well as you worked with your spouse? How could you have worked together better?
• Describe how you felt individually when the activity didn't go as expected. How did you react to your spouse when something went wrong?
• Can you think of times in marriage—your own or in general—when spouses have different expectations about the same situation? As you think of those situations, talk about what leads to the conflict. How could a couple in those situations respond constructively?

Bible Study (30-45 minutes)

Remain in your table group, and read Ephesians 4:15. Then discuss:

• This verse identifies two elements necessary to produce fruitful communication: truth and love. How do you think spouses can communicate in truth? How can they communicate in love?

• What happens when one spouse communicates to the other with honesty, but without sensitivity? Have you ever experienced this? What happened?

• What about when one spouse only considers the feelings of the other but isn't honest? Have you ever experienced this? What happened?

Read Ephesians 4:26-27, and then discuss:
• What are some ways Satan deceives us into believing our anger is justified?

• What are some common ways we react when we feel our rights have been violated?

• Describe a time when you felt deceived into thinking your anger against your spouse was justified. What did you do or say? How did it affect your relationship? How can you avoid this kind of thinking in the future?

Read Matthew 7:1-5, 12 and Ephesians 4:32, and then discuss:
• Name some principles you see in these verses that can be used as weapons against Satan's influence in your marriage. Elaborate on how you might use these principles.

• Since the beginning of time, Christ knew each wrong we'd commit. Still, he chose to die on the cross for *each* offense, willingly offering his forgiveness. How do you *forgive* your spouse when you can't *forget* an offense against you?

• Can you recall a way your spouse hurt you that you have a hard time forgetting? Have you forgiven your spouse for that offense? Why is it still hard to forget?

• How can God help restore your relationship…even when you have trouble forgetting the way you felt hurt?

Closing (15-20 minutes)

Break into couples, and give each person a red construction paper heart. Identify one attitude or action that Satan might use to gain a foothold in your marriage. This probably involves an area where friction occurs, such as finances, child rearing, work, sex, leisure time, church involvement, and so forth. On the paper heart, write a note to let your spouse know what you'll do to change this. Use principles from the Scripture passages on the previous page. You might start your note with, "I know I've been frustrated with [attitude or action], but I want to change that by [action I'll take to overcome the problem area]." Or use your own wording. Exchange hearts with your spouse.

Gather back together with the whole group, and close your study with prayer. One person can lead as follows: "As you close your eyes, I'm going to lead you in specific areas where you can pray individually and silently to God. I'll pause between each area. Take a few moments and talk to God about where you need to be more truthful in your marriage…Next, ask him to help you be more sensitive in your communication with your spouse…Ask God to give you the courage to let go of any grudges you might be holding against your partner…Ask God to show you where you might be judging your spouse and where you might be blind to your own faults…Finally, ask God to show you where you need to ask your spouse for forgiveness." The leader can then close with: "Thank you, God, for giving guidance from your Word to resolve conflict in our marriages. Help us to apply what we've learned today."

STUDY 5
Pennies and Priorities

Love might make a marriage go 'round, but financial troubles can certainly slow it down! Finances can create stress in marriage when couples have different priorities for money. This study briefly explores God's desires for financial priorities and how he can help us live out his priorities.

Items Needed
• A set of "priority cards" for each person. Create these on 3x5 index cards. On each card, print one of the following words: Tithe, Bills, Family Gifts, Ministry Gifts, Fun Stuff, Family Needs, Vacation, Clothes, Savings for the Future, Savings for Emergencies, Education, Entertainment, Eating Out.
• A pen for each person
• Optional: envelope or rubber band for each set of priority cards

Opening (10-15 minutes)
Give each person a set of priority cards, and instruct participants to put the cards in order based on their personal financial priorities. Allow three minutes for each person to look through the cards and mark each one with a number to indicate how they rank.

While we all have priorities for spending our money, our actions often don't reflect our priorities. As a reality check, have participants take the cards and put them in order (front to back) to reflect where most of their money *really* goes. Encourage them to be honest with themselves. This time, they can mark the cards by placing an R in front of new numbers to indicate "reality" ranking.

Break into couples, and have spouses compare their rankings. Discuss:
• How are your financial priorities different from each other's? How are your spending realities different?
• How well do your priorities line up with where you really spend your money? Did you find any surprises?
• Do you think your financial priorities differ from your parents'? Explain.
• Were you surprised to learn your spouse's priorities?
• Do you think married couples should share the same financial priorities? What do you think happens when we don't?

Great Discussions!

Remember to take your time as you work through these questions. Your goal isn't to finish fast, but to generate good discussion.

Here are three ways to make sure your discussion gets down to the depth you'd like:

1. When someone answers a question quickly or simply starts to move the group to the next question too fast, follow up with one of these go-deeper comments or questions:
    • "Please say more about what you mean…"
    • "I've never thought of that before—could you explain more?"
    • "That's the answer we expect—how would you explain that to someone who didn't know the 'expected' answer?"

2. If an answer is surprising or insightful, try the following:
    • To the person who answered, say, "That's an important insight. Talk a little more about what you just said."
    • Open the discussion to the group by asking, "What do others think about what [name] just said?"

3. Some of the questions are more personal than others. Because the questions sometimes focus on private matters of marriage, not everyone will feel comfortable sharing answers. However, as your group grows more comfortable with each other, you can probe deeper with more personal questions, using statements such as:
    • "That seems like the 'right answer' in theory, but does anyone have an example of how that works in real life?"
    • "If that occurred in your marriage or with your spouse, how would it make you feel?"

Bible Study (30-45 minutes)

Break into groups of two or three couples. Read Proverbs 11 and discuss:
• What principles for handling finances stand out from this passage?

• Reread verse 24. What do you think this verse means? Can you think of any examples?

• Verse 28 tells us that godly people will flourish. What do you think that means? Can you come up with any examples?

• How do you apply the principles from this passage to the finances in your life? How would you like to change that?

Read Matthew 6:19-21, 24-33 and discuss:
• What did Jesus say about our financial priorities?

• What does "the world" say our financial priorities should be? How does this differ from God's priorities regarding money?

• Do you think money can become your master? How? Have you ever felt that money—including lack of it—controlled priorities or actions in your marriage? Have you discovered any ways to keep money from running your marriage?

• If God promises to meet your needs and tells you not to worry, do you still need to make financial plans and work at being good stewards? Explain.

Closing (15-20 minutes)

Break into couples. Read Matthew 6:33. As a couple, look at your priority cards and put cards in the order you think reflects God's priorities for finances in your marriage. Spend some time discussing God's priorities for your family's finances. This time, mark the cards M for "marriage" and a number.

As a couple, discuss:

• How closely do your "realistic" financial priorities match God's priorities?

• What three actions can you take, starting this week, to bring your financial priorities more in line with God's priorities? Try to create some practical goals that you can attain so you won't be frustrated, such as arranging for your tithe or offerings to be withdrawn from your paychecks or coming up with a plan to eliminate debt.

• When you get home today, keep your discussion going. What long-term goals could help your financial priorities line up with God's priorities?

Spend a few minutes praying with your spouse about your finances. A leader can then close with prayer, asking God to give couples unity about financial priorities and discipline to reach their goals.

STUDY 6
Parenting in Sync

Why do married couples often seem to have completely different parenting styles? Of course, in spite of those differences, most parents realize they need to work together to raise their children. This lesson explores how spouses can present a united front, even if their skills, gifts, and styles are polar opposites.

Items Needed
• An obstacle course in part of the room. Use boxes, chairs, empty cans or bottles, and so forth.
• Blindfolds
• Prize for each couple

Opening (10-15 minutes)
Have couples work their way through the obstacle course. Blindfold one person to walk through the course, while that person's spouse shouts directions on how to get around the obstacles. Reward each couple as they make it through.

Once everyone has participated, gather as a group and discuss:

• If you guided your spouse, what was the toughest part? If you went through the course, what was most difficult?

• How quickly did you get into the swing of working together? Were others in the room distracting?

• Was it harder or easier than you expected to work together to achieve a joint goal?

• Let's shift gears and talk about working together as parents. What goals do you share when it comes to parenting? Why do parents need to work together in raising their kids? What happens if you don't work together?

Bible Study (30-45 minutes)
Read 1 Corinthians 12:4-27. God gives each of us different gifts, skills, and personalities that carry over into marriage and parenting.

• How can different gifts strengthen a marriage? How do these gifts strengthen the way we parent?

Great Discussions!

Remember to take your time as you work through these questions. Your goal isn't to finish fast, but to generate good discussion.

Here are three ways to make sure your discussion gets down to the depth you'd like:

1. When someone answers a question quickly or simply starts to move the group to the next question too fast, follow up with one of these go-deeper comments or questions:
   - "Please say more about what you mean…"
   - "I've never thought of that before—could you explain more?"
   - "That's the answer we expect—how would you explain that to someone who didn't know the 'expected' answer?"

2. If an answer is surprising or insightful, try the following:
   - To the person who answered, say, "That's an important insight. Talk a little more about what you just said."
   - Open the discussion to the group by asking, "What do others think about what [name] just said?"

3. Some of the questions are more personal than others. Because the questions sometimes focus on private matters of marriage, not everyone will feel comfortable sharing answers. However, as your group grows more comfortable with each other, you can probe deeper with more personal questions, using statements such as:
   - "That seems like the 'right answer' in theory, but does anyone have an example of how that works in real life?"
   - "If that occurred in your marriage or with your spouse, how would it make you feel?"

• How do you think your parenting style differs from your spouse's style? What spiritual gifts do you see reflected in your approach to parenting? in your spouse's approach?

• How have your different parenting styles caused conflict in the past? How can you use your different gifts to work together as parents?

Read Ephesians 6:1-4 and discuss:
• What does "provoke your children to anger" mean? How can parents avoid provoking their children?

• Where do you think parents find "the discipline and instruction that comes from the Lord"? Explain.

• How much time do you spend asking God to guide you in the area of parenting? In your experience, does that time increase or decrease when you face a crisis with your children? Explain. How can you and your spouse rely on God more as you raise your kids together?

Read Matthew 7:12. While this verse centers on how parents love their children, we rarely look at how it applies to parenting. Discuss:
• If you applied the "golden rule" in this verse to your parenting style, what would you focus on? How would that change the way you respond to your children?

• How does this apply to the way you respond to your spouse's parenting style?

• How can you specifically apply this "golden rule" as you respond to your children this week? to your spouse?

Read Matthew 19:13-14.

• In this passage, parents took their children to Jesus. How can you take your children to Jesus today? Why is taking your children to Jesus important?

• How might taking your children to Jesus affect their growth? your parenting style? your teamwork in parenting as a couple?

Closing (15-20 minutes)

Find a place where you can talk quietly with your spouse and discuss:

• How would you describe our parenting styles?

• Have we been working together as parents? How can we do better?

• What time each day could we pray together about and for our children, and to seek God's wisdom in our parenting?

After spouses pray with each other about their children, a leader can close the session by praying for God's blessing on each represented family.

STUDY 7
God at the Heart

Any marriage with God at the center becomes a stronger marriage. But how can you bring God into your marriage and place him at the center? This study looks at ways to make God a vital member of your marriage team.

Items Needed
- Paper for each person
- Pens or pencils
- Flip chart or white board and markers

Opening (10-15 minutes)
Start by asking couples to sit together with just their own spouse. Each couple can spend about five minutes listing all the ways they spend time together with God. These don't have to be things they do each day—even once a week or occasionally is OK. For example, you might go for a walk together as you pray each afternoon, or you might spend an hour each Sunday afternoon at a local coffee shop talking about how you sensed God working in your family during the past week.

Now spend the rest of the Opening time sharing these ideas with the larger group. Listen and jot down ideas you might want to try as a couple.

Bible Study (30-45 minutes)
Break into groups of three or four couples. Read Deuteronomy 6:1-9. This passage, a key text for the people of Israel, reminded them how to make God an important and tangible part of their daily lives. Many even repeated this text as they entered or left their homes. Now discuss:
- What physical elements in this passage jump out at you? Make a list of the actions God advised the Jews to take for making him the center of their lives.

Great Discussions!

Remember to take your time as you work through these questions. Your goal isn't to finish fast, but to generate good discussion.

Here are three ways to make sure your discussion gets down to the depth you'd like:

1. When someone answers a question quickly or simply starts to move the group to the next question too fast, follow up with one of these go-deeper comments or questions:

- "Please say more about what you mean…"
- "I've never thought of that before—could you explain more?"
- "That's the answer we expect—how would you explain that to someone who didn't know the 'expected' answer?"

2. If an answer is surprising or insightful, try the following:

- To the person who answered, say, "That's an important insight. Talk a little more about what you just said."
- Open the discussion to the group by asking, "What do others think about what [name] just said?"

3. Some of the questions are more personal than others. Because the questions sometimes focus on private matters of marriage, not everyone will feel comfortable sharing answers. However, as your group grows more comfortable with each other, you can probe deeper with more personal questions, using statements such as:

- "That seems like the 'right answer' in theory, but does anyone have an example of how that works in real life?"
- "If that occurred in your marriage or with your spouse, how would it make you feel?"

• What was the main reason for taking these actions?

• What rewards and benefits does God promise to those who follow these commands and obey them? Have you seen evidence of these in your own life?

• Reread verse 5. What do the terms *heart, soul,* and *strength* represent?

• Why do you think this passage emphasizes physical ways to make God the center of life? What physical, visual, and material items in your home might qualify as following these verses?

• Describe the ways your home might change if you apply these verses. How will your thinking change? How will your activities change?

Read Colossians 3:12-17 and discuss:
• What kind of "heart" does God want us to have in our relationship to each other and to him?

• How would you define each of the traits listed in verses 12-13?

• What steps do you see outlined for dealing with conflicts in your marriage?

• If you follow the commands in this passage, how would your marriage change? How would that place God closer to the center of everything in your life?

Closing (15-20 minutes)

Read Romans 12:9-21. While this passage lists important ways to treat one another in the body of Christ, these qualities certainly apply to marriage, too. As a large group, discuss:

• As you think of this passage and others we've looked at in this study, what are the greatest advantages of putting God at the center of your marriage?

• What are some actions you can take to apply these truths? Ask someone to write this list on a flip chart or white board.

Break into couples and discuss:

• Which action from the Opening exercise can we try in the next month to help us place God at the center of our marriage?

As a couple, pray with each other about how you can work on placing God at the center of your marriage. Ask God to help you work toward your goal and to remind both of you to make this goal a priority in your marriage. A leader can then pray, asking God to bless the efforts of the couples.

STUDY 8
Role-Playing

Real men don't do dishes? Real women don't mow lawns? Although gender roles are blurrier now than they used to be, most of us still enter marriage with expectations we hold or were raised with. This lesson helps couples keep sight of the goal—to serve together in life, marriage, and family.

Items Needed
• A set of three voting cards for each participant. These are just index cards with an initial on each card: H for husbands, W for wives, and E for either.
• A list of household responsibilities, such as doing dishes, laundry, mowing the lawn, car maintenance, changing diapers, doing finances, vacuuming, getting kids off to school, disciplining children, washing the dog, trimming bushes, and so on
• A sheet of paper for each couple
• Pens

Opening (10-15 minutes)
Give each person a set of voting cards, and read the responsibilities, one item at a time. Ask people to hold up their cards to indicate, based on social or family tradition, if they think that responsibility should be done by the husband, the wife, or either one.

Then discuss:

• What tasks or chores did your parents do when you were growing up? Did your mother or father refuse to take on certain responsibilities?

• How does your perspective reflect or differ from your parents? When you got married, did you have expectations based on gender roles? Did any of these expectations become an issue? How did you work through those?

Bible Study (30-45 minutes)
Read John 13:3-17 and discuss:
• How did the disciples respond to Jesus taking on the role of a servant?

Great Discussions!

Remember to take your time as you work through these questions. Your goal isn't to finish fast, but to generate good discussion.

Here are three ways to make sure your discussion gets down to the depth you'd like:

1. When someone answers a question quickly or simply starts to move the group to the next question too fast, follow up with one of these go-deeper comments or questions:

- "Please say more about what you mean…"
- "I've never thought of that before—could you explain more?"
- "That's the answer we expect—how would you explain that to someone who didn't know the 'expected' answer?"

2. If an answer is surprising or insightful, try the following:

- To the person who answered, say, "That's an important insight. Talk a little more about what you just said."
- Open the discussion to the group by asking, "What do others think about what [name] just said?"

3. Some of the questions are more personal than others. Because the questions sometimes focus on private matters of marriage, not everyone will feel comfortable sharing answers. However, as your group grows more comfortable with each other, you can probe deeper with more personal questions, using statements such as:

- "That seems like the 'right answer' in theory, but does anyone have an example of how that works in real life?"
- "If that occurred in your marriage or with your spouse, how would it make you feel?"

• What do you think Jesus was trying to show them?

• How does Jesus' example apply to marriage?

• Can you come up with ways this applies to your own marriage?

Read Galatians 3:28 and discuss:
• What does this verse say about roles in life?

• How does this verse affect your thinking on roles in marriage?

• When we put aside our roles and focus on a goal in marriage, how do our perspectives change?

• What's the goal of your marriage? Do you think the roles you and your spouse each take on help you accomplish that goal? Explain.

Read Romans 12:1-11 and discuss:

• How does it change your view of roles when you realize that God gives each of us different gifts?

Closing (15-20 minutes)

Break into couples. At the top of a sheet of paper, write: "Everyday Goals in Our Home." List different jobs or tasks in your home where one of you must take responsibility. The list from the Opening might help you create your own list.

Discuss who is best suited for each task in your home and why. Write your name or your spouse's (or another family member's) next to each area of responsibility. Agree that you'll revisit this list every few months. At different stages of life, one of you will probably handle certain tasks better than the other.

Close your time together with prayer. As a couple, pray that God will help you remember to keep your eyes on the goal of serving together instead of on who does what. Ask God to help you appreciate each other for the gifts you have and to give you strength and encouragement to be servants.

STUDY 9
The Purpose and the Passion

When God created male and female, he designed us to be sexual beings. His view on sex? "It is good!" This study helps couples understand God's provision of sex to help them bond and enjoy pleasure physically, emotionally, and spiritually.

Items Needed
• Construction paper cut in the shape of people (or, if possible, with men and women drawn on the paper)
• Several tubes of glue
• Pens

Opening (10-15 minutes)
Divide into groups of three to five husbands or three to five wives (with each group made up of all the same gender). Each of these small groups should read through the following scenarios, choose one, and discuss how they'd advise the individual in the situation.

• Your niece tells you that her husband wants sex much more often than she does. They've been having sex about three times a week, but he wants more. She cares for their three young children all day, and she's so tired that she prays he goes to sleep before she comes to bed. Worse, he tells her that the Bible says her body actually belongs to him, so she just needs to have faith that God will provide the energy. She wants your advice. What do you say?

• Your teenage son tells you some boys at school have been hitting on him. He's afraid he might be gay but just doesn't realize it. What do you say?

• A friend tells you he and his wife are thinking about using pornography to spice up their marital sex life. He's wondering if you think that's OK.

• Your college-aged son tells you that he and his fiancée are moving in together. They've been raised in the church and claim to be Christians, and they plan to marry after college. If they're committed to each other and the invitations are practically out the door, they wonder, "What's the big deal?" They say commitment is the real issue, not sex. How do you reply?

• A friend at work confides that she doesn't think it's necessary to have sex with her husband much anymore. After all, they already have all the children they want. She feels God primarily created sex for reproduction, so she doesn't see the point. She wants to know what you think.

• A friend tells you he's uncomfortable with some of the sexual behaviors his wife wants from him. What do you say?

After you've talked about the scenario your group chose, talk through the following questions:

• As individuals, did you have very similar or drastically different responses from the others in your group?

• Do you think the Bible offers clear guidelines regarding God's design for sex?

• In general, would you say that you agree or disagree with those biblical guidelines?

Bible Study (30-45 minutes)

Regroup into small groups of three to four couples each. Read Mark 10:6-9 and discuss:

• What do you think the phrase "God made them male and female" means? Besides physical differences, what does it mean to be male and female?

• Why did God create husband and wife to become one physically?

• Do you think a couple can be "united into one" if they don't experience sexual intimacy? Why or why not?

Read 1 Corinthians 7:2-5 and discuss:
• Why do you think the world focuses on sex so much?

• How does the world's perception of sex differ from God's design for sex?

• Would you go so far as to say that the sexual immorality we face is a spiritual battle as much as an ethical and physical one? Why or why not?

• According to these verses, how does sex offer protection to a marriage?

• Does this Scripture imply that husbands and wives should participate in sexual activity even when they don't desire to? What's the balance?

• In your own marriage relationship, have you ever struggled with what these verses teach? Explain.

Read Ephesians 5:31-33 and discuss:
• What do you think this passage means? How can marriage and sex in marriage be an analogy of Christ and the church?

• Do you think sexuality has a spiritual element? Some people say that sex within the marriage relationship can be a holy act of worship. Do you agree or disagree? Why?

• This might be an uncomfortable question, so only answer as you feel comfortable: Have you ever experienced a time of intimacy or sex that seemed like worship? Explain.

• How do we maintain sexual purity in marriage? Is this just a matter of not having affairs? More specifically, what have you done in your marriage to remain sexually pure? Explain.

• How do you think you and your spouse can keep a holy passion alive in your marriage?

Closing (15-20 minutes)

Break into couples.

God created sex in marriage. He approves of this relationship so much that his Word includes a whole book, the Song of Songs, dedicated to sex. This love note describes how Solomon was turned on by his bride! Silently, read through the eight brief chapters of this book.

On your sheet of paper, write a love note to your spouse. Get as close, personal, and specific as you want. When you're finished, let your spouse read your note.

Within marriage, sex can be like glue, because it bonds us together as couples. After you've read your notes to each other, glue your note to your spouse's (note side out). Keep this tucked in a bedroom drawer or another private place to remind you of the importance and fun of your physical bond.

Spend time praying together as a couple, asking God to help you draw closer together through times when you are intimate and particularly as you enjoy sex as God designed it within your marriage relationship.

STUDY 10
Expressions of Encouragement

One of the benefits of marriage comes from knowing that someone else is on your team. When life gets tough and situations don't go as you hope, your spouse will see you through no matter what. This study focuses on the importance of encouraging each other every day—helping each other face the emotional, physical, and spiritual tough stuff of life.

Items Needed
• Signs posted around the room that read: Compliments and Praise, Getaway, Touch, Letters and Cards, Tangible Reminders
• A sheet of paper for each person
• Pens

Opening (10-15 minutes)
When it comes to encouragement, different people respond to different things. The signs around the room represent different ways we can encourage one another.

• Compliments and Praise: Some people feel most encouraged through verbal affirmation—by hearing you directly or by hearing you tell others how wonderful he or she is.

• Getaway: When the going gets tough, some people just want to get going; if your spouse fits this description, you can encourage him or her with a surprise trip or just an evening out with friends.

• Touch: Lots of people respond most to physical affirmation. Offer hugs, kisses, cuddling, or other physical intimacy to renew energy and confidence.

• Letters and Cards: Sometimes the pen says it best. If your spouse is most encouraged by the written word, try quoting a great Scripture verse, leaving a simple love note, or taping a humorous note to the bathroom mirror.

• Tangible Reminders: Some people need something to hold; if your spouse is like this, offer a flower, a box of chocolates, a plaque, or another little gift that says, "You're special."

Walk over and stand by the sign that describes the main way you like to be encouraged. Take note of where your spouse is standing by blowing a kiss to each other! In the group where you end up, discuss:

• Tell about a time you felt discouraged and someone encouraged you this way.

• On a scale of 1 to 10, how would you rate the importance of encouragement in marriage? Do you think you and your spouse need to develop this ability? Why?

• Did the form of encouragement your spouse chose surprise you? What did you

Great Discussions!

Remember to take your time as you work through these questions. Your goal isn't to finish fast, but to generate good discussion.

Here are three ways to make sure your discussion gets down to the depth you'd like:

1. When someone answers a question quickly or simply starts to move the group to the next question too fast, follow up with one of these go-deeper comments or questions:

- "Please say more about what you mean…"
- "I've never thought of that before—could you explain more?"
- "That's the answer we expect—how would you explain that to someone who didn't know the 'expected' answer?"

2. If an answer is surprising or insightful, try the following:

- To the person who answered, say, "That's an important insight. Talk a little more about what you just said."
- Open the discussion to the group by asking, "What do others think about what [name] just said?"

3. Some of the questions are more personal than others. Because the questions sometimes focus on private matters of marriage, not everyone will feel comfortable sharing answers. However, as your group grows more comfortable with each other, you can probe deeper with more personal questions, using statements such as:

- "That seems like the 'right answer' in theory, but does anyone have an example of how that works in real life?"
- "If that occurred in your marriage or with your spouse, how would it make you feel?"

expect him or her to choose? How can knowing your spouse's preference help you encourage your spouse in the future?

Bible Study (30-45 minutes)

Now form groups of three to four couples each. Read Ecclesiastes 4:7-12 and discuss:

• Do you think encouragement is a benefit God had in mind when he designed marriage? Explain.

• According to this passage, what practical benefits do we gain when we encourage each other in our marriages? How have you experienced these benefits in your marriage?

• How does your spouse's encouragement help you grow emotionally and spiritually?

• Read Romans 1:11-12. Take a piece of paper, and rewrite these two verses to reflect a way you can encourage your spouse. If you want to, share what you wrote with your small group.

Closing (15-20 minutes)

Break into couples. Take a blank sheet, and number 1 to 10 down the side. At the top of the page, write "10 Things I Like About You." This exercise is simple—list 10 things you like about your spouse. Share the list with your spouse, and give details about why you appreciate each trait on the list. As you chat, ask your spouse how you can do better at encouraging him or her in these areas—especially using the way your spouse chose in the Opening exercise. Spend time praying together, asking God to help you draw closer together through encouragement.

fifteen

MOVIE NIGHTS
FOR COUPLES

Think of all the ways you can use a couples' movie night in your ministry! Movies can often express issues and truths (as well as lies) about marriage and family in more compelling ways than small group studies or teachings can.

Movie nights work well for small groups, couples who are close friends, or groups of couples who are relative strangers. A movie night can also be a great place to invite unchurched couples: The setting's comfortable, and the questions don't really have right or wrong answers—just each person's opinion.

Some tips for making movie nights a success:

• Meet on a regular basis—every month or two. Meet more often if you want.

• Meet in a home. When people feel at ease, they'll be more comfortable sharing after the movie.

• Make sure someone in the group previews the movie. Not every movie is right for every group.

• Urge couples to give each movie a try.

• Serve food! Do it potluck style, or pool your money for some pizzas.

• Keep it casual. Encourage people to kick off their shoes, sprawl out on the carpet, and make themselves comfortable.

• Arrange for child care at a different home. Or ask each couple to make their own arrangements. In any event, people need to relax and enjoy the movie.

• Keep discussions casual. The questions will prompt people to explore spiritual issues in the movies and talk about their own lives and marriages.

• Be sensitive to time. Some couples will need to head home to family and other responsibilities. Know what's right for your group.

• Have fun! This isn't a Bible study or a film class. So relax and enjoy the time with your spouse and your friends.

MOVIE 1
While You Were Sleeping (1995)

Genre: Romantic Comedy

Length: About 103 minutes

Rating: PG

Plot: Lucy Moderatz is infatuated with a man who comes through her subway tollbooth every day. On Christmas Day, she sees him get pushed onto the tracks and saves him from being hit by a train. But he's knocked unconscious and taken to the hospital, where he lies in a coma. When she tries to find out if he's OK, a miscommunication causes his family to think Lucy is his fiancée. Having no family, Lucy loves being embraced by this family. She doesn't want to tell them that she has no relationship with their son. In the meantime, she finds herself falling in love with the unconscious man's brother.

Discussion Questions

• While visiting Peter in the hospital, Lucy says, "Have you ever fallen in love with someone you've never even talked to?" What first attracted you to your spouse? Did you have feelings before you really knew each other?

• Lucy later learns that Peter isn't the nice person she imagines him to be. How did your view of your spouse change when you got to know him or her better?

• Lucy notes that she went from having nothing to being a fiancée, a daughter, a sister, a granddaughter, and a friend. What roles do you have in your marriage and family? How do you feel about each role?

• Peter's family immediately embraced Lucy. Has your spouse's family warmly welcomed you? How do you feel about your relationship with your in-laws? What would you change? What parts would you like to make stronger?

MOVIE 2
What Women Want (2000)
Genre: Romantic Comedy
Length: About 127 minutes
Rating: PG-13

Plot: Nick Marshall, a stereotypical ladies' man, is more interested in what women can do for him than in what they think. After a freak accident, he can hear the thoughts of every woman around him. At first, it drives him crazy, and he learns that most women don't think he's all that great. But then he realizes that he can connect easily with women when he knows their thoughts.

Discussion Questions
• Would you want to know what people of the opposite sex are thinking? Explain. What advantages and disadvantages would that ability give you?

• What are your communication strengths as a couple? How can you strengthen weaker areas? Since God doesn't give us the ability to read each other's thoughts, how can you better communicate your needs, thoughts, and feelings to your spouse?

• Why is it so hard for men and women to communicate with each other? What did Nick learn by being able to read women's thoughts?

MOVIE 3
Yours, Mine, and Ours (2005)
Genre: Comedy
Length: About 90 minutes
Rating: PG

Plot: Widower Frank Beardsley, a Coast Guard admiral, runs his family like he runs his ship—with rules, charts, and organization. His eight kids are kept orderly and appropriate at all times with discipline and direction. Helen North has raised her 10 kids with a free-spirit and free-expression attitude. Her house is in constant chaos. When high school sweethearts Frank and Helen meet again at a reunion, the sparks return and they get married right away—without telling their families. But problems begin immediately when they try to bring the two families together under one roof. The only thing bringing the kids together is a mutual desire to break up their parents' new marriage.

Discussion Questions
• What differences between your families have you worked through? What strengths did your families bring to your marriage family?

• If you've been married before, what was it like to join two families into one? How have you worked to bring your children together into a new family? How did they feel about your new marriage?

• What differences do you see between getting married the first time and getting remarried with children? How much influence should your children have in your new relationship? How do you determine when to follow your children's opinions and when you need to just make decisions as adults?

• Helen and Frank try to get the kids to help remodel their house. Compare what builders need to construct a house with what you need to construct a family. How are these lists similar and different?

• In the movie, the kids conspired to break their parents apart. What forces try to tear your marriage apart? How can you combat them? How can you guard your marriage against all the things that can work to break it apart?

MOVIE 4
Facing the Giants (2006)
Genre: Drama
Length: About 111 minutes
Rating: PG

Plot: In the six years that Grant Taylor has coached the Shiloh Eagles high school football team, they've never had a winning season. Now a group of parents and administrators plot to replace him. Then he learns why he and his wife have been unable to have the children they desire. Overwhelmed by failure and defeat, Grant cries out to God. He decides to lead the team in a new way—based on faith and believing that God can do the impossible. Soon a revival sweeps through the school, but the Eagles face their toughest challenge yet against a stronger team—the Giants.

Discussion Questions

• Grant and Brooke Taylor face several large stresses—job difficulties, infertility, and a faith crisis. What difficulties have you faced as a couple? How did you each react to them?

• What effect did these times have on your marriage? Did you feel distant and divided from each other, or stronger and part of a team? How do you look back on these difficult times?

• When the world seems to be against you, how do you and your spouse support each other? How can your spouse show support when you need it?

• What part does faith play in your marriage? How can you pray for your spouse? How can your spouse pray for you? Share a time when your family has seen God do the "impossible."

MOVIE 5
Father of the Bride (1991)
Genre: Comedy
Length: About 105 minutes
Rating: PG

Plot: George and Nina Banks are surprised when their daughter, Annie, returns from Rome and announces her engagement. George becomes stubborn and irrational in his determination to dislike Annie's fiancé and the wedding. As the wedding planning progresses, George begins to accept his future son-in-law, the prospect of giving his daughter away, and the transformation of his little girl into a young woman.

Discussion Questions

• What did you find most humorous in the movie? What did you relate to?

• How did George and Nina balance each other? How do you and your spouse balance each other?

• George admits he doesn't like change. How does he deal with the prospect of change? How do you deal with change in your family?

• George often reflects on how fast the time with Annie has gone. What memories did he cherish? What do you want to remember as you reflect on your children's time at home?

• What can you and your spouse do to make sure your child chooses a spouse with solid character and who wholeheartedly loves God? What can you do to make sure your child will be a spouse with those traits?

MOVIE 6
Cinderella Man (2005)

Genre: Biography/Drama
Length: About 145 minutes
Rating: PG-13 for brutal boxing violence

Plot: *Cinderella Man* tells the true story of Depression-era boxer James Braddock. Braddock loses all his possessions in the stock market crash of 1929. In 1934, he returns to the ring to feed and provide for his family. With character, courage, and determination, he becomes a symbol of hope and perseverance to a hopeless nation as he fights to save the family he loves.

Discussion Questions

• Why was the life of James and Mae Braddock so powerful? Why did his story become an inspiration to the country?

• How did Mae deal with her fears for her husband's safety, yet support him and his choices for their family? How do you face fears about your marriage and family?

• What issues did James Braddock struggle with as he tried to provide for his family? How did he respond to discouragement? How do you respond when trials bring discouragement? How can you support your spouse in hardship?

MOVIE 7
My Big Fat Greek Wedding (2002)

Genre: Romantic Comedy

Length: About 95 minutes

Rating: PG

Plot: As a Greek woman, Toula is expected to marry a Greek man. When she turns 30, she hears with increasing frequency that she looks old. Breaking from the cultural mold, Toula quits working at her family's restaurant, goes to college, and begins working at her aunt's travel agency. She meets Ian Miller, a non-Greek, and falls in love. As they plan their wedding, Ian, Toula, and their families learn to understand and appreciate what makes each of them unique.

Discussion Questions

• Describe the differences between your family and your spouse's family.

• What do you most appreciate about your in-laws? What have you learned from them? How have they influenced you?

• What examples of miscommunication and misunderstanding did you see in the movie? Do you ever feel that you and your in-laws speak different languages? How have you learned to speak the language of your in-laws?

• Remember the wedding toast given by Toula's dad? How can your attitude and your view of your in-laws affect your thoughts and actions?

MOVIE 8
The Incredibles (2004)
Genre: Animated Action Comedy
Length: About 115 minutes
Rating: PG for action violence

Plot: Former superheroes Bob and Helen Parr, along with their children, Violet, Dash, and Jack, live average, anonymous lives. Lawsuits have banned all superheroes from active duty. But Bob, formerly known as Mr. Incredible, yearns for the "glory days." Discouraged with his life, he jumps at the opportunity to be a "super" again when he receives a top-secret assignment. However, it turns out to be a trap. They must all come together to save their family and the world.

Discussion Questions

• What are you passionate about? What do you feel you were created to do? Can you be content with who you are, yet long for something greater?

• What lessons of honesty and communication did you see in the movie? What repercussions of dishonesty and lack of communication did you see?

• Violet says to Dash, "Mom and Dad's life could be in danger. Or worse… their marriage!" As a culture, do we grasp truth in this statement? Explain.

• Mr. Incredible experienced a turning point when he thought he lost his whole family. What moments or circumstances in your life helped you realize what's most important to you?

• What does this movie communicate about unity in marriage and family life?

MOVIE 9
Pride and Prejudice (2005)
Genre: Drama/Romance

Length: About 130 minutes

Rating: PG

Plot: *Pride and Prejudice* tells the story of the five Bennet sisters: Jane, Elizabeth, Mary, Kitty, and Lydia. With no male heirs, at least one sister must marry well to support the family when Mr. Bennet dies. When the wealthy Mr. Bingley arrives in town, Mrs. Bennet is confident of a match for her oldest daughter, Jane. However, Bennet's best friend, Mr. Darcy, disapproves of the match. Disgusted by Mr. Darcy's apparent pride, Elizabeth vows to "loathe" him forever. The main story centers on the evolving relationship between Elizabeth and Mr. Darcy amid the social structure of 18th-century England.

Discussion Questions

• How did you and your spouse meet? What were your first impressions of each other?

• What characters in the movie did you identify with most? What did you find refreshing in the movie? What didn't you like?

• How do modern-day customs compare to the 18th-century social norms portrayed in the movie? How did Mr. Darcy and Elizabeth approach relationships and marriage?

• What role do you think pride plays in relationships? Explain.

• What effect did Mr. and Mrs. Bennet's marriage have on their daughters? What occurs in marriage and family life when a spouse disengages from situations or operates on his or her own agenda?

MOVIE 10
Cheaper by the Dozen (2003)
Genre: Comedy
Length: 98 minutes
Rating: PG

Plot: Tom and Kate Baker have 12 children and live a simple, happy, yet chaotic life. When Tom receives his dream job—coaching football in Chicago—he uproots his family from their small-town life. As Tom begins his new job, Kate leaves for a book tour to publicize her first book. Soon, the family begins to unravel. A family crisis forces Tom and Kate to reevaluate and remember what defines true success and happiness.

Discussion Questions

• Have you ever experienced moments when you felt you were experts at managing chaos in your home?

• What priorities hurt the family, and what priorities benefited the family? Talk about God's priorities versus the world's priorities in relation to family.

• What aspects of Tom and Kate's marriage do you admire? What actions can you and your spouse take to be sure you still "got the heat" years from now?

• What do you admire in their parenting? What weaknesses do you see?

• When Tom resigns, he says, "If I screw up raising my kids, nothing I achieve will matter much." Is this a true statement? Why or why not?

MOVIE 11
Joe Versus the Volcano (1990)
Genre: Allegorical Fantasy
Length: About 100 minutes
Rating: PG

Plot: Joe, a downtrodden copywriter and hypochondriac, is diagnosed with a terminal "brain cloud." Because Joe doesn't have long to live, a businessman hires Joe to throw himself into a volcano on a small South Pacific island. This will appease the gods the islanders believe in and secure a business deal. Joe's adventure changes his life.

Discussion Questions
• In the beginning of the movie, can you relate to Joe? Why or why not?

• How is Joe's life at the beginning of the movie like the lives of other people you know?

• How does Joe's adventure change him?

• In the movie, Patricia Graynamore says, "My father says almost the whole world's asleep. Everybody you know, everybody you see, everybody you talk to. He says only a few people are awake. And they live in a state of constant, total amazement." In what ways are Christians "awake"?

• Are there ways you live your life asleep?

• Do you have a sense of adventure together as a married couple?

• As a couple, how can you live together in a state of amazement?

MOVIE 12
Life Is Beautiful (1997)

Genre: Drama/Comedy

Length: 118 minutes

Rating: PG-13 for Holocaust-related thematic elements

Plot: An Italian Jew uses his sense of humor to win the heart of the woman who becomes his wife. Later, during World War II, his humor and ingenuity save the life of his son in a Nazi death camp.

Discussion Questions

• Guido, the protagonist, found beauty in simple things. Rank yourself from 1 to 10: At what level do you find beauty in daily life?

• The characters of this movie discovered beauty in life by finding joy in the small things together. How can you experience a beautiful life with your spouse each day, no matter what circumstances you face?

• Guido focused on his family's well-being. Describe a time your spouse sacrificed for you or your family.

• Describe a challenging time in your life. How did living through that period affect your ability to feel joy and to enjoy life?

• Do you believe God works through difficult situations in our lives? Why or why not?

MOVIE 13
Kramer vs. Kramer (1979)

Genre: Drama

Length: 105 minutes

Rating: PG

Plot: Ted Kramer had no idea how to care for his young son—until Ted's wife, Joanna, walked out the door and didn't come back. Ted discovers how to care for his son—and how to fight for custody when Joanna reappears.

Discussion Questions

• Divorce touches most of us in some way. How has it affected your life?

• What kinds of battles in the movie reflected battles you've witnessed in divorce situations?

• As you watched Ted and his son, did it remind you of your own relationships with people you're close to? Explain.

• What did you think of Joanna's actions and attitudes? How did you see her change as the story progressed?

• If you could snap your fingers and eliminate the possibility of couples getting divorced, would you do it? Why or why not?

MOVIE 14
City Slickers (1991)
Genre: Adventure/Comedy
Length: 112 minutes
Rating: PG-13

Plot: Mitch, Phil, and Ed are middle-aged guys having midlife crises. Their solution: Experience an action-packed, two-week cattle drive from New Mexico to Colorado. On the drive they meet Curly, a weather-worn trail boss who challenges Mitch to find the "one thing" in life that matters.

Discussion Questions
• Which character did you connect with most in the movie? Why?

• What adventures have you undertaken to find meaning in life?

• Whether or not you've had a midlife crisis, tell about a time you felt restless.

• What are some positive ways you've dealt with restless feelings? What have you tried that *didn't* work?

• If Curly stuck his gnarled finger in your face and asked you to identify your "one thing," what would it be? Why?

MOVIE 15
The Family Man (2000)

Genre: Comedy/Fantasy

Length: 125 minutes

Rating: PG-13 for sensuality and some language

Plot: Jack Campbell, a fast-lane investment broker, doesn't have a single regret. He has it all: fast car, fast career track, gorgeous girlfriend. But one day, he wakes up to the life that might have been—if he hadn't broken up with his college sweetheart. In this new life, he has kids, a van that won't start, and a less-than-spectacular career. For Jack, which life offers the most satisfying rewards?

Discussion Questions

• This movie focuses on values. What does Jack value? How do his values compare with yours?

• Who do you relate to in this movie—Kate (the wife) or Jack? Why?

• Tell about a time you had to make a tough choice between what seemed glamorous and what was best for your marriage or family.

• If you could see how your life would turn out if you'd made different choices, would you want to know? Why or why not?

twenty ideas FOR CONNECTING WITH OTHER COUPLES

While serving together provides a great way for individual couples to grow closer to each other and to the Lord (see Section 2), couples who take the step of becoming a part of your church's organized marriage ministry program might want to serve together as a group— perhaps accomplishing something on a larger scale that comes from strength in numbers. Whether it's an official marriage ministry group of couples—or just a number of couples who want to explore new ways to serve—the following ideas can help them connect with each other and reach out to other married couples and families in your church, community, and beyond.

10 SMALL GROUP IDEAS

To help couples in your church connect with other couples, why not add to your church's small group ministry? Establish small groups just for couples, for parents, and for whole families. This is another way to expand the area you call "marriage ministry." Some couples might get active in a small group, but they'd never come to a marriage ministry event. Yet you're helping them strengthen their marriage and family relationships and increase fellowship with other Christians.

IDEA 1
first meeting do's and don'ts

You've launched a small group for couples or families. You'll be taking a diverse group of individuals and forming them into a community. They come from different backgrounds and families, have different likes and dislikes, span a range of ages, and possess different spiritual maturities. How can you create an atmosphere that allows people to blend comfortably and not feel threatened? Set the right tone by following these ground rules as you lead the group's first meeting.

Don't begin with preconceived expectations. It takes time for couples to trust you and other couples in the group. So do the best job you can to lead, but avoid setting unrealistic expectations. Take what you get and build from there.

Don't allow people to feel pressured. Give them freedom to participate as they feel comfortable. Be careful not to put anyone on the spot. Each person will have different levels of comfort.

Don't ask people to read aloud until you know they're comfortable. Someone might have a reading disability. The last thing you want to do is embarrass anyone.

Don't assume everyone will want to pray aloud. Urge people to pray if they want to, and then you can close. It often takes time for people to feel comfortable praying in front of others. The same goes for comfort level when spouses pray together. You might need to help people get to that level.

Don't ask people to give spontaneous "testimonies." Some people might just be shy, while others might not be Christians or know what a testimony is (in fact, it's best to avoid using church lingo completely).

Do ask people to let you know if they feel uncomfortable praying or reading aloud. They can enjoy and learn and grow in your group without fear that you'll put them on the spot. Tell people to inform you if they change their minds as they feel more comfortable with other group members.

Do ask people ahead of time if they're willing to share their faith stories. This gives people time to prepare what they want to say—and lessens the chance they'll ramble on and on.

Do ask for volunteers to read Scripture. Simply ask, "Would someone like to read verse 28?" This gives people a chance to read aloud if they want to. If no one volunteers after a few seconds, say "OK, I'll go ahead and read that passage."

IDEA 2
front-burner focus

The coffee is lukewarm, the cookies gone, and people are heading for the door. While your small group meeting has officially ended, what will the couples or families who attend do until you meet again? During the week ahead, how can what they've studied stay on the front burner?

There are many ways to keep your small group alive and functioning between meetings. Some are as simple as encouraging couples or families to sit together in church or to work together at a volunteer event. Others require more organization, like forming chili cook-off or trivia night teams. Use the dynamics of your group to promote togetherness. For example, if the families have young children, urge them to organize play dates and picnics.

Modern technology can also help. During the week, contact people through e-mail and phone calls. For those intimidated by the small group setting, your personal connection might be what keeps them coming back. And don't forget couple to couple or family to family connections. If all agree, supply the group with phone and e-mail listings so people can contact each other.

All types of social interaction, from casual cookouts to morning coffees, can also benefit families. But as you encourage people to mix, remind them about maintaining boundaries. For example, all group members should be invited to events to avoid cliques. And discourage the husband of one couple from meeting with the wife of another, and stress same-gender or couple meetings only.

IDEA 3
beyond connecting

Getting to know other couples can be hard. Even in a small group setting, deeper and meaningful relationships can be elusive.

This activity can help couples in a small group connect by getting to know others on a deeper, personal level—without being too invasive.

Each couple should write down one or two things they enjoy doing as a couple. Or they might list something unique about the way they celebrate an important event such as an anniversary. The idea is to list something meaningful to their relationship—something that says, "This is us."

Have couples share what they've written. As you listen, be looking for ways the whole group together can do what each couple answers.

For example, if a little cafe downtown was the spot of one couple's proposal, your small group might meet there for dinner or dessert. While at the cafe, urge that couple to talk about themselves. The spotlight is on them. How does the memory or the place or what they enjoy reveal who the couple is and what they value?

Your group doesn't need to do this connecting time every week. Perhaps intersperse these outings once a month until every couple takes a turn.

We establish bonds and start close friendships when we share experiences together. Inviting others into our world to share what we care about, what we dream, what makes us a "couple," opens up our lives to others.

IDEA 4
create a group covenant

Every small group needs guidelines to function effectively. Your small group's covenant is a formal agreement that lays out the parameters of the small group. A covenant is binding on all parties—but only as long as parties choose to be bound. Your small group covenant helps hold members accountable to each other. Use these ideas to help your group create its covenant.

What to Include in a Group Covenant

Some items belong in almost every small group's covenant. Members of your group might suggest these items, but if no one does, you can suggest the ones that seem appropriate for your group to consider.

• Meeting time and location. This statement should include times the meeting will begin and end, the day of the week when your group will meet, the group's meeting place(s), and how often the group will meet.

• Policy for dealing with exceptions to regular meeting time. What will your group do during severe weather, holidays, or an all-church function? Who will make calls or send e-mails to group members?

• The purpose of your group. Yes, you know that you're a couples or family group. But will you primarily study the Bible, focus on fellowship with each other, or study a non-Bible book? What's the purpose of the activity? Is it for young married couples to develop relationships with other young married couples? Is it to learn more about faith? If you don't have a clear purpose, the group can easily veer off course. Listing the purpose in your covenant will help keep the group on track.

• Commitment to starting and ending on time. This allows members to make your small group's meetings a priority and plan their schedules around the meeting. If you consistently wait for people who run late, you run the risk of giving others "permission" to be late, too. If your group's meeting consistently runs longer than you agree to, some members might stop participating, especially if they're dealing with a job or baby sitters.

• Attendance accountability. Agree that group members will contact you (the leader) if they can't attend a meeting. This lets you know how many members of the group to expect. If you face an unusual case of many absent members, you can even decide to cancel the meeting. This honors your time.

• Commitment to confidentiality. Group members should be able to bring up issues and express opinions without fear that anyone outside the group will hear them. This builds trust. What's said in the group should stay in the group.

• Agreeing to participate in group discussions. Some shy members won't talk at all. Urge all participants to share, but don't embarrass those who can't think of anything to add at a particular point in the discussion.

• Agreeing to take turns. One or more members might monopolize your discussions if you don't agree to give each other time to speak. Occasionally, as the leader, you might need to give a gentle reminder. Say something like, "What do others think about what [person's name] is saying?" or "Do others have thoughts about that topic?" Using the word *others* reminds the person dominating the conversation that it's time to be quiet for a while. Another way to build participation is to agree that your group will regularly use smaller subgroups for discussion.

• Agreeing to attend meetings and social activities regularly. For members of the group to form relationships, they need to be as faithful in attendance as possible. Those who attend inconsistently will feel like outsiders as the group grows together over time.

• Commitment to pray for one another. Praying together can take many forms—prayer request lists, praying as God leads during corporate prayer times, or praying for each other between meetings.

• Be a facilitator, not a dictator. As couples or families gather to form your small group and then put together a covenant, you'll have more "buy-in" if you act as a facilitator while members generate ideas. A top-down list of rules simply isn't as effective as an agreement that the group as a whole creates.

• Record all ideas from group members. Ask members of your group if they agree that drawing up an agreement for the small group is beneficial. Discuss how having a covenant would be better than not having one. Ask if anyone has been in a small group previously, if those groups had covenants or ground rules, and what items were included. This can help initiate brainstorming about what your group's covenant should include. Stimulate the discussion, if necessary, by suggesting items as fundamental as time, place, and confidentiality.

• Divide and conquer. You can involve more people and move almost twice as fast if you split your group into two to work on elements for your covenant. One subgroup can work on the meeting details of the group (time and place), while the other subgroup focuses on valued qualities (being on time, confidentiality). Facilitate the activity by recording ideas generated by each group on a flip chart or white board. The whole group can then decide which items to include in the covenant.

• Ask group members to prepare in advance. Encourage them to come to the meeting with a written list of ideas they believe should be incorporated in the group's agreement. Suggest that individuals leave their names off their lists. Write all the items on a flip chart or a white board, and decide as a group which items to include in your covenant.

IDEA 5
encouraging actions

Encouragement is an integral part of the church and small groups. What would happen if families in your small group encouraged other families every day? The result would be stronger individuals, stronger families, a stronger small group, and a stronger church! Try the following suggestions:

• Follow up on prayer requests. Many times a prayer request is for an event on a specific date. Doctor appointments, medical tests, or even awkward family gatherings are some examples of things group members might request prayer for. Call the other family on that day to say that you were praying and to find out how things went to remind the other family that you care.

• Make a phone call before an event. This is similar to the previous idea, except that you call *before* the difficult experience. Make a brief phone call the evening before, and let the other family know that you'll be praying for them. You can offer to pray on the phone together, too.

• Remember children. The children of the families in your group are involved in sports, music, and church events. Send kids a note of congratulations or recognition of a job well done. It will probably mean more to the parent than the child, but that's OK.

• Buddy chores. Give one of the families in your group your assistance for a morning. Ask when you can come over and help with a task. Most jobs go better when people work together.

• Send an article or cartoon. If you see an article or cartoon that somehow relates to one of the families in your group, send it. It might mirror a funny situation a parent described about their kids. Or maybe it's a helpful parenting article. Just attach a sticky note saying, "I saw this and thought of you."

• Sit together at church. A new family might feel all alone in a large crowd. Invite them to sit with you. Or simply invite other families from your group: "Let's all sit together in the fourth and fifth rows on the left side next Sunday."

• Initiate a group project for one family. Gather the whole group together to tackle a job for one of the families in your small group. A group of people can accomplish a lot of yardwork or a needed home improvement in a short time. Your children will have a blast helping, too.

• Invite someone to your child's event. Because most biological families are scattered, the families in your small group can serve as your extended family. Invite other families to your child's concert or sporting event, and attend their children's events as well. Your kids will be delighted with the extra attention.

• Make a long-term commitment to pray. Let other families know that you intend to pray for them each day for a specific length of time. Pray for children away at college for the school year. Or pray each day for someone out of work until he or she finds a job.

• Meet a financial need. God might make you aware of a family in your small group going through a difficult time. Depending on the circumstances, your family or several families in your group might be able to provide a financial gift. It could be cash for a night out, a supermarket gift card, or setting up a temporary fund to cover significant expenses during a crisis.

IDEA 6
worship strength training

Scripture contains many stories of families standing together among the assembly of God's people. For example, before the Israelites passed into the Promised Land, Moses held a great assembly to remind them what God had taught since the exodus from Egypt. This was just one of many assemblies where the people gathered to listen to God's spokesperson talk of his Word and the difference it would make in their lives. In the midst of it all, God's people worshipped him. This picture occurs in the New Testament as well. Look at the epistles, and remember that the church wasn't a building; it was a gathering of families meeting in a home.

The dynamic of families worshipping side by side takes place today both in "big church" and small groups as well. When children are part of your small group, they can bring a wonderful, fresh perspective to worship.

Take advantage of what's "in" about worship today, such as:

• A longer worship time. Often, people would sing a song or two before the teaching and call it worship. If possible, have your small group's worship time be a mixture of several songs, with prayers and testimonies sprinkled in. Again, don't forget to include kids—you'll be amazed by the simplicity and depth of their prayers and stories of how they're living out their faith.

• Focused toward God. In the past, children in Sunday school sang songs worlds apart from the ones adults sang in church. Children sang about Father Abraham who had many sons, and about being in the Lord's army. Adults sang hymns about God as "Holy, Holy, Holy" and "A Mighty Fortress." Take advantage of worship choruses that your small group can sing *to* rather than *about* God. Most likely, the children and adults in your small group will already know many of them from church.

• More instruments in the band. Think how fresh your small group worship time would be if parents and kids both brought the variety of instruments they play to your worship time!

You'll discover how great it is to have whole families involved in small group worship.

The way children pray and praise will touch hearts and strengthen the bonds of marriages and families.

IDEA 7
child-care solutions

Before long, most small groups face the issue of what to do about child care. In fact, some couples might say they can't join your group because they can't find anyone to care for their children. So be proactive and help solve the problem before it starts. Try these ideas in your group:

• On-site child care. If you meet in a home or other location where this would work logistically, urge group members to bring children along to your meetings. Parents can pool their money to pay for on-site child care. Of course, you'll want to prescreen any potential child-care worker who watches children as part of a church-sanctioned activity. Check to see if your church has a screening process in place that your group can use.

• Older kids care for younger ones. If some small group members have preteens and teenagers who are mature enough to watch younger children, your group can pay these kids to watch the younger children during your meeting.

• Recruit from the youth group. Check to see if the high school group has interest in providing child care as a youth group fundraiser. Of course, any teen who watches children should be certified, screened, or under adult supervision.

• Piggyback with existing child care. Could your small group meet at church when child care is already available? Try not to take advantage of volunteers who provide this care. For example, you might need to adjust how long your group meets each week to fit the child-care schedule.

• Rotate among group members. If most or all of your group members have young children, rotate the child-care responsibility among group members. Ideally, this would take place on-site where the group meets. This means no extra stop to pick up kids on the way home. Plus, when the meeting is over, everyone—including children—can enjoy the group's informal fellowship time.

IDEA 8
progressive dinner

Plan a progressive dinner for a social event to kick off a couples or family small group. The meal is easy to plan, and it will draw people together in greater unity.

• Recruit four or five couples from your new group who are willing to host everyone at their place for the progressive dinner. If your group starts in the fall, host your dinner at the end of the summer. This allows families to spill into backyards. If possible, give every couple in the group a chance to host one of the courses. Possible courses are appetizers, soup, salad, main course, and dessert.

• Hold a planning meeting. Pick a date, choose a menu, and decide who'll serve which course. Be sure to discuss budget, because the family hosting the main course might incur greater expense than the couple hosting the salad course. But two or three couples can pitch in for the more expensive parts of the meal.

The couple serving appetizers might want to have some fun get-to-know-you questions or games for families to do at the first stop. The couple serving dessert might plan a short devotional for a good way to end the night.

• Use disposable plates, cups, and flatware to minimize cleanup. This allows families to move on to the next home before the night gets too long. Encourage each home to decorate creatively. At the first home, arrange the seating so families can meet people they don't know well yet.

• Be sure to ask God's blessing for the evening, and thank him for the food. Encourage families to continue getting to know the people they met at this event.

IDEA 9
intergenerational and family small groups

Have you ever wished that you could lead a small group composed of entire households and families? Why can't whole families pursue the same spiritual things together? Think how great it would be to come together on purpose to experience the benefits of multigenerational family life!

When multiple generations and families connect, a continuity of passing on faith occurs that can't happen when generations don't interact with one another. Modeling becomes a primary part of the process God uses to transfer faith from generation to generation. Psalm 78:1-7 gives a beautiful picture of generations coming together and continuing to pass on the faith to future generations.

If you want to start or join an intergenerational/family small group, keep these basic principles in mind:

• Keep it simple! This isn't brain surgery. You're encouraging families and multigenerational groups to do the same things we encourage individuals and couples to do: study God's Word, pray, sing praises, fellowship, and reach out.

• Believe it and live it! Encourage church leaders to embrace, adopt, and model this concept. Recruit members of the pastoral staff and/or lay leaders and their families to commit to being a part of intergenerational/family groups.

• Don't suggest replacing age-segregated groups. Family and intergenerational groups provide another option for people in your church; there's nothing at all wrong with people continuing in their more typical groups *and* participating in an age-integrated family group as well.

• Integrate your "family group" into the church's overall small group ministry. Again, present it as an option. A lot of people might not think to ask for this option, but they might choose these groups if given the opportunity.

• Pass it on! Communicate your commitment to the body. Encourage people in your sphere of influence to embrace, adopt, and model these groups.

• If your small group is successful, start new groups. Encourage other thriving groups to spawn new groups.

When your group begins, communicate both subtly and clearly the reasons and expectations for having this type of group. Some suggestions:

• Encourage families to sit together at your meetings. Don't meet together only to then segregate once you're in the same room or the same home.

• Parents are in charge of their own kids. No need for child care!

• Remember that you're breaking new ground. This will take your commitment and the commitment of the families who give it a shot. It's not easy or simple, and it probably won't look "perfect." Offer each other plenty of grace.

IDEA 10
fresh prayer

While your couples or family-oriented small group will naturally spend time praying for the needs of family members who are part of the group, don't limit yourself to these self-directed prayers. Try mixing in these topics to bring freshness and energy to your prayer times.

• Pastor and staff. Ask your pastor and ministry staff at your church to make your group aware of specific prayer requests. Let them know that you want to teach your families the importance of prayer. You'll have no shortage of items for your prayer lists. Remember to follow up when God answers these requests.

• The church directory. Bring in directories of church members, and encourage families to pray for other families by name. Also, use these times as a reminder to pray for individuals and families who visit your church.

• Missionaries. Request a list of the missionaries your church supports. Compile information about them, their families, the country where they serve, and specific prayer requests they've made recently. What a great way to teach children in your group about how God works in families all around the world.

• Newspaper or newsmagazine prayers. Bring in daily newspapers and weekly newsmagazines, and have family members clip out items the group can pray for. Pray specifically about each situation, need, or person by name.

• Influence. Take time to talk about various influences in the world today. Pray about each of these as you see fit, asking God to do his will in circumstances that sometimes seem too complex to understand.

10 OUTREACH IDEAS

While small groups oriented toward couples and families provide connections to other people in your church, the following ideas offer a way to reach out beyond the people in your congregation and the walls of your church to the couples and families of your neighborhood, community, and world.

IDEA 1
the cause of orphans

Offer an adoption conference to minister to your church and community. Here's a basic plan for a conference:

• Plan several large group sessions. Primary speakers can share vision, with topics such as God's heart for adoption, the church's responsibility, and barriers to adoption. These speakers might be church leaders or invited guests from adoption ministries. Ideally, they've gone through the adoption process themselves.

• Organize a number of seminar sessions. The number of sessions depends on how many people you expect to attend. Aim for just a dozen or so people—six couples—to end up in each seminar session. Keep these groups small enough so couples can choose topics related to their situation and feel comfortable asking individual questions. Seminar speakers should have personal experience with the workshop's topic (for example, foster parents speaking at a foster care seminar). For a finance seminar, adoptive parents can share their story, while a representative from a financial aid organization answers questions. Other seminar ideas include domestic, international, and special needs adoptions; infertility and adoption; and orphan ministries.

> Check out the following Web sites for additional information.
> • Family Life's Hope for Orphans — www.familylife.com/hopefororphans/
> • Shaohannah's Hope — www.shaohannahshope.org
> • Dave Thomas Foundation for Adoption—www.davethomasfoundation.org

• Provide resource tables and displays. Use this area to provide information not covered in sessions and to distribute supporting material related to seminars and large group sessions. Include books, related messages on CDs, and handouts at resource tables. Handouts might include lists of Web sites, books, necessary documents, financial aid organizations, and companies providing adoption benefits, as well as country profiles, adoption tax credit information, and questions to ask prospective agencies. Invite adoption organizations to set up booths as well.

• Create conference folders for each couple attending. Include a church map, name tag, schedule, seminar options, and outlines for large group sessions.

• Recruit volunteers to serve as hosts to greet people, do registration, and answer questions throughout the event. Label seminar rooms to ease movement between sessions. Other volunteers can organize food and refreshments.

IDEA 2
footloose and fancy free

Give parents an evening out, with free babysitting and a fun-filled night for their kids. While you can offer this event any time of year, you might consider Christmas to allow parents to shop without their kids in tow. Here are some ideas for organizing and holding a successful event:

• Make sure parents feel safe leaving their children in your care. Use claim tags with an assigned number for each child. Parents must present the tag at pick-up time. Create a check-in sheet where you can list each child's name, the assigned claim-tag number, parents' names, contact information (cell phone), special instructions, and allergies. All kids should wear name tags. Label bags, coats, or bottles accompanying the children. Check with your church's Christian education director to follow policies about background checks for volunteers and other safety and security policies.

• Make sure all workers know which children have food allergies. Write the allergy directly on the child's name tag. Check snack labels, and to avoid potential hazards, don't allow children to bring in food. Graham or Ritz crackers and bananas or apples make good allergy-free snacks.

• Group kids by age into separate classes. Begin with play time to allow the children to get comfortable in their environment. Use supplies such as cardboard boxes, chairs, and blankets to create obstacle courses or build forts.

• Pick a theme for your planned activities. *Children's Ministry in the 21st Century* (Group) has great ideas for snacks, crafts, and games centered on biblical themes and holidays. Tailor

If you're looking for a great resource to reach out to couples and strengthen marriages at the same time, check out Group's *Couples' Night Out* kits. Couples gather at your church for 20 minutes of "rally time." In this high-energy party atmosphere, they'll enjoy a comedy clip and discover biblical principles for marriage. Then couples head out on the town for dates with a few discussion questions in hand.

Each kit includes a Rally Guide with a script and practical helps, Date Question Cards to get couples talking, publicity materials, and child-care programming.

the activities for each age group, and make a tentative schedule.

• Break each age group into two or more subgroups for craft time. One group can work at the craft while others play. Then switch. Smaller groups within each class provide children with individualized attention.

• End the evening with a snack, an organized game (check www.familyfun.go.com), and a movie. To choose a video, check www.pluggedinonline.com for detailed movie reviews.

IDEA 3
shall we dance?

Partner dancing is more popular than ever. Dancing is a great way to build relationship, interact, spend time together as a couple, and have a lot of fun.

Host one event or a series of evenings where couples can learn skills for different styles of dancing. Structure the time so that couples receive instruction during the first hour or first class, and the remaining time or next get-together is a dance event—allowing the couples to dance together using what they've learned.

Arrange for experts to teach each style of dance, such as the waltz, ballroom dancing, square dancing, swing, or line dancing. Feature one style of dancing at a time. Schedule events once every two or three months.

Encourage couples within your church to invite outside couples to come as guests. Offer door prizes at the dances for guest couples, such as dinner certificates or movie tickets. Decorate the dance area according to the style of dancing. For example, for a square dance, set up outside with a barn-style décor, using bales of straw and wooden crates. Hang twinkle lights around the dance area. Urge participants to wear appropriate attire. Serve lemonade and pie.

IDEA 4
"i'm fondue of you"

Help couples rediscover the need to spend time together by hosting a date night event, complete with ideas on how to enhance their relationships. Provide an elegant evening of fondue dessert and entertainment, plus a short talk by a leader on the benefits of dating your spouse and how to accomplish it. Here are some thoughts on putting together this event:

• Take reservations to obtain a head count.

• Collect fondue pots. Many people have one tucked away in storage. Ask people in your church to loan their pot for the event. Label them in some manner for easy return.

• Decorate with tablecloths, candles, and centerpieces—such as a single rosebud for each couple to take home. Seat only two or three couples per table, if possible. Arrange the room with an ambience of romance and serenity.

• Prepare chocolate fondue, pound or angel food cake, and fruit.

• Begin the event with the leader talking about the benefits of dating. Help couples see what hurts communication, such as TV or too much socializing with others. Stress the importance of romancing each other, whether married 18 weeks or 18 years. Encourage couples to identify what they enjoyed about their spouses when they first fell in love. While they enjoy their fondue, challenge couples to spend time reminiscing and sharing what they cherish then and now.

• Follow the leader's comments with a lounge-type performance—a live pianist, guitarist, or harpist to provide background music while the couples enjoy their dessert and talk about the speaker's thoughts.

> For ready-to-go dating ideas for married couples, see "Section 1: 20 Nights Out and Weekends Away" beginning on page 15.

• Provide lists of date ideas. Encourage couples to look over the lists, choose activities they'd like to try, and plan their next date. Suggest they spend time communicating during each date. For example, they might share with each other why they fell in love and what they love about their spouse today. For additional creative date ideas, set out copies of these books by FamilyLife: *Coffee Dates for Couples* and *Dates on a Dime*.

Use the following ideas to help you compile a list of local and specific date ideas. Call it something like *101 Creative Dates*. Prior to the event, brainstorm with other couples in your church to create a printed list couples can take home.

• Local museums, galleries, aquariums, planetarium, art exhibits
• Nature walks, historical walking tours, trails, parks, gardens
• Bowling, mini or Frisbee golf, biking, skating, swimming, croquet
• Hiking, picnicking, flying a kite, square or line dancing
• Reading aloud to each other, listening to music together
• Attending a play, concert, book signing, karaoke club, amusement park
• Shopping at garage sales, antique stores, flea markets, thrift stores
• Getting away to a bed and breakfast, weekend trip, camping, cruise

IDEA 5
home and marriage improvement

Large, difficult home improvement projects might not be for everyone, but learning to work together—even if only on a small job—can benefit any couple.

Provide a workshop so couples can work on a project together while learning healthy ways to support each other, avoid frustration, and share the satisfaction of a home improvement project well done. Here are some guidelines:

• If the workshop will teach several different skills—such as laying tile, changing or fixing a faucet, hanging window coverings, painting rooms with decorative techniques, or refinishing wood floors—arrange for specialists to teach each topic and demonstrate the methods involved. Set up stations where participants can practice the process. Rotate every 30 minutes or so.

• If just one project will be offered—such as finishing a piece of unfinished furniture—decide if all couples will work on the same type of piece or have a choice of items.

• Determine what materials your church will provide and what couples need to bring. Make sure any supplies and tools are on hand.

• Before beginning the project, provide a questionnaire about working together. Ask couples to fill it out together. Ask questions that will allow each participant to identify strengths, expectations, and fears. Through the questions, encourage couples to explore previous experiences of working together on home improvement projects. What worked? What caused frustration, conflict, or anger? How did they react?

• Present a short devotional on Nehemiah 2:17–3:5. In the face of oppression and ridicule, Nehemiah led his people to rebuild the wall around Jerusalem. They depended on God to give them success. They dedicated their work to the Lord, and tackled it together. Help couples understand that even when they face adversity in life, relationships, or marriage, they can depend on God to give them success. Encourage them to approach their home improvement project with Nehemiah in mind, remembering that God called them to work together.

• Help couples approach this workshop with open minds. For example, they might try sharing the workload differently than they normally would. Encourage couples to explore new ways to work together and to let the emphasis be on unity and enjoyment, not on final results.

IDEA 6
laser tag

To help couples explore some dynamics in their marriages, use laser tag along with a relational workshop. Couples will enjoy plenty of laughter, too!

Reserve a party room at a local laser tag facility. Arrange with the facility to have two laser tag sessions, with a break between the two. Request private tag sessions for your group, if possible. Couples will gather in the party room about 30 minutes before the game begins, again between the two sessions, and once again after the second session of tag.

Provide food, such as soda and pizza, during the last portion together in the party room.

Before the first round of laser tag, break into small groups of about three or four couples, with one of the couples acting as facilitator for the discussion. Talk through these questions:

• How well do you think you work together as a couple?

• Are you competitive as individuals or as a couple? In what ways do you compete against each other?

• Do you communicate well with each other? Do you think your spouse understands you well?

• Who usually makes decisions in your household? How did you establish your system of decision-making? How well does it work for each of you?

After about 20 minutes, tell participants that they'll be playing tag in teams of two—married couples. They should work together to accomplish their goals. Then head to the gaming area, and play according to the facility's rules.

Gather in the party room after the first game for a debriefing. Rejoin the same small groups as before, and talk about the following:

• How did the game go for you as a couple? How well did you work together? What worked? What didn't?

• What could you do better? What could your partner do differently?

• Did any aspect of your relationship come out in a way that contradicted what you discussed and believed earlier? Explain.

• In the second game, how will you improve the way you work together?

• What characteristics of your marriage show as you play laser tag together? Which do you like? Which would you like to change? (Couples might choose to talk about this question on their own after the event.)

Play the next game, then return to the party room for snacks and fellowship.

IDEA 7
take a hike!

Sponsor a mountain or scenic hike for married couples, using prompts along the way so each couple can explore growing together spiritually as a couple.

Structure the hike to last half a day, with a picnic meal break. You could also plan a bike ride instead if that will draw additional participants.

Gather as a group at the trailhead before starting. Or share breakfast at the church or a restaurant before the hike, and distribute the instructions for the hike there. Ask each couple to bring a small Bible, notebook, and pen, in addition to any supplies they might need, such as water, sunscreen, food, or extra clothing.

Start with a morning devotion, perhaps from Psalm 121, and prayer. Use the opportunity to model how to meditate on a passage. Ask questions such as:

What stands out in this passage to you?

What do you think God is saying?

What is he saying to you personally?

Have participants write in their notebooks their thoughts about the passage.

During the hike, encourage couples to travel with just their spouse, devoting the time to each other and to God. Each couple can leave the trailhead in staggered increments of time to allow some distance between each pair.

Provide each couple with a handout that outlines the structure of the hike or bike ride. Structure the time as follows:

• Stop at least once each hour, and find a restful place to sit.

• Take turns choosing passages in Psalms to read during each rest period. Read out loud to your partner.

• Pray together, asking God to teach you and help you hear him. Even if you normally don't pray out loud or together, do so now. Even if you just say a simple sentence, sharing a prayer together is a step toward developing a deeper spiritual connection and surrendering your will to God.

• Meditate on each passage you read. Spend time in silence. Write your impressions in your notebook. Then share what stands out to you. What do you think God is saying to you? What does this passage mean to you as a couple?

• During the silent times of your hike, quiet your mind and thoughts, and allow God's Spirit to speak to you. Share any insight you gain with your spouse.

You might want to gather again after the hike to debrief. In place of opening the event with breakfast, organize a dinner gathering following the hike. Participants can relish the peace of the day and share their experiences.

IDEA 8
open secrets

Celebrate the wedding season with a springtime event for engaged and newly married couples. Organize a panel of four to six long-married couples who feel comfortable talking about their marriages—the challenges they have overcome; the benefits of commitment; the value of marriage in today's world; their "secrets" for a happy, lasting marriage.

• Decide on the specific topics your event will cover: budgeting, setting priorities, forgiveness, respect, arguments, stepfamilies, lasting love.

• Identify couples who might be willing to sit on the panel. Visit each couple in their home, and explain the purpose of the event and the topics. Say, "Your marriage is an inspiration to us, and we're hoping you'll share your insight and experience with others." Then ask for their commitment to join the panel.

• Ask some younger couples to prepare short skits to introduce topics. For example, piles of bills provoke an argument about spending; hectic work schedules clash with a need for time together; the honeymoon's over, so now what?

• Publicize the event in your community. Put a note in your local newspaper. Emphasize that the event is open to couples of all ages, and encourage couples from your church to bring their friends.

• Recruit a couple who can be moderators for the event. Introduce the couples on the panel with their names, how long they've been married, and something interesting about them. Introduce the topics along with the skit performers. Keep track of time so you cover all the planned topics.

• After the event, invite panelists and the audience to stay for fellowship. Encourage young couples to maintain ongoing relationships with older couples they find particularly helpful. Distribute fliers that highlight your marriage ministry program, or the church's service times, ministries, and contacts.

IDEA 9
long-term money ministry

Many couples face financial troubles that create serious stress in their marriages. Your church can help meet these couples' needs by setting up a money management ministry.

Kick off this ministry with a one-time seminar on managing finances, or hold a multiple-week study on finances. A good resource for a multiweek Bible study is FamilyLife's HomeBuilders Couples Series: *Mastering Money in Your Marriage*, while resources for the entire church include Crown Financial Ministries and Financial Peace University.

For the long-term ministry, set up financial mentors. Enlist one couple to mentor each couple that signs up to receive help. This aspect of the ministry can help couples at various levels.

For example, mentors might help couples understand basics such as bills and checkbooks. Or if participants are in serious debt, mentors can help make financial and purchase decisions, even setting up a payment plan to reduce and eliminate the debt.

IDEA 10
wedding workshop

One of the best moments to establish meaningful contact with the young adults in your community is when a couple gets engaged. Try something a little different—offer an entire wedding planning workshop.

• Plan a half-day event for a weekend afternoon. Invite local bridal shops and wedding planning services to set up displays. Give a tour of your building, highlighting areas of interest for couples getting married. Hold drawings for items like a wedding planning book, a unity candle, or a free floral arrangement.

• Introduce your pastor or pastoral staff or a counselor with experience in premarital counseling. Urge them to talk about the premarital counseling they offer and what's included. The pastor or counselor should also address practical issues every young couple needs to think about—money, children, in-laws, sex, and dealing with conflict. Schedule 10- to 15-minute breaks between each session and a half-hour open forum at the end for couples to ask questions of your experts and discuss these topics with each other.

• Provide theme-related snacks for the event, such as wedding cake and punch. Or keep things simple with snacks like a box of chocolates, heart-shaped sugar cookies, or conversation heart candies.

• Advertise the workshop on the wedding announcement page of your local paper, as well as at local bridal shops, florists, and wedding planning companies.

section eight

twenty ideas
TO CARE FOR
MARRIAGES

As you lead and serve in your church's marriage ministry, you'll inevitably be called on to work with people in all kinds of relationships. Marriage ministry involves more than just ministering to traditional married couples. At some point, you'll probably work with and counsel engaged couples, newlyweds, people in troubled marriages, and couples going through separation or divorce. This section provides ideas and tools to help you with each of these situations.

10 IDEAS FOR STARTING MARRIAGES RIGHT

When couples get married in your church, you have a unique opportunity to connect with them on a regular basis. In addition to providing counseling for an engaged couple, you might want to put together small groups or Sunday school classes specifically for engaged couples or newly married couples. You can easily adapt most of the following ideas for use in any of these settings.

Keep in mind that many couples need some "alone time" together during the months leading up to their wedding. And many newlyweds want to spend the first months and even years of their marriage just getting to know each other. With that in mind, you'll also find a few ideas that are more informational—items that you can simply pass on rather than using in a counseling or group setting. Use these any way you like! Copy these to hand out after a counseling session with an engaged couple or at the end of a couples' small group or Sunday school class. Or you might want to reprint the ideas in a "Just for New Couples" column in your church newsletter.

IDEA 1
how to fold a towel

Most challenges that couples face early in marriage aren't about big issues like the existence of God or the needs of sub-Saharan Africa. Instead, couples argue about how to fold towels or when to pay bills.

You can help engaged couples and newlyweds realize that the home they create won't look like either of their childhood homes. Start by assuring the couples that you aren't judging their families but simply comparing their views of "normal" in the home. Ask each partner to tell his or her story of "growing up in my house" as you ask the following leading questions:

> For forms that might help you with engaged couples and their weddings, see "Traditional Wedding Service Order" on page 222 and "Wedding Information" on page 223.

• What were the husband/wife roles in your family? Who served as primary disciplinarian? Who managed the money in your family?

• How did your parents handle conflict resolution? Did they shout? Did they negotiate behind closed doors away from you and your siblings? (Oddly, most couples tend to repeat the very patterns they *hated.)*

• What were your family's "house rules"? In your parents' house, how "clean" was clean? Did your meals involve planned weekly menus or daily spontaneity? Did your family view possessions as personal or as family property? What about scheduled chore times?

• What was your family "cheap" about? When were they extravagant?

• What family traditions did you grow up observing? Did your family make a big deal out of birthdays, Christmas, or other holidays? Were your parents tight with extended relatives? Did you take a big annual summer vacation?

Just getting these issues out in the open helps engaged and newly married couples learn and laugh about these issues outside the heat of the moment. Instead of pushing for a *compromise,* encourage couples to examine the strongest traditions of each family and to take the best from both. This will help them begin to come to a *consensus* about how they'll do their own marriage and family.

IDEA 2
deciding to love

Most engaged couples and newlyweds experience a naive excitement about their time together. Yet in the months before and right after their weddings, they'll inevitably face moments when tension and stress simply dampen their spirits. Here's how it often plays out: One minute everything is fine, and the next minute they're so upset with each other they can't agree on anything. During the worst of these times, they'll question why they're getting married (or got married) at all.

When decisions stress out an engaged or newly married couple, they can easily lose that loving feeling and forget why they decided to marry in the first place. Help them learn to turn things around, guiding them to *purposely* decide to love each other regardless of how they feel at any given moment. As they practice this technique now, it can be valuable long after the wedding bells ring.

Give couples the following situations, and have them spend some time role-playing how they might respond:

1. Your uncle is a photographer, so he assumes he'll take your wedding photos. To avoid ruffling the family feathers, you agree. However, your fiancé has someone else in mind. Before you know it, you're fighting over nothing.

2. You meet your new spouse's boss for the first time. Your spouse suddenly turns into someone you don't know, laughing at the boss' lewd jokes and agreeing with the boss' strange views on social issues. On the way home, you confront your partner in the car.

After couples spend some time acting out the argument that results from one of these situations, encourage them to talk about how they might resolve it. How can they take the step of encouraging each other after a situation like one of these occurs? What insights do they have about choosing to love each other?

Whether this kind of tension occurs during the engagement period or after the wedding, love gives couples permission to step away from the stress. Often, an activity as simple as eating a meal together, taking an afternoon hike, or enjoying a weekend of solitude can relieve the pressure. Make sure engaged and newly married couples understand that they don't need to feel guilty about making each other a priority.

IDEA 3
as you are

When an engaged or newly married couple first met—whether they locked eyes across a crowded room or were thrown together on a blind date—something took place that made them want to meet again and again. After the engagement and certainly after the wedding, surface talks about favorite colors and preferred cuisine become passé. Even though couples might be tempted to skirt tough subjects, you can help them really get to know one another— warts and all. If they can learn to accept each other now, their ride through marriage will be much smoother. Urge engaged couples and newlyweds to head out to their favorite coffee shop or bookstore to work through these topics.

• Ask each other, "What's your idea of a perfect spouse?" No fair answering "You!" Then ask, "What imperfection or quirk do I have that you *like*?"

A bit of advice: Realize that marriage is a journey, not a destination. Along the way you'll both grow and change. What seems important now might be totally forgotten in a few years. Don't dwell on negative details; they won't last forever.

- Ask each other, "When you were growing up, what did your dad do that your mom tried to change? What did your mom do that your dad tried to change?" Then ask each other, "What one thing about me do you hope never changes?"

A bit of advice: When you focus on each other's appealing traits, you'll more easily dismiss the qualities that aren't your favorites.

- Ask each other, "Do I have any habits or behaviors that irritate you?" It might be knuckle-popping, nail biting, or driving too fast. Then ask, "If you had to choose, what one habit would you like me to work on for you?"

A bit of advice: While habits usually aren't deal-breakers in marriage, talking about them right before and after married life begins can make it easier to accept them down the road. And many habits can be broken.

Some other tips to help engaged couples deal with each other's warts:

- Ask tough questions now, and don't be afraid to hear the answers. Accepting people for who they are doesn't mean you agree with everything they do or say. It simply means you willingly take the good with the bad. (And hopefully, the good far outweighs the bad!)

- Don't look at acceptance of each other as being joined at the hip. You'll disagree on issues because you're two different people.

- Accepting one another for who you are might mean you realize that you can't change the other person. But you can still work together to prompt change in your relationship, which will require a little fine-tuning from time to time.

IDEA 4
old and new

Pair engaged couples and newlyweds from your church with longtime married couples for a dinner. Give the new couples permission to ask any and all questions about marriage, married life, and going the distance over time.

This offers experienced couples in your church the opportunity to serve in an important ongoing ministry. Choose couples based on strengths you see in their relationships, such as the depth of their faith, their commitment to each other, and their hospitality to others. These longtime married couples essentially will wait "on call" to host engaged and newly married couples in your church.

Ask the experienced couple to plan a dinner, invite the engaged or newly married couple over, and host the evening. The couples can arrange the dinner for a time that's mutually convenient. The new couple simply needs to think of questions they'd like to ask about marriage.

You might offer the engaged couples and newlyweds some suggested questions, such as:

- Why has your marriage lasted so long?
- Is there anything you wish someone had told you before you were married?
- Are there any conflicts that you can share with us that surprised you?
- What are some of the healthiest marriage habits the two of you practice?
- What outside influences were toughest on your marriage?
- What should we do as a couple in the future when things get difficult?

- What role does your faith play in your marriage?
- How did children affect your relationship with each other?
- What kinds of preparations should we make for the years ahead?

Be sure to write thank-you notes to the couples hosting the dinners, and ask if they'll be available for future dinners as engaged couples and newlyweds come to you for counseling. Also, ask the engaged and newly married couples for feedback about how to improve the time for future participants.

IDEA 5
trust for a lifetime

We want to spend our lives with someone who doesn't make us worry about faithfulness. When you're counseling an engaged couple, you can help them establish a strong basis for trust by encouraging them to hold back on physical expressions of affection during their engagement.

This might seem old-fashioned to some couples. After all, so many people live together outside of marriage that it seems silly to urge engaged couples to back down on physical contact. But that's exactly the point: Restraint in the face of this widespread indulgence offers the foundation for a lifetime of trust.

Engaged couples often comment that Satan turns up the fires of temptation to sexual indulgence as soon as the engagement ring is on the finger. "We're already committed to each other," one whispers. "What difference does a piece of paper make?" Yet, when an engaged couple caves in to their hormonal urges, they prove to each other that breaking the rules is sometimes OK. But later in the marriage when the couple faces challenges, one or the other might wonder, "Is he or she breaking the rules again?" Even if the fears are unfounded, the doubt, suspicion, and anxiety can be overwhelming.

On the other hand, when a couple holds the line and celebrates marriage with their first sexual experience together, by then they know that passions can run hot and temptation can be difficult to resist. But they also know that they've married a person of strength and integrity who can face the heat and still make the right choice. What a gift!

> Many engaged couples and newlyweds will benefit from being matched with a married couple who serve as mentors. For guidance on launching a marriage mentoring ministry in your church, check out "The Sleeping Giant in the Church" on page 187.

So how can a couple stay celibate until marriage? While these suggestions might sound like a junior high sex talk, they provide good talking points you can use to help engaged couples establish a long-term trust:

- Urge engaged couples to set clear boundaries about physical touch and stick to them.
- Suggest that each person find an accountability partner (other than the future spouse) who cares enough to ask tough questions.
- Encourage engaged couples to keep themselves away from circumstances where premarital sex might take place—such as decorating their new apartment or taking an overnight trip together.
- Pray with the couple—and suggest they pray together—for discipline and integrity and trust in their relationship.

Counsel engaged couples that holding back on physical expressions of affection doesn't need to be a burden for already stressed people to bear. Instead, it can be a wonderful tool to show trust and loyalty to one another.

IDEA 6
great expectations

One of the toughest parts about the early years of marriage is dealing with expectations: what will marriage really be like, what is your spouse like to live with, who will do what around the house, and so on. Use this activity to help engaged and newly married couples talk about expectations and keep unfulfilled expectations from chipping away at their marriage relationship.

Gather a group of engaged couples or newlyweds, and serve an unusual food for a meal or snack (see box for some ideas). Make sure that whatever you serve offers a surprising taste—tasting good when it looks bad, a yummy-looking treat that doesn't taste yummy, or a surprisingly intense taste.

Allow each person to taste the food—have fun with it! Then use the experience to lead into a discussion about expectations in marriage. Talk about the following questions.

• What did you think of the food I provided? Did you like it or not? Why?

> ### unexpected food ideas
> • A cake-shaped meatloaf "frosted" with mashed potatoes
> • Harry Potter Bertie Bott's Every Flavor Beans (jelly beans)
> • Lemonhead candies
> • Hot cocoa "cupcakes" (recipe at www.foodnetwork.com)
> • Dirt cake (recipe at www.allrecipes.com)

• How did the taste of the food differ from what you expected, based on how it looked? How did you feel about not having your expectations met? How did it make you feel about me when I said I was giving you something good?

SAY: No matter how long we know our spouse before we get married, during the first year or two of marriage most of us get hit with a clash between expectation and reality. Sometimes these expectations are minor or even funny. But sometimes marriage turns out to be so different from what we expected that we question if we really should get married (or if we married the right person).

• What expectations do (or did) you have about marriage and your spouse? What expectations does (or did) he or she have about you?

• How do you think the reality of married life will compare (or does compare) to your expectations about it?

• How do you and your fiancé (or spouse) react when you run into issues that don't meet your expectations?

• What ways of dealing with these clashes would hurt your marriage? What are some positive, relationship-strengthening ways to deal with unmet expectations in marriage?

IDEA 7
the honeymoon's over

Photocopy this idea to give couples at the end of premarital counseling sessions, or hand it out after a small group meeting or Sunday school class for engaged couples or newlyweds. Or reprint

it as a column in your church newsletter.

Your thank-you cards are mailed, your Caribbean tan has a few days left, and you can't wait to use the fondue set from Aunt Rita at your next party. Newlywed life truly is blissful; but unfortunately, nothing lasts forever! Soon the real world will be pounding at your door, with deadlines to meet and people to please. So, how can you make the transition from the wedding hoopla to real life and still keep that honeymoon glow? Here are a few suggestions:

• Take care of the basics, but take everything else slowly. Pay your bills, go to work, keep up on car maintenance, mow the lawn, and do anything else that must be done. But don't be in a rush to settle down. You have the rest of your lives to be married, but only a short period to be newlyweds.

• Be yourselves. Newlyweds often feel that they're under a microscope, and family and friends are watching every move. So they try to be perfect, with the perfect house and the perfect life. Don't let the outside world pressure you to be something you aren't. In the end, you'll only let each other down.

• Dream now while anything seems possible. Imagine the possibilities now and remember them later, when you can make them come true. Dreams can be your springboard to future goals.

• Spend your time and money carefully. Don't fall into the trap of thinking you need to be where your parents are now. It took them years to achieve the level of comfort they have—it might take you just as long. For now, don't rush the clock, or you'll look back and lament the time (and credit card interest) you lost.

• Make pressing decisions now—like what groceries you need this week. But don't rush into long-range planning—like where to retire. Enjoy being newlyweds and give yourselves a chance to settle in for a while. Don't start your marriage with homegrown stress; plenty of that will find its way into your lives without any effort on your part.

• Focus your energies on issues that are important to both of you. This might include your faith, your family, your values, or any of a hundred different things you're both passionate about. Work to keep these important people, issues, or causes a part of your marriage, and you might just keep a bit of the honeymoon feeling you have today for many years to come.

IDEA 8
who does what?

Photocopy this idea to give couples at the end of premarital counseling sessions or after a small group meeting or Sunday school class for engaged couples or newlyweds. Or reprint it as a column in your church newsletter.

In the 1950s, household and family responsibilities were pretty clear: The husband went to work and brought home the bacon, while the wife stoked the hearth fire and had dinner on the table at 6 p.m. But for married couples in the 21st century, this template usually doesn't work. Both spouses probably work outside the home, and dinner is often balanced on knees in the car rather than served off placemats at the dining room table.

While *all* families struggle with home and family responsibilities, newlyweds discover this abruptly once the wedding is over and life as a couple truly begins. Suddenly, bills, laundry, car maintenance, and grocery shopping all need attention. And not too far into the future, PTA meetings, soccer practice, and homework could follow. But by seeing your new life together as a journey, mapping out home and family responsibilities before you begin, you can more easily smooth out some of the bumps along the way.

Here are a few ideas to help you chart your course.

• Recognize that each of you has preconceived notions—based upon individual upbringing, other couples modeling certain behaviors, and even TV sitcoms—that need to be addressed. If Dad always took out the trash when you were growing up, don't assume your husband will do the same. Talk now, before chasing the trash truck later.

• Approach household and family responsibilities the same way you approach your marriage—with love. More will get done and you'll have less anger and resentment if you treat household chores and family responsibilities as a loving gift to each other rather than as duties.

• Watch out for unsolicited advice. Family and friends can be great resources when you need to change the furnace filter or buy a new car. But sometimes their advice comes with strings. Remember, advice is something you sift through to collect only the grains you can use as a couple. The more things you tackle together—even with mistakes—the stronger your marriage will be.

• Respect each other's opinions. Keep the master/servant monster at bay. Marriage is a joining of souls, not a contest to see who wins.

• Leave room for change. Life isn't stagnant. Down the road, one of you might become sick or disabled, or you'll simply need to re-evaluate responsibilities as your family grows.

• Finally, don't let your home become more important than your family—even when that family is just the two of you. Furniture and belongings will wear thin or go out of style, and those lovingly planted tulip bulbs will be left behind when you move. But the time you invest in your family will reap a bountiful harvest long after your final mortgage payment reaches the bank.

IDEA 9
money matters

Photocopy this idea to give couples at the end of premarital counseling sessions or after a small group meeting or Sunday school class for engaged couples or newlyweds. Or reprint it as a column in your church newsletter.

Money: the root of all evil and the cause of many arguments! It can sure seem that way when you first marry. When you're single, you spend your money and face the consequences alone. But married money has two masters: two opinions on what to spend, what to save, and what to give away.

However, if you address your individual expectations from the start, you can avoid many money arguments. These tips can help keep the money monster at bay, avoiding hurt feelings now and serious money problems down the road.

• Recognize that your philosophies on spending may vary widely. If you ignore your money-spending differences now, one of you will end up feeling like you have no voice in money management. This tension and stress grows and festers over time, negatively affecting other areas of your married life.

• Discuss your spending expectations: How will your marriage reflect your joint vision of money? Talk about the philosophies each of you has about saving, spending, and giving. For example, what constitutes a major purchase, and what do you really need at this time in your lives? Re-evaluate your expectations from time to time.

• Bring up tough questions, such as these: How much would you like to save so that both of you feel comfortable? How do you feel about church tithing and giving to other organizations? Who will oversee the bill paying and checkbook keeping? Listen without judgment, remembering that the two of you come from different backgrounds and have different histories.

• Discuss your feelings on debt and credit cards. Debt can quickly put a strain on your married life, but you might try to agree about times when going into debt will be necessary, such as for a home purchase. Just make sure you both discuss and agree on how much debt is acceptable. Then work hard to pay it off sooner rather than later.

• Budget for the future. Devise a money plan you both agree on. Make sure your budget includes money for basic necessities, savings, and giving. Allocate extra for a first house, graduate school, starting a family, and so forth, and then stick to your plan.

• Finally, don't let money issues become bigger than the two of you. If you make your money work for you and spend it in ways that represent your values, you'll avoid arguments and serious money problems well into the future.

IDEA 10
make room for god

Photocopy this idea to give couples at the end of premarital counseling sessions or after a small group meeting or Sunday school class for engaged couples or newlyweds. Or reprint it as a column in your church newsletter.

Couples often discuss their personal beliefs of God when they're dating or engaged. But once the wedding rings are in place, God and faith easily take a back seat to more pressing matters, such as household and work schedules.

Don't let this happen to you. Take time to seriously consider what role God will play in your lives, both now and in the future.

• Take individual faith inventories. This simply means examining your own personal relationship with God and talking about it with each other.

• Share your spiritual upbringing. You each have different faith histories, so share what God means to you, and really listen to one another.

• Examine God's presence in your lives as a couple now—whether you attend the same church, attend different churches, read the Bible daily, pray together, or serve together. How will those practices change or continue once you're married?

• Explore your prayer practices. If one of you prefers private prayer while the other prays aloud whenever the Spirit leads you, how will you incorporate these differences into meal times, church events, and end-of-the-day routines?

• Plan now for God's role in your future. Life isn't stagnant, and both good times and tragedies will come and go. But God can be your stronghold. Make time to explore the Bible together, seek other couples of faith to socialize with, and echo your faith in God to your children as your family grows.

5 IDEAS FOR HELPING COUPLES THROUGH ROCKY TIMES

As a pastor, marriage ministry leader, or counselor, you have the joy of guiding engaged couples and newlyweds through times of marital bliss. However, you might have a premarital counseling appointment with an engaged couple at 10:00 a.m. then abruptly turn the corner for a counseling appointment with a married couple facing serious troubles at 11:00. The following ideas can help prepare you to guide couples through these times of marital crisis.

IDEA 1
separation tactics

When a couple finally comes to you for counseling, they've probably been enmeshed in conflict for years. For most couples, counseling is a last resort. By the time you see them, their hostility can be intense. When couples throw emotional poison at each other, they place additional stress on you and damage rather than improve their own relationship.

Give both the husband and wife a chance to express their frustrations confidentially without the other spouse present. When counseling begins, meet with each spouse individually for two or three visits, allowing them to vent complaints, pray, and work toward forgiveness.

> Counseling situations can consume your time and drain your emotions. Be sure to protect your time, your family, yourself, and the people you counsel using the invaluable advice in "The Disciplines of Marriage Counseling" beginning on page 203.

Or prior to your first session, arrange for the spouses to meet with mature Christians of the same sex to work toward the same goals. James 5:16 urges, "Confess your sins to each other and pray for each other so that you may be healed."

When you first meet with each spouse, listen patiently to that individual's list of complaints. After you listen and the conversation becomes less intense, let him or her know that God can provide the grace necessary to forgive. If the person is willing, spend time praying through the complaints with each spouse to clear the hurts they're holding against each other.

As you pray, guide each spouse to ask God for grace to forgive and to ask forgiveness for any emotional damage they've caused the other person. As the couple forgives each other, the marriage can begin to heal. Forgiveness is key for a stronger marriage. When the spouses reach the point of forgiveness, then they're ready to meet with you together to start the process of reconciliation.

IDEA 2
rescued by christ

Couples in troubled marriages suffer mental and emotional stress. Serious emotional trauma can go unrecognized in marital counseling. Trauma from chronic and unresolved marital battles can cause spouses to be discouraged, depressed, and even suicidal. Both spouses need time to heal from trauma in order to restore their marriage. If they don't heal this trauma from the past, emotional poison continues to erupt from within. This means the downward spiral of ongoing arguments must stop before a couple can move forward.

In order to help a couple stop magnifying their problems, help them focus on hope, faith, and love. With God nothing is impossible.

Spouses can drive each other crazy trying to squeeze the love they want out of each other. Yet their focus should be on Christ. As humans, we're limited creations, incapable of fixing others no matter how much we want to. Even as a counselor, you only can be a guide to point hurting people toward answers. And the only real answer is Christ. Only he loves us enough to mend our hearts.

> ### recommended reading
> • *Love Must Be Tough: New Hope for Marriages in Crisis* by James Dobson
> • *Telling Yourself the Truth* by William Backus and Marie Chapian
> • *Forgive and Forget: Healing the Hurts We Don't Deserve* by Lewis B. Smedes

While experts try to offer many answers to cope with problems, only Christ can provide complete freedom: "So if the Son sets you free, you are truly free" (John 8:36). In a troubled marriage, the goal should be emotional and relational healing, not just covering up problems. Christ not only saved us from sin, he carried our sorrows on the cross (Isaiah 53:4). A couple in a troubled marriage can find emotional healing through faith in Jesus' sacrifice, which paid for our restoration.

Guide both spouses to invite Christ to rescue them from their hurts and misconceptions. Ask Christ to invade their hearts with his light and love, as he promises in Revelation 3:20-22: "Look! I stand at the door and knock. If you hear my voice and open the door, I will come in, and we will share a meal together as friends. Those who are victorious will sit with me on my throne, just as I was victorious and sat with my Father on his throne. Anyone with ears to hear must listen to the Spirit and understand what he is saying to the churches." The healing and holy presence of Christ can restore every dark and wounded part of our hearts and minds.

A couple in a troubled marriage can only hope to enjoy their relationship again when they experience emotional healing. While this restoration takes time, urge the couple to release their burdens each day as they pray for Christ's guidance for their marriage and life together.

IDEA 3
radical forgiveness

The strongest marriages occur when couples learn to accept each other completely. They love each other enough to stay calm during disagreements and accept each other's differences of opinion. Ongoing forgiveness and acceptance is the only way to create a strong and happy marriage.

You can help troubled couples address each other's unrealistic expectations. These expectations can cause spouses to not accept each other. Until they let go of perfectionist standards, husbands and wives continually compare their partner to a "fantasy spouse," and they'll never be content.

A fantasy wife is always available to help. A fantasy husband is never too busy to care. Fantasy wives are slim and gorgeous. Fantasy husbands are handsome, ambitious, and never lose their temper. Many spouses have a hard time accepting their mates because reality doesn't match their dreams.

The reality of married life—with bills, responsibilities, and adjustments—brings disillusionment that many marriages never recover from. Chronic disillusionment results in a

---

negative cycle of criticism and complaining that couples find difficult to stop.

As a counselor, help couples annihilate their fantasy spouses. Only by ridding their minds and hearts of these unrealistic expectations can they learn to appreciate each other. They need to stop comparing their marriage partners to those who seem more successful or to idealized bodies and romantic ideals in the media. Urge them to get rid of things that deepen their discontent. For example, sometimes romantic novels and movies can create false expectations of the perfect relationship, the perfect spouse, the dramatic moment. Talk to the couples you work with, and find out if they habitually resort to these fantasy-producing sources to escape reality. For other people, pornography serves as a destructive medium that creates abnormal fantasies and impure thoughts. Ask the couples you work with if pornography is an issue in their lives (you'll want to ask this to each spouse individually).

When spouses let go of their ideals, they also have to grieve that loss. While couples might find it silly to receive grief counseling about giving up images or fantasies that bring discontent to their marriage, walk them through the stages of grief, including denial, anger, bargaining, depression, and acceptance.

Spend time praying with the couple, asking God to help them forgive past, present, and even future offenses that lead them to live in fantasy instead of reality. Encourage the couple to ask Christ for the grace to continue to forgive and accept each other. Forgiving each other in the future will be easier when they've already decided to release these offenses now.

IDEA 4
the art of communication

When you counsel couples going through troubled times, you can't teach new communication skills until they break the cycle of fighting. Constant bickering causes anxiety levels to soar and prohibits couples from thinking objectively. Emotional pain and anxiety freezes thinking abilities. Anxious couples attack or retreat and can't resolve disagreements. They even lose track of what they're arguing about, yet can't communicate effectively because of anxiety.

When couples fight for years, you face a difficult challenge trying to get them to work through sensitive issues together. At first, simply ask them to stop criticizing and attacking each other and to pray for wisdom about how to communicate in more positive ways. Urge them to wait on the Lord for answers and to heal emotionally before they start addressing painful issues again.

After a couple works through emotional hurts and reaches forgiveness, they can start to communicate in more positive ways. With a sense of peace restored in their relationship, they can communicate without raising defenses.

God wants us to exercise self-control so we don't hurt others with our words and actions. Self-control is a fruit of the Spirit. Both husband and wife need to know their spouse won't attack when they discuss difficult problems. After a time of healing, the couple can begin communicating about small problems. Remind them to speak in a calm and loving manner about how they feel and to discuss ideas for resolving the problem being discussed.

Suggest some basic communication skills, such as calmly asking the other person to clarify his or her meaning to prevent misunderstandings. For example, "When you said _____, what did you mean?" Couples can avoid most arguments when one spouse asks the other what a comment means. Often, the spouse doesn't mean to cause insult or hurt.

Another helpful skill involves communicating one partner's emotional response to a comment or behavior, but only when the spouse is in a calm and positive frame of mind. "When you said or did [specific words or actions], I felt [hurt or frightened], because [I care about you and our relationship]." After the spouse communicates the words or actions and the emotion it prompted, the couple should drop the subject before an argument starts. The spouse can think about the other person's feelings without getting upset and can make needed adjustments without undue pressure.

When a couple trusts each other not to attack with hurtful words, they can discuss larger and more sensitive problems without hurting each other emotionally.

IDEA 5
accentuate the positive

A healthy life comes when we focus on what's good in our circumstances. Use these ideas to help couples focus on the positive aspects of their lives.

• Encourage couples to be thankful for blessings. A great exercise involves having each make a list of positive qualities of their married life—including what they appreciate about each other—to fill the void of arguing. Instead of complaining about each other to family or friends, they can praise each other using items on this list.

• Have the couple brainstorm both together and separately about positive interests they'd like to pursue. Remind them to shut down their inner censors and write down anything that sounds like fun. After they make their lists, think together with them about how to include these interests in their life without spending too much money. Having fun together is crucial for an enjoyable marriage. When married adults incorporate wishes, dreams, and fantasy vacations into marriage, they're less likely to look elsewhere.

For a list of great date ideas for married couples, see "10 Date Night Ideas" on page 16.

• Encourage the couple to date at least once a week. Remind them not to discuss problems during dates. They should focus on the food, entertainment, or project and simply enjoy each other's company.

• Suggest that the couple take up a sport such as volleyball or bike riding, or even just walking together. Too many couples become sedentary and unhealthy. Walking in the evenings is a great way to relax, enjoy each other's company, and catch up on daily events.

• Encourage couples to find a project to work on together or a place where they can serve in the church or community. Working together creates a synergy that benefits both the couple and the people they serve. God loves to use Christian couples in various types of ministry.

• Urge couples to pray instead of arguing. Praying together provides one of the most powerful ways God can change a couple's relationship. As they trust Christ to be in charge of their problems, he'll lift their burdens and worries and provide peace of mind. As the couple leaves their concerns with Christ, they can enjoy their time together. The Apostle Paul wrote, "Don't worry about anything; instead, pray about everything. Tell God what you need, and thank him for all he has done. Then you will experience God's peace, which exceeds anything we can understand. His peace will guard your hearts and minds as you live in Christ Jesus…Fix your thoughts on what is true, and honorable, and right, and pure, and lovely, and admirable. Think about things that are excellent and worthy of praise" (Philippians 4:6-8).

5 IDEAS FOR MINISTERING TO COUPLES GOING THROUGH DIVORCE

Perhaps one of the greatest challenges of marriage ministry involves dealing with couples contemplating or already proceeding with divorce. As you provide guidance at this stage, remember that you don't need to give every couple the same advice. Urge couples to seek God's will for their unique situation, including the possibility of reconciliation. However, if a divorce seems inevitable, you can also provide godly support both during and after the process.

IDEA 1
urge reconciliation

Unlike divorce attorneys—and sometimes even a couple's friends and family—you can offer couples on the brink of divorce a last ray of hope. Encourage them to explore the possibility of reconciliation, seeking God's will for their situation. Remind them that many divorces create at least as many problems as they solve. Many couples who weather the storms of life enjoy stable and fulfilling relationships afterward.

Romance and commitment both serve important roles in marriage. Commitment carries people through the stresses of life—such as geographic moves, job changes, and the loss of loved ones. When a couple faces severe stress, they might not feel loving, even if their love is strong. They might not feel romantic until they alleviate the stress. Encourage them to stick it out.

The main goal as you counsel a couple considering divorce—or as you counsel just the husband or the wife—is to teach them to communicate without emotionally insulting or damaging each other. You might have the couple attend separate sessions with you or with mentors of the same sex. Listen to their concerns, and pray with them to ask God for grace to forgive. When they can speak to each other calmly, ask if they're willing to come to sessions together.

Before that first session, ask the spouses to each list their goals for your time together, as well as ways they believe the marriage could be repaired. When you meet with them, read each list aloud and comment on each issue without allowing them to contradict. Discuss guidelines based on Scripture, and work with them to create options for following through with their own goals. Ask them not to discuss the lists when they leave the session, but to pray separately for Christ to enable them to forgive and respond well to each other's requests.

If the couple wants to continue meeting with you, set guidelines that they can't argue during those times. Ask them to sign an agreement that they'll work on communicating after the session without fighting. As they communicate with each other without attacking verbally, they'll be under less stress—a better situation for deciding whether to divorce or to give the marriage another try.

IDEA 2
recruit mentors

Multiply your efforts by enlisting compassionate mentors who can guide and support reconciling or divorcing couples. Look for mature Christians who have a heart to help troubled couples. Mentors must also demonstrate a humble attitude, compassion, and accountability.

Of course, mentors won't help much if they regard troubled couples as "inferiors." The term "prayer partners" might work better than "mentors" to avoid any prideful attitudes. This can also help the mentors establish friendships that can be far more helpful and last longer than a true mentoring arrangement. Mentors who have overcome their own marriage struggles can help by simply listening and praying with a couple going through troubled times.

Ask potential mentors the following questions to help you determine if they have the right attitude for this important ministry:

• Will you study God's Word and pray together?

• Will you be open to training?

• Will you be willing to learn how to minister by working alongside me and other experienced mentors?

• Will you accept the couples you mentor as equals rather than projects?

• Will you include the couples you disciple in your social life if appropriate?

Once you have mentoring couples in place, meet with them periodically for training. A few important issues to emphasize:

1. Hurting people must depend on God rather than mentors and friends. Mentors simply point the way to God's resources. While a couple might lean on mentors temporarily, it needs to be just that—temporary. Only God can heal hearts.

2. Train mentors how to maintain a positive attitude and healthy emotions for themselves as they help other couples. This includes maintaining and growing their own relationships with each other and with God. Remind mentors that helpers are only called to carry a light burden when they serve.

3. Remind mentors that they can't help everyone. If you ask them to mentor another couple, the mentors should pray first before making a decision. Some divorcing individuals could cause chaos in a mentor's life. Only God knows whether people are sincere when they ask for help. Urge mentors to not help anyone they don't have peace about working with.

> ## recommended resources for mentors
>
> • Isaiah 61. This section of Scripture focuses on the person, character, work, message, and hope of Jesus, and his promise to restore and rebuild.
> • *The Bondage Breaker* by Neil T. Anderson
> • *Boundaries* by Dr. Henry Cloud and Dr. John Townsend
> • *Healing for Damaged Emotions* by David A. Seamands
> • *Keys to Emotional Freedom* by Robin Martens

IDEA 3
offer mediation

If there's nothing more you can do, and a couple has clearly decided to move forward with divorce, offer to work with them on their settlement. If you don't feel equipped to do that, refer them to a mediation service. When a couple cooperates to work out finances, custody, and visitation schedules, they avoid destructive and expensive court battles that typically increase hostility and create an adversarial relationship.

If the couple agrees to mediation, the divorcing spouses should each decide what they'd like the divorce settlement to include; you or a mediator can then help the divorcing couple find a middle ground. This lays a foundation for a more peaceful time both now and down the road, when the couple needs to deal with visitation of children and other family issues.

Financially, consider the needs of the spouse with the lowest income, as well as the spouse who is taking primary care of the children. Primary caregivers of young children might have a hard time earning income, and they might also face costly child-care expenses. The settlement must also provide for the future needs and expenses of children.

Work with the divorcing couple on how to handle visitation—especially the stress of dropping off and picking up the children. Both spouses need to observe boundaries and not invade the other's private life. Remind divorcing couples that it's normal for children to act out and become sad or stressed when they go back and forth between homes. This normal grief process usually doesn't mean children are being abused. Children will be sad to leave each parent, and the ex-spouses should respect those feelings. Both parents need to let children know it's OK to enjoy themselves at the other parent's home.

If one of the spouses feels threatened before you begin mediation, the couple will probably need to consult lawyers rather than a mediator. A mediator can't protect the interests of an abused spouse as well as a court of law. Also, if a couple can't agree on a settlement that provides adequately for the needs of the custodial parent and children, then the divorce will instead need to be handled through the court system.

If a couple does agree on the terms of the divorce during mediation, all agreements need to be finalized in legal documents. Urge both parties to have their own lawyers review all documents before signing a final agreement.

IDEA 4
support after divorce

If you took a survey of the adults in your church, you'd be surprised to discover the percentage of church members who are divorced. Spend some time evaluating and improving your church's ability to encourage, support, and accept people who've been through a divorce. You might start by gathering a group of divorced individuals, treat them to pizza and soda, and simply ask what your church can do to better help them feel accepted and supported.

A few basic pieces of information can guide your discussion:

• Keep in mind that many divorced singles who attend church aren't the ones who sought the divorce.

• Divorced individuals need to be accepted on their own merits and not prejudged. Remind them that they're a valuable and worthwhile part of the congregation, equal to anyone else in the church.

• Divorced people don't want to hear that God gave them the "gift" of singleness. Divorce isn't a gift. It's a loss. Divorced people obviously had a desire to be in a marriage relationship.

• Divorced individuals need to hear that whether they stay single or marry again is between them and God. Provide objective resources they can read to draw their own conclusions. No matter where you stand theologically, you don't want to drive people away from church. All people need God's forgiveness and grace.

• After divorce, wounded Christians need to find a church home where they feel welcomed, accepted, and appreciated. After they begin to heal emotionally, help them find places where they can minister to and serve others.

IDEA 5
positive connections

While recovery groups provide some short-term benefits, divorced individuals should graduate into normal life as soon as possible. Retelling sad stories over and over by commiserating with other divorced singles for years can feed discouragement and depression, slow emotional and social healing, and prevent a return to normal life. Encourage divorced men and women to seek out positive and healthy Christian relationships. Often, this means associating with families rather than other emotionally wounded singles. Here are some other ways you can help divorced singles "return to normal life":

• Encourage newly divorced men and women to continue friendships that provide accountability. These friends should be mature Christians of the same sex who have overcome the trauma of divorce.

• Urge divorced singles to re-enter normal life as soon as possible. Suggest developing new interests by returning to school or joining a photography class or hobby group.

• Respect divorced singles for their gifts and areas of expertise, and recruit them to minister to others. When you focus on people's strengths, you help them remove their own focus from their weaknesses. Ask for advice in areas where they excel. When you have faith in the capabilities of others, they'll likely rise to the level of your expectations.

• Be understanding about the limitations of singles. For example, single parents might be overwhelmed with caring for children and a home on their own. If divorced singles are too busy to serve directly, ask for their advice. This helps them feel needed and appreciated.

• Establish an online church bulletin board to help divorced singles—and all church members—with different subjects and needs. Post requests for help, roommates, jobs, items to sell or give away, as well as helpful resources.

fifteen ideas
FOR LATER-IN-LIFE
MARRIAGES

In your effort to have your marriage ministry connect with all the married couples in your church, have you considered unique issues that older couples in your congregation face? As couples get way down the road in their marriage, they might be dealing with a newly emptied nest, retirement, relocation, grandkids, health issues, or how to keep their marriage alive. Pass along these ideas to long-term couples to help their marriages survive and thrive.

5 TRANSITION IDEAS

IDEA 1
the empty nest

Imagine a house filled with excitement as your child packs up to head off to college. Yet your emotions catch you off guard after your child drives away. You wonder how the years slipped away so quickly. You and your spouse get up one night and quietly walk down the hallway to your child's room, sit on the bed, and reminisce. At that moment, you realize life has changed forever—you've entered what's often called the empty nest.

Major components of your marriage have changed. After many years when parenting was your highest priority, you now find yourselves in a house alone. How you adapt will determine the success or failure of going through this transition. Talk through the following questions with your spouse:

- With our children gone now, how will we use our time?
- How will we each view our marriage now? How can we mutually work at making our marriage stronger as we move into this new stage of life?
- How do we feel about our children being "on their own"?
- How will we develop a new kind of intimacy with each other now that we can focus more on each other?

As you ponder the questions, think about how meeting the following needs can help you through this difficult time:

- Reach out to people your own age, and establish new friendships. Not only do you miss your children, you miss their friends. Reconnect at church, join community organizations or hobby groups, or volunteer for service projects.
- You need to develop new communication skills. The house is suddenly a lot quieter. You probably joked about sending kids on their way and enjoying the peace and quiet. But an empty house offers deafening silence if you don't re-establish good communication with your spouse. Seek out things to talk about—join a book discussion group, invite a group of friends over to watch an uplifting movie and discuss it afterward, or reminisce about your dating and early marriage years, before the kids came along.
- Develop new spiritual intimacy. Try a new approach to worship, spend time serving the Lord together inside and outside of your church, and spend quality time together.
- Learn more about each other. Again, you need to talk. Share the qualities you most admire in your spouse. What words do you love to hear your spouse say to you? When did you feel the most supported by your spouse? How can you resurrect some of those favorite moments?
- Cherish each day as a gift from God. You'll naturally cherish the days when your children were young and when they moved through adolescence and into adulthood. And perhaps someday you'll be blessed with the joy of grandchildren or even great-grandchildren. But you can learn to cherish "now" as a gift from God, too.

IDEA 2
grandkids and beyond

While you probably think of marriage in the present, when your children are grown and God blesses you with grandchildren and even great-grandchildren, how will that affect your marriage?

Here are four questions to think about if your marriage involves grandkids:
- What actions can we take to help nurture our grandchildren?
- How can we share our family history—both joys and sorrows—in a positive way?
- What will we need to do to mentor our grandchildren?
- What values do our grandchildren see in us? How can we strengthen those values in their lives?

Grandparenting takes a team effort, beginning with a strong marriage. This permits your grandchildren to "see in action" what a biblically sound, godly marriage is like. If your marriage is God-honoring, you can share God's love with your grandchildren. Try these practical tips for communicating your love:
- Accept your grandchildren for who they are. Respect each grandchild as a special person. Discover something unique about each grandchild, and provide an opportunity to encourage his or her development. Believe in your grandchildren. Never ridicule them and compliment them often.
- Take time to be with your grandchildren. Plan a day together to just have fun. Go hiking, fishing, camping, or to a park. Spend time together having fun.
- Do activities together. Prepare a meal. Bake a cake or brownies together. Go grocery shopping and let your grandkids choose some foods. Young children love to scramble eggs, plus they get to enjoy a good breakfast after the work is done!
- Be patient, fair, consistent, firm, and forgiving. Children have an amazing way of moving on without holding grudges. They respect discipline and learn great lessons.
- Show affection to each grandchild. In addition to a lot of hugs and kisses, be sure you're modeling a loving marriage. As your grandchildren see your love relationship in your marriage, they'll grow to love and respect others.

IDEA 3
retirement readiness

Retirement is a major transition in life and will inevitably put a great deal of stress on your marriage. Even after years of planning, this transition can come early or late. Sometimes it's the culmination of a long-awaited goal, and sometimes it's the shock of "forced" retirement.

As you and your spouse age, your needs change. By the time you retire, your needs and desires are quite different than they were in earlier stages of life. Like most people, you probably look forward to your retirement years, when you can pursue new opportunities, travel and do everything you put off earlier in life, and simplify your daily routine and enjoy life to its fullest.

Retirement also has its own stresses. Whether you liked your job or not, it gave you a sense of who you are and how you fit into society. In a culture that identifies people by what they do, retirement can make you feel like you've been stripped of your worth. The routine, the familiar pressures, the fun of accomplishing tasks, and the comradeship with co-workers are all gone.

Although many retirees remain active and independent, they desire a simpler lifestyle with fewer responsibilities and more social activities. Today's retirees enjoy not just motor homes and travel, but also motorcycling, rock climbing, and in-line skating.

How will you deal with your retirement years? These ideas can help you along the way:

1. Change the way you define retirement. Think of it as a starting point for accomplishing new goals rather than the end of your career.

2. Create an identity away from work. Start a hobby or tackle projects with your spouse. Work on a novel you always wanted to write. Or start a new business you've been dreaming of.

3. Renew relationships with friends and extended family members. You and your spouse can take a long trip and spend time with people you haven't seen for years. Be sensitive to their schedules, and move on before your hosts want you to leave. That way, they'll invite you back again!

IDEA 4
changing energy and interest

Most of us grew up eating fast food and living a fast-paced life. In the early years of marriage, you ate junk food, drank good-tasting sugar-filled drinks (jumbo size), and might not have been all that active.

It's never too late to start eating healthy, drinking more water, and exercising. As you age and your energy and interests change, you face new challenges and new opportunities. The Apostle Paul wrote that our bodies are the temple of the Holy Spirit (see 1 Corinthians 6:19).

No matter how long you've been married, *now* is a great time to face the challenge and get healthier. Most couples know academically the simple keys to a healthier lifestyle, but it takes motivation. Why not set that goal together, holding each other accountable for living healthier? Here are some accountability statements to get you started:

• We'll be accountable to each other as we begin to eat healthier and maintain our proper weight.

• We'll be accountable to each other as we begin to exercise on a personal program, as a couple, or in a group setting.

• We'll be accountable to each other as we work on getting enough rest.

• We'll be accountable to each other as we drink plenty of water and balance our work and our play.

• We'll be accountable to each other as we are faithful in worship, study of God's Word, and service for the Lord.

• We'll be accountable to each other as we assume a sense of responsibility for our own health; we'll be proactive, not passive.

• We'll be accountable to each other as we learn to manage stress and conflict in our marriage.

• We'll be accountable to each other as we learn to grow in a circle of Christian friends and establish relationships for love and caring for one another.

IDEA 5
law and order

Elder law is a relatively new area of legal practice that focuses on the legal needs of older adults, incapacitated people, and their families. As you grow in your marriage, you need to look seriously at not only the financial and health issues ahead, but also take steps to ensure that things are in order legally.

Some of these issues in the legal realm include long-term care planning, planning around public benefits such as Medicare and Medicaid, estate planning, advance planning for incapacity, elder abuse, elder financial exploitation, and guardianship and conservatorship court proceedings. All of these are important in later-in-life marriages.

Perhaps long-term care planning tops this list. Long-term care planning involves determining if you can afford to pay for future care in a skilled nursing care center or assisted living center. If you don't have sufficient income and savings to pay for this care, you need to seek legal and financial planning so you can preserve your assets while also qualifying for Medicare and Medicaid.

A central part of elder law involves estate planning. Estate planning involves written documents that express how you want your assets to be owned, managed, and preserved during your lifetime, and how you want assets allocated after you die. Wills and trusts are common ways to distribute your assets after you die. Trusts have the added benefit of avoiding probate.

You might also want to establish legal relationships with individuals who will guard your interests. For example, a financial power of attorney appoints an agent to manage your financial affairs in the event you become incapacitated. A healthcare power of attorney appoints an agent to make healthcare decisions for you in the event you become incapacitated.

You can find elder law attorneys by contacting the Area Agency on Aging, the National Academy of Elder Law Attorneys, and the Alzheimer's Association, or by consulting your local yellow pages.

5 IDEAS FOR COPING WITH HEALTH ISSUES

IDEA 1
changing emotions

Along with the joys of being together for many years, later-in-life marriages also bring health challenges. The aging process might raise a variety of psychological, social, spiritual, and physical health concerns for you. For example, your concerns might include dealing with chronic illness or disability, the loss of friends and family members, and your own impending mortality. You might also feel that you don't have the resources, coping skills, or social support to shape your lives according to your needs and desires.

Depression is one of the most common mental health challenges. But you might feel that depression is just a normal part of aging, so you don't seek treatment for this illness. Depression can be caused by poor eating habits, not getting enough rest, reaction to drugs (toxic depression), physical depression related to glands, infections of the brain and nervous system, hypoglycemia, repression of anger and anger turned inward, self-pity and self-blame or poor self-image, or faulty behavior and faulty thinking. Simply being aware of situations that can put you or your spouse at risk for depression can help you make sure you seek treatment if needed. These situations include:

- Retirement or other changes in role or status
- Financial issues
- Loss through death or relocation of family, friends, or pets
- Loss or perceived loss of function or capabilities
- Chronic illness or pain

Also, take note if you or your spouse shows any of these signs of depression:

- Constant or pervasive sadness
- Difficulty concentrating or making decisions
- Loss of interest in hobbies, friends, or activities
- Change in sleeping habits
- Sudden weight loss or gain
- Frequent visits to the doctor
- Statements such as "You'd be better off without me" or "I don't want to be a burden"

You can take some specific positive, practical steps to climb out of depression—especially if you're simply not experiencing the joy you once knew. If that statement describes how you or your spouse feels, try these ideas:

- Give praise. Rejoicing in the Lord is closely linked in Scripture with praising the Lord: "May all who are godly rejoice in the Lord and praise his holy name!" (Psalm 97:12). It's easy to become nearsighted and see only your "problems." Getting outside, even if only for a simple walk around the block, can be a very healthy experience. Being with friends at church, singing praise to the Lord, and engaging in good fellowship can do wonders.

- Read positive Scriptures. Jeremiah is often called the weeping prophet. He wrote in Jeremiah 15:16, "When I discovered your words, I devoured them. They are my joy and my heart's delight." Many of the psalms also lift the discouraged and depressed heart.

- Pray. OK, so this sounds clichéd. Yet prayer is an amazing means of fighting depression and increasing joy in your life. Jesus said, "You haven't done this before. Ask, using my name, and you will receive, and you will have abundant joy" (John 16:24).

- Obey God and serve him. Again, Jesus pointed out the benefits: "When you obey my commandments, you remain in my love, just as I obey my Father's commandments and remain in his love. I have told you these things so that you will be filled with my joy. Yes, your joy will overflow!" (John 15:10-11).

Additionally, take some practical actions, such as exercising, abdominal breathing, mental relaxation, meditation, muscle relaxation, a warm bath, listening to music, doing something for others, talking it out, family support, revising a daily schedule, or just being with good friends for some fun.

IDEA 2
filled with love

Maybe you're acquainted with the various Greek words for love. The three most common are *eros, philia,* and *agape.* Love is about far more than sex. Later-in-life couples can make sure their expressions of love for each other are well-rounded, encompassing all that these three words mean.

Eros is the love that seeks sensual expression—romantic love and sexual love. It's inspired by the biological part of human nature. In a strong marriage, you'll love each other romantically and erotically. Yet in later-in-life marriages, sexual challenges can arise. So if your marriage has been built only on eros, you could be in trouble.

If your marriage is strong, you and your spouse are also good friends. Friendship means companionship, communication, and cooperation. That's philia love—true friends who enjoy each other.

Then there's agape love. Agape is the self-giving love. It's the love that goes on loving even when the other person is unloving. This sort of love doesn't come naturally. You and your spouse must work at making this kind of love be a part of your marriage.

Love in your later-in-life marriage will suffer if you and your spouse don't have a clear understanding of these three biblical concepts of love. In addition, you must be willing to communicate deeply and have an absolute commitment to each other. If you and your spouse suddenly declare that you no longer love each other, the real question is, "When did you choose to *not* love each other?"

What kills love? Love dies when you spend little or no time together and when you stop sharing activities that are mutually enjoyable. You create or destroy love by deciding to or not to have pleasurable activities (not necessarily sex) over a period of time together. Your marriage relationship diminishes when either you or your spouse (or both of you) stop smiling, caressing, complimenting, showing compassion, and spending time together.

Here are some questions to discuss if you're facing these challenges:

• What do you do to reinforce the behaviors you enjoy?

• What can you do to increase feelings of friendship and deepen the love relationship with your spouse?

• How can the presence of Jesus in your life help you love your spouse through eros, philia, and agape love?

IDEA 3
serious illness

Serious illness changes lives and changes marriages. If you or your spouse is facing serious illness, these reminders can bring hope and comfort:

• Find someone to talk to about the illness. Talking is one of the best ways to face feelings. You might think it's too difficult to talk about deep hurts. But it's far more difficult to experience the hurt and not talk.

• Accept reality. While it can be tough to face the reality of aging and its challenges, make a conscious effort to find its joys as well.

• Look at each day as a gift from God. Focus on the positive as much as you can. God can put a song in your heart even if you or your spouse is lying on a bed in a hospital room or at home sitting in a wheelchair.

• Remember that all life is fragile. You have this moment in time, and the future is in God's hands. That truth hasn't changed during your whole lifetime! Try to thank God for the blessings you've enjoyed over the many years you've had together as a couple.

- Pray. Prayer is a powerful experience. Just talk to God. He's big enough to hear your anger and fears. The Holy Spirit dwells in believers, providing comfort. Jesus promised, "I will ask the Father, and he will give you another Counselor to be with you forever—the Spirit of truth" (John 14:16-17, NIV).

- Keep on keeping on. Ultimately, you'll learn to comfort yourself. No matter how many people are around someone with a serious illness during the day, reality can be tough to face in the loneliness of the night. You must learn to cheer yourself to move forward with God's help.

- Set goals. No matter how small, any goal can help you feel a sense of achievement. For example, if you're healing from hip surgery, those first five steps with a walker are huge accomplishments.

- Keep a sense of humor. Learn to laugh at yourself and the funny things around you. See humor and laughter as gifts God provides to offer relief from your difficult times. Remember the simple words of Solomon: "A cheerful heart is good medicine, but a broken spirit saps a person's strength" (Proverbs 17:22).

- Be thankful for each day, and greet it joyously. God is the giver of joy.

- Accept comfort offered by friends and family. The strong support of all the people who love you might be the strongest medicine.

- Claim God's strength and fill your heart with Scripture's promises. Meditate on verses and passages such as Psalm 119; Romans 5:3; 8:28; 11:33-36; 1 Corinthians 10:13; James 1:12.

IDEA 4
changing lifestyles

Most couples in later-in-life marriages face decisions about where to live. Maybe you've owned your home for years, or maybe you decided to buy a motor home and you spend your days traveling across the country. Chances are, you've been around long enough to know that no living situation is permanent.

As you and your spouse face the possibility of changing your living situation—whether now or many years down the road—it helps to know the language. Here's a brief list of some key vocabulary words:

- Independent living. Requires little or no assistance with the activities of daily living.

- Telephone reassurance. Provides a daily call for those who live alone, who are anxious about safety or security, or who face health challenges.

- Transportation services. Offer rides to elderly or disabled persons who don't have private transportation or who can't use public transportation.

- Home-delivered meal services. Services that bring healthy meals right to the home of the homebound.

- Home support. Provides assistance within the home by external agencies or persons who manage daily living tasks such as housekeeping, laundry, limited maintenance, meals, bathing, and so forth.

- Self-care. The individual self-manages the simple and complex activities of daily living and a certain limited amount of medical care.

- Assisted living. Similar to home support services, but generally provided within an apartment or patio home in a retirement center setting.

- Continuing Care Retirement or Life Care. A retirement center provides shelter, care, and services (including nursing services) for as long as the resident lives in the facility in return for a one-time entrance fee and monthly fees.

• Counseling services. Individuals or agencies that provide families with guidance and support in solving problems and making decisions.

• Friendly visiting services. Provides regularly scheduled visits for the homebound or isolated; provides companionship and expresses concern for the individual's well-being.

• Adult day care. Provides planned, supervised activities and meals in a group setting for adults all or part of an entire day.

• Intermediate care. Is the medium level of care between personal care and skilled nursing care.

• Adult foster care. Enables people to live with families or individuals who are willing to share their homes.

• Alzheimer's care. Usually provided in a hospital or skilled nursing facility setting.

• Group home. Refers to a residential house converted to accommodate several senior adults in a home setting and atmosphere.

• Hospice care. Medical and support service for individuals diagnosed with a terminal illness and who have a short life expectancy.

• Occupational therapy. Medical service that promotes rehabilitation of social, recreational, and body mechanics needed for the activities of daily life.

• Personal care. The lowest level of care provided within a skilled nursing care center.

• Physical therapy. A medical service that promotes rehabilitation of the body through exercise and other types of stimulation.

• Residential care. Provided in a retirement center setting with 24-hour supervision.

• Respite care. Provides residential care, usually for less than a month.

• Skilled care. Provided in a skilled nursing setting by licensed nurses on a 24-hour basis.

• Speech therapy. A medical service promoting rehabilitation of speech.

• Subacute care. The highest level of medical care given in a skilled nursing setting.

• Supervisory care. Another term for residential care.

For a simple checklist of activities of daily living to help determine if a later-in-life couple needs to consider assisted living or skilled nursing care, see *Senior Adult Ministry in the 21st Century,* Wipf and Stock Publishers, 2006, pp. 25-26.

IDEA 5
loss of spouse

One of the biggest challenges you might ever face in your marriage is finding your way after losing your spouse. No words can explain the emptiness.

Certainly your spouse would want you to become what some call a "creative survivor"—seeking ways to go on in spite of your loss and grief. The truth is that you must press on, and with God's help you will survive. Life will never be the same, but you must move ahead. While the pain you feel is excruciating, these keys can help you move ahead when you're ready:

• Take one step at a time. You have this moment in time—right now. You can't do much about yesterday, and you have no guarantees for tomorrow. You have today. Take a small step forward each day. It might help to write out your steps by keeping a journal of your feelings, getting involved in a grief group, or taking that first step of going to church the first time after the loss of your spouse. If you've been involved in a church together, going back after your spouse's death is a huge step. It's a bit easier if you go with someone and don't sit alone.

• Don't make quick decisions. Most counselors encourage people to not make any big decisions for at least a year, and that's good advice. You might feel inclined to sell your house or move across the country. But whatever decision you make, time will greatly help you make it wisely. Feelings change and you may make decisions that you regret later.

• Remember that healing takes time. You might find the book with that title, *Healing Takes Time* by David Gallagher (Collegeville, MN: Liturgical Press, 2005), to be a helpful resource. Or if you're more of a reflective soul, you might find comfort from *God in the Dark* by Luci Shaw (Vancouver, BC: Regent College Publishing, 2000).

• Take steps to relieve loneliness. Loneliness can be crippling. It will take real effort to begin to get back on the road of socialization. Don't drop out of church or social groups you and your spouse enjoyed. In fact, if you've stayed away because your spouse battled a long illness, think of this as a time to reconnect.

• Let others help. It is amazing how God can use people to help you rebuild your life. In addition to family members, look to grief groups, activities, fellowship groups, care groups, and other ministries in your church and community to provide help you need.

• Find ways to ease the adjustment. You need to do a lot of talking, so resist your urge to withdraw. Again, reconnect with family members and friends. Ask your pastor if you can meet for coffee. Don't be afraid to seek professional counseling help if you feel like you're not getting over your grief in the ways you expected to. As you tell your stories of pain, it will begin to lessen over time.

• Try not to dwell on regrets. After the loss of your spouse, you'll naturally think about the past. Even if you faced conflicts or spoke hurting words during your marriage, focus on the many happy times in your marriage.

5 IDEAS TO KEEP LONG-TERM MARRIAGES ALIVE

IDEA 1
pursuing new interests

An important key for keeping your long-term marriage alive is clear and simple communication. You and your spouse need to communicate not just your thoughts and ideas but also your feelings. Try using I-messages and reflective listening:

• *I-messages* means stating the effect on you: "I feel [name the emotion]."

• Reflective listening means stating what you heard your spouse say: "What I understand you saying is that you are feeling… because…"

Another important element to keeping long-term marriages alive is doing new things together. Try these ideas to help cultivate new interests:

• Help beautify the church (inside or outside).

• Volunteer at a local hospital or hospice.

- Help in Sunday school, small group ministry, children's ministry, youth ministry, or young adult ministry as a team.
  - Volunteer as a couple at a skilled nursing care or assisted living center.
  - Offer your services at the library, sports arena, Little League, and so on.
  - Provide transportation, prepare meals, and take food to the homebound.
  - Telephone members of your church on their birthday or anniversary.
  - Help in a local school or at an after-school program.
  - Volunteer at the American Red Cross, YMCA, or YWCA.

IDEA 2
new uses of time

Keeping long-term marriages alive with new uses of time is an amazing opportunity for outreach. Your church might have a drama team without actors, small groups without leaders, or a library without librarians. Why not jump in and help? By volunteering, you not only provide service but you strengthen your marriage as you serve the Lord together.

The list of ways you can serve together is almost limitless. Tap into your common interests. For example, if you and your spouse love to travel, serve on a short-term mission trip. Here are some other ways you can serve together:

- Small group leaders
- Pastoral assistance
- Home repair
- Church library
- Kitchen and cooking
- Cleaning and yardwork for homebound who need assistance
- Financial planning (provided by those who have such ministry gifts)
- Missions and outreach
- Music and drama
- Facilities
- Worship leaders
- Tele-Care ministry
- Prison ministry
- Tutoring

IDEA 3
a new view of marriage

Marriage has cycles. Most couples begin their marriage with high expectations. Marriage vows, easily spoken when you're at the altar, can be challenging to live out over the test of 30, 40, 50, 60 or 70 years. When things get rough, it takes hard work to invest in your marriage. Don't be afraid to seek counsel from your pastor or even a professional marriage counselor. Some issues you might be facing include:

- The need for affection and sexual intimacy
- The need for companionship
- The need for family (especially if your children have moved out of the area and you're

facing severe health challenges or your spouse is deceased)

- The need for financial security as you grow older together
- The need for spiritual intimacy together with God

How can you rediscover the fulfillment you'd hoped for in marriage? The bottom line is commitment—focusing on the covenant you and your spouse made to each other before God.

You might want to go out to your favorite breakfast spot or just sit on your patio or deck and talk about how you can make the following commitments together. Probe a bit beyond the surface—instead of just words, decide what actions you can take to live out each commitment in your marriage. Ask your spouse what you do or don't do to *show* each of the following statements to him or her:

- Our disappointments can be steps of growth as we face disappointments together honestly and give them to God.

- Our relationship with each other must be based on our relationship with God. He is the giver of life and able to keep our marriage alive and give us a new view of our marriage.

- Our dependence on God strengthens our interdependence with each other.

- Our commitment will be strengthened as we recommit ourselves to absolute faithfulness to one another and to God.

IDEA 4
new roles

Keeping long-term marriages alive by understanding new roles will involve facing some new realities:

- We've both changed through the years; we need to work hard at communicating our feelings as equals.

- We must both make a new commitment to absolute faithfulness to one another and to God.

- We both need to evaluate our use of time. Now that we have more time, how will we use it, and what will we do together?

- We both must accept the fact that we need to spend time together in reading Scripture, in prayer, and in worship with the family of God.

With these thoughts in mind, approach your pastors about offering a preaching series not just on marriage enrichment for young couples, but on marriage enrichment for the later-in-life marriages as well. Your pastor can help later-in-life couples answer the following questions:

- How can we develop new intimacy with each other?

- What new roles do we have during this time and stage of marriage, and what do we each need to do to function happily in our new roles?

- How have friendships changed—what family members and friends have moved away? Whom do we feel comfortable with as we try to make new friends?

- What's our new relationship with each other, with our children, with our grandchildren?

- What service or ministry opportunity is God calling us to as a couple?

IDEA 5
new opportunities

Long-term marriages offer amazing and wonderful opportunities for growth. As a couple, you just need to learn your new roles and learn good communication.

You also have a new relationship with your children during these times. While your children have moved on into careers, they can share with you meaningful things going on in their work and family life. Often children seek their parents' counsel about parenting. Amazing doors of opportunity can open as you share your wisdom and experience.

New opportunities can arise in other areas as well. Here are some simple and practical suggestions to help you enjoy new opportunities together:

• Keep your faith strong by maintaining a fresh, personal, vibrant relationship with God.

• Maintain godly character traits through constant evaluation and dialogue with your spouse who sees your blind spots.

• Be faithful in worship and fellowship at your church. Worshipping together has amazing power to draw two people together.

• Get involved in a good small group for accountability and support.

• Live a godly life through obeying the commands in Scripture.

• Serve the Lord together; work together in helping others. For example, consider mentoring a younger married couple (to get started, see Chapter 10, "Marriage Mentoring," starting on page 187).

Couples in later-in-life marriages who are successful in their relationships generally display these four characteristics:

1. They set priorities together and work hard at putting God first and each other second, followed by the many pressing needs and pressures of life.

2. They balance their lives with a good blend of time for each other and time together with mutual friends.

3. They keep a close watch for signs of their marriage relationship slipping by observing any nagging, sarcasm, communication breakdown, or jealousy.

4. They develop their own areas for using spiritual gifts and help their spouse develop his or her spiritual giftedness.

Do these qualities define you? If not, what can you do to claim them?

the sleeping giant
IN THE CHURCH:
WHAT EVERY PASTOR
NEEDS TO KNOW ABOUT
MARRIAGE MENTORING

by Drs. Les and Leslie Parrott

In his book *Did You Spot the Gorilla?* psychologist Richard Wiseman described an experiment where volunteers watched a 30-second video of two teams playing basketball and were asked to count the number of times one of the teams passed the ball. However, the researchers didn't tell the volunteers that halfway through the video, a man dressed in a gorilla suit would run onto the court, stand in front of the camera, and beat his chest. Amazingly, only a few of the volunteers spotted the man in the gorilla suit. Most of the volunteers, focused on counting passes, completely missed the gorilla.

Wiseman concluded that most people go through life so focused on the task at hand they completely miss what would otherwise be obvious. Has the church fallen victim to this phenomenon? Are we blind to the gorilla of marriage mentoring? This slumbering giant makes itself visible in every congregation—a team of couples who have what it takes to make a powerful impact on marriages around them. And yet, for the most part, what they could offer remains untapped.

We'd like to change all that. We want to awaken the sleeping giant of marriage mentors in the local church and help them to seize an opportunity neglected for too long.

Would It Make a Difference?

Think of the painful divorces you've witnessed where no one suspected trouble. Think of the couples in your church who are stuck in a rut, not reaching their full potential. Now, think of what would happen if you could link these couples to more seasoned and experienced couples. Would it make any difference? Yes! How do we know? Because we've been recruiting, screening, and training couples to become marriage mentors for more than a decade. We've heard their stories. We've done the research. Marriage mentoring works.

Just do the math. Nearly 400,000 churches exist in America. If just a third of these churches recruited and trained 10 mentor couples each, the result would be more than one million marriage mentors. Think of the difference that would make! With this mighty band of marriage mentors, certainly we could save half of the 1.2 million marriages that end in divorce each year. And think of the marriages that could move from good to great if only they had a more experienced couple to walk beside them.

Truth be told, every congregation—no matter how large or small—can awaken the marriage mentors in its midst. Too many marriages suffer in silence, and too many couples merely get by. So we need to do something. And we can.

Our Story

Fifteen years ago, we first began using the term "marriage mentors" as part of a program we developed called *Saving Your Marriage Before It Starts*. Through a seminar launched in Seattle, we began helping hundreds of newlyweds get started on the right foot. Before long, we started to wonder if the information we taught made a difference. We wondered how we could build in accountability for the couples who went through our program, to be sure they actually put the information into practice.

The number of couples didn't allow us to follow up on each one personally. So we began to recruit older, more experienced couples to meet with these newlyweds. Without much training at first, we asked them to check in with their assigned couple every so often to see how things were going. It didn't take long before we realized that something exciting was happening because of this fledgling notion. We started to hear remarkable stories that convinced us to apply the time-honored tool of mentoring to marriages.

Tom and Wendy, a typical newly married couple, were among the first to experience our program. In their mid-20s, they'd dated for nearly two years before getting engaged. They had the blessing of their parents, attended premarital counseling, and seemed to be on their way to living happily ever after—or so everyone thought.

Marriage for this couple, like most newlyweds, wasn't all they hoped for. For different reasons, each of them felt a bit slighted. However, unlike the majority of newlyweds, Tom and Wendy talked openly about their feelings. Their expectations about marriage weren't being met. Determined to do something about it, on a cold January day eight months after their wedding, Tom and Wendy asked for help.

The Guinea Pig Couple

When they came into our office, they began to shed their coats. Wendy sipped hot coffee to thaw out. "We've asked friends and family about what's going on," she said. "But we both realize we need more objectivity."

Tom joined in: "Yeah, people who know us say 'just give it time' or something like that." He went on to say that their marriage wasn't suffering a major trauma. It didn't need a complete overhaul, just "a little realignment."

We met with Tom and Wendy for nearly an hour, listening to their experience. We gave them a couple of exercises to help them explore their misconceptions about marriage, and we recommended a few resources. Then we talked about the idea of linking up with a marriage mentor couple.

"What's that?" they both asked.

We told them that meeting from time to time with a more seasoned married couple could give them a sounding board—a safe place to explore their questions about marriage. Like most newlyweds we talk to, Tom and Wendy eagerly wanted to find such a couple. After a bit of discussion, they suggested a married couple in their church. Neither of them knew the couple very well, but they had respected their marriage from afar and thought they'd fit the bill. After a couple of phone calls and a little more exploration, we made the connection for Tom and Wendy. Over the course of several months, they met several times with their mentors, Nate and Sharon. Tom and Wendy found the marriage mentoring so helpful that they wrote a letter to us back then:

> *Dear Les and Leslie,*
>
> *How can we ever thank you for helping us find a marriage mentor couple? Before coming to you, we'd never even heard of such an idea. But our mentoring relationship with Nate and Sharon ended up being the most important thing we've ever done to build up our marriage. It was so nice to have another couple know what we're going through yet remain objective at the same time.*
>
> *We've since moved to another state, but on our wedding anniversary, Nate and Sharon always call to celebrate our marriage.*
>
> *Anyway, we wanted to say thank you and to say that you should tell more people about the benefits of marriage mentoring. Someday, we hope to give back the gift that Nate and Sharon gave to us by mentoring some newly married couples. We think every couple just starting out should have a mentor.*

We thought to ourselves, *That's not a bad idea!* Ever since, we've made it standard practice for every newlywed couple who takes part in our *Saving Your Marriage Before It Starts* program. We've linked thousands of newlyweds with mentors over the last decade.

How They're Doing Today

As we were writing this, we got curious about Tom and Wendy. So we tracked them down. Now living in Portland, Oregon, Wendy and Tom have been married for 15 years and have two children. They're not the perfect couple, but they are madly in love and happier than they ever imagined. Just this week, we received an e-mail from Wendy revealing a "secret" to their success.

> *As one of the first couples in your group to go though the mentoring process, we became quick converts. We immediately saw the advantage of having Nate and Sharon, a couple we didn't even know at the start, in our lives. They made a world of difference for us.*
>
> *You'll be pleased to know that we followed up on our intentions to give back what they gave us. A few years ago, we decided it was time for our church to have a mentoring program, so we started one! We now have six other mentoring couples who work with us, and we have a blast. Tom often says, "It's the best thing we do all year for our own marriage." He's right. Meeting with the couples we mentor brings us closer together, and it feels so right to know we're doing some good... just like Nate and Sharon did for us.*
>
> *By the way, they still send us an anniversary card every year!*

As you might imagine, we were certainly encouraged by this e-mail. Because of Tom and Wendy and thousands of couples we've met with just like them, we come to the enterprise of marriage mentoring with great conviction and passion. And with a vision for what might be.

What Is Marriage Mentoring?

Why do trades have apprenticeships and professions require internships? Because the personal attention of experienced practitioners helps those just starting to master essential skills, techniques, attitudes, and knowledge. In every culture throughout human history, mentoring served as the primary means for passing on knowledge and skills. The Bible contains many examples of mentoring: Eli and Samuel, Elijah and Elisha, Moses and Joshua, Naomi and Ruth, Elizabeth and Mary, Barnabas and Paul, Paul and Timothy. And, of course, Jesus provided a supreme example of mentoring with the disciples.

Here's a pop quiz question:

A mentor is:

a. A model

b. An encourager

c. An imparter of knowledge

d. All of the above

The answer is "d." A mentor might wear many different hats, but all mentors share the ability to listen and encourage. A mentor provides a brain to pick, an ear to listen, and a push in the right direction.

Over the years, we've helped coordinate thousands of marriage mentoring relationships. During that time, we've come to the conclusion that no single way exists for being a marriage mentor, and every mentoring relationship takes on its own personality. Yet the variety in these relationships still operates within certain parameters, and that allows us to define our terms. So here goes.

A marriage mentor is a relatively happy, more experienced couple purposefully investing in another couple to effectively navigate a journey that they have already taken.

A marriage mentoring relationship can be short term or long term. It can be consistent and predictable or spontaneous and sporadic. While every marriage mentoring relationship has its own style that unfolds as the relationship develops, some potential confusion can be spared if the mentors and those being mentored discuss their initial expectations of the relationship. This discussion, of course, means that the mentoring couple needs to be somewhat clear about their own "style" before meeting with the couple they plan to mentor. To understand what a marriage mentor couple does, it helps to start with a representative list.

A marriage mentor couple:

- willingly shares what they know (in a noncompetitive way).
- represents skill, knowledge, virtue, and accomplishment because they've gone before the couple they are mentoring.
- takes a personal and heartfelt interest in the other couple's development and well-being.
- offers support, challenge, patience, and enthusiasm while guiding other couples to new levels of competence.
- points the way and represents tangible evidence of what another couple can become.
- exposes the recipients of their mentoring to new ideas, perspectives, and standards.
- has more expertise in terms of knowledge, yet sees themselves as equal to those they mentor.

How to Launch a Marriage Mentoring Ministry

While we can't cover every detail here, these are some basic steps:

1. Read *The Complete Guide to Marriage Mentoring* by Les and Leslie Parrott. This book guides mentors through three major sections: The Big Picture on Marriage Mentoring, The Marriage Mentoring Triad, and The Essential Skills for Marriage Mentoring.

2. Select a "lead couple" who can manage this ministry in your church.

3. Have this lead couple study the "10 Essential Skills of Marriage Mentoring" in *The Complete Guide to Marriage Mentoring*.

4. Help the lead couple recruit and train three other mentor couples in your congregation so each couple can coordinate the different aspects of marriage mentoring outlined in *The Complete Guide to Marriage Mentoring*.

5. Announce to your congregation that you're launching a marriage mentoring ministry, and invite couples interested in being mentored to sign up.

6. Log onto www.RealRelationships.com and sign up for free mailings to help you maintain and grow your marriage mentoring ministry.

7. Pray for God to direct and bless the couples in your church who get involved in this lay-led ministry.

What's Your Excuse?

We both grew up in parsonages and have been in church work our entire lives. We also speak to hundreds of pastors each year. So we know you might hesitate, saying, "I don't need another program to run." You're right. But marriage mentoring really is low-maintenance because it belongs to the lay people in your church. Or maybe you're saying, "I can't get volunteers to teach classes, let alone mentor other couples." We understand. But recruiting mentor couples is easier than you think. Perhaps you're saying, "I don't want to detract from the marriage counseling program we've built." It won't. In fact, marriage mentoring will augment it. Or you argue, "For now we're putting our energies into children's ministry and youth work." Worthy indeed, but marriage mentoring might be the most important thing you ever do for the young people in your church. Marriage mentoring can literally increase the spiritual vitality of your entire congregation.

The truth is, we can't think of a legitimate excuse for not having a marriage mentoring ministry in every church, large or small. Couples of every age and stage benefit from marriage mentoring, and it's easy for churches to get going.

In addition, the Bible calls us to this kind of action. Marriage mentoring is a primary way you can fulfill your job as a pastor "to prepare God's people for works of service" (Ephesians 4:12, NIV). What works of service could be more valuable to the people in your church than marriage mentoring?

The Dream

We have a dream that one day a massive network of marriage mentors will undergird the state of marriage across North America and around the world. Serving as a type of safety net, mentors will lift up and support couples at crucial crossroads—those just starting out, about to have a baby, in crisis, raising teenagers, and in just about any stage and phase of married life.

We've talked about this dream wherever we can—on national radio and television, at dozens of conferences, and in numerous magazines and newspapers. Just a few years ago, the governor of Oklahoma invited us to move to his state—where they have one of the highest divorce rates in the country—for a year. And we did, because it provided the opportunity to meet with hundreds of clergy and thousands of lay couples just to talk about our dream of marriage mentoring. We've preached "marriage mentoring" for so long in so many places with so little repercussion that we sometimes wonder if anyone's listening.

But no longer. We're very encouraged, because more than ever, we see the church catching on to this dream. In fact, we receive e-mails every day with requests for more information on marriage mentoring. If you search "marriage mentoring" on the Internet, you'll find more than a half million Web sites dealing with the idea in some fashion. More and more churches identify themselves as having a marriage mentoring ministry. And in a recent survey, 62 percent of couples said they'd like to find a mentor couple in their church, and 92 percent said they'd especially like a mentor to help them through times of conflict.

Times are changing. We hear the rumblings of a sleeping giant about to wake up. And we'll do everything we can to meet its needs.

Drs. Les and Leslie Parrott are co-founders of RealRelationships.com and the authors of *The Complete Guide to Marriage Mentoring.*

second thoughts:
REMARRIAGE AND BLENDED FAMILIES

by Dr. David and Lisa Frisbie

"**M**y daughter *loves* him," Zoe says as she laughs, pointing at Jared, her husband-to-be. "Kayla climbs up in his lap and then she won't leave. It's like she wants to stay there forever."

Jared, still shy at 28, smiles. "I was married before, but we didn't have any kids," he says softly. "Until I met Zoe and Kayla, I never realized how much I missed that, how much I wanted to be a dad."

Zoe and Jared stayed around to chat after the "Preparing for Remarriage" class we teach at a church in southern California. Now engaged, they plan to marry in a few months. The class helps couples like them sort out their feelings, learn how to communicate better, and look ahead to building a strong, lifelong relationship. Increasingly, couples preparing for marriage resemble Zoe and Jared, bringing something to the altar that wasn't part of most weddings a generation ago: prior experience, plus maybe a few children.

As the millennial clock struck 2000, married life was changing in the United States. Today, first-marriage couples no longer make up a majority of American families.

Zoe, never married but raising a daughter, and Jared, married before but without having children, are more than just a 20-something couple taking a class at a large church. As they plan a small-budget wedding and a Kayla-included honey-moon, they are surprisingly representative of engaged couples today, both within and outside of the church.

How well is the church adapting to this new social landscape? As we travel around the country, we encounter busy and highly committed pastors and other church lead-ers who tell us they don't feel prepared at all for the changes they need to make in pre-marriage counseling. Many feel unsure of themselves as they counsel couples marry-ing for a second or even third time.

Dan, the pastor of a conservative evangelical congregation, asked us, "How can I offer meaningful help to a bride and groom who have been married before?" As an afterthought, he added, "I'm not even sure what my theology about remarriage after divorce is right now. I'm still working through that."

Some pastors openly wonder if they're "weakening" or "abandoning" a high view of marriage by agreeing to perform a wedding for a couple entering a second or third marriage. One pastor rhetorically asked us, "Should I send these people right back to their original marriages? And what if their original spouse is already married to someone else?"

Other pastors, equally respectful of the sacrament of marriage, more easily under-stand the broken world they minister in. "My philosophy is simple," notes a senior pas-tor in Arizona. "I want to come alongside these couples with support, encouragement, and wise counsel. God's grace gives all of us the chance to start right where we are."

As churches wrestle with the theological implications of adults entering a second or third marriage, pastors must deal with the daily reality of remarried couples mak-ing up more and more of the people in their congregations. As a result, these church leaders want help in understanding the issues that previously married adults bring to a remarriage situation.

Unique Strengths of Previously Married Adults

In 25 years of working with divorced adults, remarried couples, and blended families at The Center for Marriage & Family Studies, we've learned that men and women with prior marriage experience can bring several particular strengths to a new marriage. Some come from simple demographics, while others are responses to the nature of their own histories and relationships.

A Little Maturity Helps

Generally, adults considering remarriage are older than those approaching a first marriage. While higher age doesn't guarantee greater discernment or personal matu-rity, most of us do learn and grow as we get older.[1]

A man who marries at 19 might have a very different temperament, character, and outlook on life when he remarries at 32. The passing of more than a decade, with experiences of earning a living and caring for a family, might make him a wiser, more disciplined, more patient husband and father.

A woman who marries just out of high school might be far more selective as she chooses a partner in her late 20s. She's likely learned to evaluate her options more carefully rather than rush ahead based on emotions, instincts, or perceived needs. As an adult who has lived through a relationship—even a troubled one—she is wiser and has better decision-making skills.

Learning How to Choose a Partner

Adults considering a remarriage will more likely base their attraction and attachment to each other on rational factors such as common interests, shared values, and compatible temperaments. They're less likely to repeat the mistakes of youth, marrying in a rush of surging hormones or during an emotional moment. They've learned that not everyone is a good fit; they've also learned how a husband and wife who share similar interests and strong values—including religious faith—can be a much more unified couple.[2]

As Emily approached her second marriage, she told us, "I never realized how much I missed having a spiritual leader in my home. Don left me; I didn't leave him. I would have stayed with him forever. But now that we're divorced, I realize how much I missed by not having a husband who shared my commitment to Christ, my involvement in the church, and my passion for others."

When men remarry, they often tell us that they're simply looking for a positive person rather than a negative one. "I just want someone who sees the brighter side of life," Aaron told us. "I made such a big mistake by marrying a critical, negative person who was never satisfied."

Both men and women tend to approach new relationships from a wiser and more grounded perspective than how they viewed their first marriage. They're less likely to be "swept away" by good looks or a good line. Instead, they're looking for stability, more maturity, and evidence of personal character in their next spouse. And they'll simply stay single until a good fit comes along.

Out of Brokenness, a Teachable Spirit

Men and women considering a remarriage often bring humility and a teachable spirit as they sit down with counselors, pastors, and friends. They realize that their previous marriage involved failure at some level; the more mature ones realize their personal share of the responsibility for that failure.

These adults also seem more open to learning about the ways their own temperament and character traits or their own lack of problem-solving or communication skills contributed to the end of a previous relationship. They know they need help, and willingly learn, grow, change, and adapt.[3]

Divorce might not be a welcome teacher, but it can be a useful one. The end of a marriage often provides enough trauma to shake people out of their old unhelpful routines and practices, showing them where they need to grow. After more than two decades of working with divorced men and women, we can boldly claim that some of the wisest and most mature people we know, and some of the most godly people we know, have a divorce in their history.

Areas of Remarriages That Need Special Attention

As you work with couples considering remarriage, consider referring them to trained counselors familiar with the specific issues likely to emerge when forming a post-divorce union. You can often find qualified help from a Christian perspective. A nearby larger church might already provide an on-site counseling center. If you know of a church-based counseling center within driving distance of your own community, stop by for a visit. Get to know the men and women who serve there. Find out how they approach remarriages. Look for counselors who are both biblically sound and clinically competent.

When adults seek to remarry following divorce, the following challenges will likely be present.

Feelings of Guilt and Shame

Following a divorce, people will likely exhibit guilt, shame, and some level of anxiety based on their own role in the process. In some cases, these feelings are clearly valid and connect to specific sins. And other times the feelings result from vague but deeply rooted shame and failure, resulting in lower self-esteem and self-confidence, particularly in women.[4] These feelings of shame may not be rooted in any specific sins but in the ordinary frailty that's part of being human, whether a marriage remains intact or not.

Unfortunately, churches sometimes feel like discouraging and shame-placing environments instead of grace-filled fellowships. Divorced adults often change churches when a marriage ends, mostly to get away from the shame they sense because of ending their union. This seems to take place less often in large churches where people feel a bit more "anonymous."

However, churches hold a unique position in offering help to divorced adults. In a church setting, these individuals can process the spiritual implications of their previous experiences. If unconfessed sin and personal irresponsibility remain, a gracious pastor can help a divorced man or woman make essential, life-giving spiritual choices.[5] Many churches are insisting that their counseling be pastorally based, centered in biblical foundations, and aimed at restoring those who have erred.

Pastors and other counselors will wisely look past the bland assurances that "everything's OK" when counseling with post-divorce adults. The more recent the experience of divorce, the more likely a good counselor can help a hurting adult discover repressed or unprocessed feelings of shame or anxiety. Looking at these issues honestly and openly helps a couple contemplate remarriage from a more revealing and more accurate perspective.

Dealing with the "Ex" Factor

After divorcing, adults often experience complex, multilayered relationships with their ex-partners. These relationships create ambiguous, frustrating, and often unhelpful emotional baggage and distress. Even in a reasonably amicable and agreeable divorce, one or both parties might experience sudden bursts of anger or depression.

"I thought I was past all that," Heidi told us as she described a recent communication breakdown involving her ex-husband. "When he didn't get there to pick up the kids for his scheduled weekend, I was a lot angrier than I expected. It was like I was angry for a lot of things, all rolled into one." Heidi's reaction is common.[6]

Divorced adults might gloss over the feelings, especially as they form new relationships. Regarding their ex, they assure their new partner, "I've gotten over my feelings for her" or "I'm not angry with him anymore." Usually, these adults aren't consciously lying. They're trying to please someone or seem attractive to a new mate. Yet in many cases, the prior relationship continues to have troubling, surprising, suddenly emerging overtones for years into the future, even if someone remarries happily.

Again, wise pastors and counselors will help a divorced man or woman realize that life will be like this for a while—filled with emotions that pop up from nowhere. Responses such as anger or depression are normal and natural; admitting them and facing them is a big part of moving forward.

If the divorced couple has children, some level of interaction with the ex-partner likely will be present for a long time. Interaction, both positive and negative, might take place with parents and extended family members of the ex-partner. Divorced adults preparing for remarriage need to understand that they'll be juggling divided loyalties and balancing conflicting interests for a long time to come—and things won't necessarily get easier.

Generally, a new spouse who understands the dynamics of the previous relationship and who steps in with consolation or a calming presence when needed is most helpful. One divorced and remarried woman told us, "Gary keeps me from losing my mind. Without him around I would have *killed* my ex-husband Richard by now."

While she spoke figuratively and would never intend actual murder, this woman's statement points to a truth: The calming presence of a new partner helps her cope with an anger that still surfaces from time to time.

Raising the Kids: A Source of Conflict

The presence of school-age or younger children within a blended family places significant pressure on a remarriage. Statistically speaking, when the adults who remarry have children who are themselves adults—no longer living at home—the risk of divorce decreases substantially. These empty-nester adults will more likely form a lasting union.

But when remarriage partners both bring young children or adolescents into a new household, the results are often disastrous. Children rarely bond and connect into a loving and cohesive unit. More commonly, they show outbursts of jealousy, resentment, and even open warfare. The parents, who expected things to turn out a lot better, seem surprised by these reactions among the kids.

The most difficult connection seems to involve two teenage females from separate families thrown together in a new home. But other combinations can be equally troubling, particularly when the children's ages are close. Simpler connections might involve younger children from one partner and older children from the other, or males from one side and females from the other. Ironically, the "blending" is easier when the children are less alike and less close to their new stepsiblings in age. But in any case, remarried couples can expect difficulty.

Although first-marriage couples need to come to agreement on matters of discipline and raising children, these parents can form and even change their opinions over time as they learn by observation and interaction. Differences of opinion can exist for a while without derailing the unity of the marriage.

However, differences of opinion in a remarriage family about how to raise or discipline the children can be—and often are—lethal to the relationship. So when post-divorce adults remarry, they absolutely must have open and well-rounded discussions about how to train, admonish, and raise the children.

When we travel to speak to remarried couples and blended families, this topic usually dominates the question-and-answer times after we speak. Successful blended families often say that "letting the birth parent be the boss parent" can be the wisest approach, especially in the early years of a new union.[7]

Grateful for the Process

Perhaps the most helpful perspective we can have when counseling couples planning to remarry is realizing that God is providing an opportunity to minister his grace where it's much needed.

As we research the key dynamics that contribute to healthy, thriving remarriages, we continually encounter the theme of grace. Couple after couple, while sharing openly about their struggles, failures, difficulties, and problems, eventually bring the discussion around to their experience of encountering a gracious and forgiving Savior, finding hope in the presence of an unexpected but welcome mercy from God.[8]

Where would any of us be without God's mercy? All of us are lost without the redemptive message that Christ's sacrifice finds us where and as we are; Christ's resurrection lifts us up into new life, transforming our relationships.

This perspective guides J.D. Larson, a pastor at North Coast Church in Vista, California. His responsibilities include young married couples and helping couples prepare for marriage, including remarriage. He describes the opportunity he has to interact with couples considering remarriage: "It's an honor to stand with a couple who is ready to make a vow before God. Each one of them is in a unique situation, and I know that God is in the business of healing the past and giving us an opportunity to be transformed through it. I have the privilege of joining couples on a small part of that journey."

As a pastor, counselor, or lay leader working in marriage ministry, you might have that same privilege: joining with a couple at a challenging stage along their journey and becoming a friend and helper. You can guide and lead them through a careful process that fills their prior history with the redemptive, life-giving force of God's love.

Dr. David and Lisa Frisbie serve as executive directors of The Center for Marriage & Family Studies in Del Mar, California. Frequent speakers at conferences, retreats, and seminars, they are the authors of numerous articles and eight books, including *Happily Remarried* and *Raising Great Kids on Your Own.*

---

1 One study, for example, shows that women marrying after age 25 (as opposed to age 18 or earlier) reduce their risk of divorce by 24 percent. (Matthew D. Bramlett and William D. Mosher, *Cohabitation, Marriage, Divorce and Remarriage in the United States,* National Center for Health Statistics, Vital and Health Statistics, 23 [22], 2002).

2 For a useful discussion about forming this kind of unity in a remarriage relationship, see our recent book *Happily Remarried.* (David and Lisa Frisbie, *Happily Remarried,* Harvest House Publishers, pp. 22-35.)

3 You may enjoy learning from two case studies that perfectly illustrate this kind of response to the crisis and trauma of divorce. We discuss these at some length in our book *Moving Forward After Divorce.* (David and Lisa Frisbie, *Moving Forward After Divorce,* Harvest House Publishers, pp. 31-42).

4 For a brief but useful discussion of the ways in which divorce can cause unhelpful kinds of shame, read a few pages of this book by Jeff VanVonderen. (Jeff VanVonderen, *Tired of Trying to Measure Up,* Bethany House Publishers, pp. 53-54).

5 A very useful and positive discussion can be found in "Managing Stress in Marriage" by Roy Rotz. (Roy Rotz, chapter in *Making a Marriage,* Beacon Hill Press, edited by Larry Morris, pp. 92-93).

6 We discuss this at length in a chapter called "The 'X' (ex) Factor," which has become one of the most quoted and commented-upon portions of *Happily Remarried.* (David and Lisa Frisbie, *Happily Remarried,* Harvest House Publishers, pp. 155-170).

7 We discuss this idea in helpful detail in the pages of our recent book, *Happily Remarried,* which examines the healthy habits and best practices of successful second marriages.

8 This was our working method and process for *Happily Remarried.* We sat down with medium- and long-term remarried couples whose relationships exemplified stability, maturity, and spiritual strength. Over a period of several years of reflective listening, we were able to identify patterns and common themes that formed the basis for the book as well as our seminars and workshops.

the disciplines
OF MARRIAGE COUNSELING

by Doyle Roth

When I began pastoring a church in Littleton, Colorado, more than 30 years ago, I never would have guessed how much time I'd dedicate to counseling married couples. I expected preaching, teaching, and other leadership responsibilities to take up the bulk of my time. I never anticipated the enormous amount of time or emotional investment necessary to minister to needy people through counseling.

In the trenches of a consistent counseling ministry, I've learned a lot about the process. And I've gained some biblical disciplines that help me manage an intense counseling load. These disciplines will equip you for a more effective counseling ministry and maximize the time you need to care for a hurting flock.

The Necessity of Self-Discipline

A vital ingredient in healthy counseling is the self-discipline of the counselor. The Holy Spirit provides an essential ingredient in the counseling process, bringing conviction of sin, illuminating the Scriptures, and enabling us to live the Christian life. But the Bible also clearly directs Christians to be self-disciplined. The Apostle Paul wrote, "God has not given us a spirit of fear and timidity, but of power, love, and self-discipline" (2 Timothy 1:7). Counselors can easily have a "spirit of timidity" or careless indifference instead of "power, love, and self-discipline." In fact, many pastors conduct counseling in a haphazard manner, thinking of it as a less significant ministry than others. However, pastors who nonchalantly kill an hour under the guise of "counseling" will be ineffective. So we need to bring a sense of discipline into our offices.

To understand discipline, let's consider what it's like to be undisciplined. Scripture addresses this topic as well: "A person without self-control is like a city with broken-down walls" (Proverbs 25:28). In other words, an undisciplined person remains unprotected against the many enemies in life and counseling: time, fear, disorganization, and so on. Without good boundaries, counselors easily become victims of other people's problems and confusion. As counselors, we must build "walls" that protect us. These walls include appointment books, clear priorities, a good watch, and people who help us stay focused.

The late D. Martyn Lloyd-Jones, who served as minister of Westminster Chapel in London, observed: "I defy you to read the life of any saint...without seeing... that the greatest characteristic in the life of that saint was discipline and order. Invariably it is the universal characteristic of all the outstanding men and women of God...Obviously it is something that is thoroughly scriptural and absolutely essential" (*Spiritual Depression: Its Causes and Cure*, Grand Rapids, MI: Wm. B. Eerdmans Publishing Company, 1965, p. 210). Whether you're young or old in the faith, you need discipline and self-control if you plan to minister to others through counseling.

I face challenges during every counseling appointment. In order for my counseling to be effective, I practice several important personal disciplines. I'd like to share these with you, in the hopes that they'll keep your counseling ministry effective, too.

The Discipline of Time

Time is one of the most important commodities in life and ministry. The Apostle Paul urged us to "make the most of every opportunity in these evil days" (Ephesians 5:16). Counseling can easily eat up most of your week. If you counsel five couples in a week, you'll use up close to a solid day of work. In-office appointments for those couples will take a total of five hours. In addition, you'll spend about 15 minutes preparing for each case, another 15 minutes summarizing your session for each couple, and other bits of time getting the five appointments scheduled.

If you don't have a way to manage your counseling appointments, you'll find yourself frustrated. People who are suffering easily lose track of time. So I suggest these helpful time-saving disciplines:

• **Use voice messaging and e-mail.** As much as possible, minimize your counseling phone work unless it's serving as a substitute for an in-office appointment. In other words, don't get caught off guard and spend 30 minutes on the phone confirming an appointment with someone you're counseling.

• **Return phone calls rather than taking every call.** When you make a phone call, you'll be able to end it more easily. Another hint: Return phone calls just before another appointment so you can politely end the conversation.

• **Set a particular day for counseling.** For example, use the entire afternoon of one day for counseling appointments instead of scattering appointments throughout the week. This mentally frees up the rest of the week to concentrate on other ministry obligations. If you can't schedule counseling appointments back to back, schedule counseling toward the end of the day or just before lunch to contain the appointments to one hour.

• **Limit the length of counseling appointments.** Scheduling appointments each hour will help you stay on time. At times, you might run over an hour. But discipline yourself to stay within the hour. Ending a session when the counselee is still struggling can be difficult. However, feelings aren't a good gauge for determining the success or failure of a counseling situation.

• **Be careful about walk-ins.** Discourage so-called "urgent" appointments, such as "I need to see you this afternoon and at the latest, first thing in the morning." Yes, exceptions exist. But the majority of counseling issues can wait. I've saved many hours not getting caught in the "tyranny of the urgent."

You can handle "urgent" requests in a couple of ways:

1. Set up appointments one to two weeks in advance. Even if you have openings in your schedule, you don't need to fill those with additional counseling appointments. Your time will also be more productive when the people you're counseling aren't on emotional overload and have had time to calm down.

2. Ask the couple you're counseling to call you back in a few days to schedule an appointment. After a cooling-off period, many people with "urgent" problems won't call back at all. Be careful not to become a "Band-Aid specialist," merely covering wounds for the short term. Instead, be a counselor who sees practical sanctification as a matter of time and growth.

• **Scheduling additional appointments doesn't always equal more progress.** Be aware of the investment the people you're counseling make in the process. In other words, ask yourself: Are they working hard toward counseling goals? following your advice? doing the homework? growing spiritually? Some people will take advantage of you; they might want to talk about their problems, but have little interest in dealing with them.

• **Follow up after a period of time.** I want the people I'm counseling to know I truly care. Sometimes I call a week, a month, or even a year later. Often, I try to merely leave a voice message expressing my love and encouraging them to continually grow in their

Christian lives.

• **Be careful about evenings.** Your family needs you, too! Use voice messaging to screen calls, and return most calls the following day. Train people to respect your family time.

• **Be prepared to refer long-term counseling cases.** I consider myself a "short-term, solution-based" counselor. After working with someone for six weeks, I either see good progress or the person needs another level of counseling. I personally avoid working with "professional patients"—those who just want to go over their problems endlessly. I keep a list of other counselors who take long-term counseling cases.

The Discipline of Hope

When I was younger, my wife and I saw a counselor. I wasn't sure what to expect, but I assumed I might feel better after the session than before it. Deep down, I wanted someone to assure us that pressing forward toward reconciliation and renewal in our marriage made more sense than ending it. The counselor we saw failed in the "hope" department—he couldn't cheer up a circus clown.

When people come in for counseling, they're discouraged, disappointed, depressed, or uncertain. They benefit a great deal if you're light-hearted, positive, and hopeful. After all, they come to you because something has compromised their hope. The loss of hope gives way to despair and anxiety. With no end in view to their troubles and an unquenchable thirst for the "water of life," your office might be the only place where they can find an ounce of refreshing hope.

Failing to discipline our spirit can lead to hopelessness. When someone begins to unpack his or her concerns, unbelief can be a real temptation. We might mumble to ourselves, "This thing is over" or "I'm just wasting my time." Perhaps Genesis 18:14 should be a plaque on every counselor's wall: "Is anything too hard for the Lord?" In the midst of severe difficulties, we can forget that we have a great God who specializes in broken lives and hurting people. Thankfully, we offer hope rooted in Christ's sacrifice and God's sovereignty.

Sure, sometimes we need to be more sober when counseling. People will shed tears when clouds of pain and suffering roll in. But the sun is still there. Jesus says, "I will never fail you. I will never abandon you" (Hebrews 13:5). God accomplishes his purposes and grows people through suffering. When people trust us, they need to see the discipline of hope alive and well within us.

Let me suggest a few ways to focus on hope and to communicate God's loving plan:

• **Put out some breath mints.** Just place a dish of mints on a table in your office. Something sweet helps bitter medicine go down.

• **Start your time by talking about something positive.** Learn about their family, work, hobbies, or children. What do they enjoy?

• **Develop a list of Scriptures that stress God's ability to change any and every situation.** Add some Scriptures that teach this message: "For God is working in you, giving you the desire and the power to do what pleases him" (Philippians 2:13). Keep these nearby and use them at the beginning of your session.

• **Improve your sense of humor.** Humor releases tension in tough counseling situations. Learn to make fun of yourself. Look for humor in every situation. You're not making fun of anyone; rather you're having fun learning and growing together: "A cheerful heart is good medicine" (Proverbs 17:22). Yet be sensitive: "Singing cheerful songs to a person with a heavy heart is like taking someone's coat in cold weather or pouring vinegar in a wound" (Proverbs 25:20).

• **Share personal victories.** I love sharing how God spared my own marriage and how he works in my life. Tell how God has conquered sin in your life. People need to see your transparency.

The Discipline of Investigation

I use the first portion of counseling sessions to gather information so I can properly understand the problem. Counselors need the skill and discipline to ask questions. When we went for counseling many years ago, I wanted the counselor to genuinely try to understand our situation. Yet he couldn't get there in five questions or in five minutes. He needed to follow the adage, "Spouting off before listening to the facts is both shameful and foolish" (Proverbs 18:13). Through the years, I've learned that properly asked questions uncover essential information. Use questions that start with *How? When? Why? Where?* and *What?*

The discipline of investigation involves asking questions until you gain adequate information to understand what's really going on. The more you learn, the more targeted your counsel will be. Look at Jesus—he asked questions of almost everyone he dealt with.

A few practical suggestions to follow:

• **Use the first 15 or 20 minutes for investigation.** Don't be tempted to stop after a question or two to suggest a clichéd solution.

• **Learn to ask tough questions.** These might be shameful or embarrassing for the people being questioned. But don't be afraid to tighten the knot through questions. Confession is good for the soul.

• **Don't be afraid of silence.** Be patient. If you don't get an answer, ask if the person understood the question. Then ask the same question again with slight revision. Silence might also alert you to an area that needs more digging.

• **Ask specific questions.** Don't be satisfied to ask, "How do you feel?" Go on to ask questions such as: Why do you feel like that? When do you get those feelings? How intense are your feelings? What spiritual issues do you think surround those feelings? What do you think God has to say about the way you feel? The more specific it is, the better the question.

• **Avoid asking questions with "yes" or "no" answers.** If you blow it, follow up. Say "Why?" or "Could you explain?" Or ask one of the questions above.

• **Ask questions that provoke conviction and godly sorrow.** Jesus asked Martha, "Do you believe this?" (John 11:26). That must have been a convicting moment in her life.

• **Ask questions that challenge or provoke commitment.** For example, if you want to give someone a homework assignment, ask: Will you do the assignment? Will you memorize that verse? Why is it important for you to do the assignment? What's our next step if you don't do the assignment?

The Discipline of Hearing

Have you ever gone to sleep during a counseling session? Or lost track of time or caught yourself staring into space? Maybe you were just preoccupied. I've done all these things. This raises another important discipline for counselors—the discipline of effective hearing. People need to know you're not just listening but "hearing." How many times do you listen to your spouse or children but don't really hear what they've said?

When I speak at a conference, nearly everyone listens. But I often wonder how many people hear me. When your pastor teaches, you might listen to the message from God's Word, but do you hear it, too? It takes energy to be a good hearer—an acquired ability and a disciplined skill: "You must all be quick to listen, slow to speak, and slow to get angry" (James 1:19). As people pour out their story of heartache and confusion, do you really hear? You might listen to the words, but do you hear the anger, disappointment, and failed expectations?

Here are some practical tips that can help you be a determined hearer:

• **Hear tones of voice.** This might lead you to say, "You sound frustrated and overwhelmed. Tell me why" or "You sound discouraged. What's that about?"

• **Pay attention to descriptive words, and ask for clarification.** For example: "You used the word *abusive*. What does that mean to you?" or "You spoke of being afraid. What happens when you become afraid?" or "You threatened to take action. What would that look like?"

• **Repeat back what you hear.** This lets people know that you're paying attention instead of daydreaming. But it also provides clarification. Discipline yourself to hear what people mean, not just what they say.

• **Hear if the counselee is withdrawing.** People have many different reasons for not responding. I often hear a wife say, "I'm not sure what I think." That might mean "I really don't know." Or it can mean "I'm afraid to say because my abusive husband is sitting right next to me." Good hearing skills help identify fear, manipulation, control, and so on.

The Discipline of Scripture

The Apostle Paul's words nearly jump off the page when he proclaims, "All Scripture is inspired by God and is useful to teach us what is true and to make us realize what is wrong in our lives. It corrects us when we are wrong and teaches us to do what is right" (2 Timothy 3:16-17). As a biblical counselor, you must settle the matter of Scripture. It's either adequate or not. It's either sufficient or not. It either communicates God's plan for us or it's an inadequate, trite, and incomplete treaty filled with clichés.

Counselors need to develop a discipline of Scripture—using the Bible effectively and targeting emotional and behavioral problems from a scriptural perspective. Many counselors hesitate to use Scripture and resort to the latest fad of psychological solutions. However, Hebrews 4:12 tells us that "the word of God is alive and powerful. It is sharper than the sharpest two-edged sword, cutting between soul and spirit, between joint and marrow. It exposes our innermost thoughts and desires." Don't we want the people we counsel to grow? Then God's Word is the answer: "Like newborn babies, you must crave pure spiritual milk so that you will grow" (1 Peter 2:2).

Allow me to suggest the following about the discipline of Scripture:

• **Let people know your convictions before you start.** Tell them that you hold the Word of God over other forms of wisdom. No secrets, revelations, or scientific discoveries can change what God promises and declares in his Word.

• **Ask about their beliefs regarding the Bible.** You might as well get this discussion underway if you want your counseling to be effective. If people doubt the validity of Scripture, then you need to discuss that before moving forward.

• **Develop a scriptural paradigm.** Get *The Christian Counselor's Manual* by Jay Adams (Grand Rapids, MI: Zondervan, 1986). This will help you think through emotional, marital, and other issues biblically.

• **Keep a Bible on your counseling table.** Refer to it often, and open it frequently. Remember that during a counseling session, the only perfect counsel will come directly from the Scriptures.

• **Develop a library of Bible-based materials.** *Quick Scripture Reference for Counseling* by John Kruis (Grand Rapids, MI: Baker Books, 2001) provides an easy way to look up issues and find appropriate Scripture texts. Also, collect articles and books that deal with patterns of thought and behavior. Use these materials for homework assignments, Scripture memory, and so on.

The Discipline of Confrontation

The ministry of confrontation—reproving, rebuking, and exhorting—is a mandatory ministry in the counselor's office. This ministry implies direction. When a couple comes to your office for counseling, one presupposition will generally set the tone for the meeting: the work of confrontation. Yes, people need comfort, encouragement, and a loving pat on the back. But problems often revolve around sinful patterns of thought that lead to undesirable actions and emotions.

I use the last part of every session for confrontation. Remember, being blessed by God is for those who "hear God's word and obey it" (Luke 8:21). Christian counselors can't support sinful behavior. If you sense sinful attitudes or actions, you must confront them. I firmly believe that the Holy Spirit supernaturally uses loving confrontation to bring conviction, repentance, and growth. Sin is sin, and only spiritual truth promises real deliverance. Confront the behavior of the people you counsel, and give them biblical reasons for confession of sin and repentance.

Here are some ideas you might find helpful:

• **Speak the truth, but in a loving manner.** Don't sound judgmental or prideful. While you must speak truth, be careful about how you speak it.

• **Tell people that God's opinion is what really counts.** Sure, I have opinions about the circumstances of people I'm counseling. But what God thinks about their situation, behavior, and attitudes is what matters. Your attitude will improve when you see it through God's eyes.

• **Ask people if they care what the Bible says about their situation.** You don't need to hesitate. Once they say "yes," you have permission to confront their problems biblically. You can openly discuss what God's Word says about their situation and apply his treatment plan. If they say "no," close with prayer. Invite them to return if God changes their heart about listening to his Word.

• **Ask questions.** These include the following: Do you understand what these verses say? Do you agree with this passage of Scripture? Do you have any questions?

• **Communicate with eye contact and body language.** Look into people's eyes. Speak slowly and emphatically, but also speak tenderly with compassion and understanding. You have the authority of God's Word behind you, but you don't need to be a hard-nosed, dogmatic legalist. And don't act as if you have it all together and never need an occasional rebuke from Scripture or a loving friend.

• **Show compassion with appropriate physical touch.** A touch on the arm or a pat on the back might be very kind and reassuring under the right circumstances. Counselors need to be careful about physical touch. But at times, I've placed my hand on a person's shoulder. When counseling a husband and wife, I sometimes hold their hands to pray. Again, be very careful about this point.

• **Let people know you understand their pain.** Confrontation and conviction hurt. However, God can heal and restore the joy of their salvation.

• **Pray together.** Urge the people you're counseling to renew good communication between themselves and God. Only through the work of the Holy Spirit can people challenge and change sinful behavior and thoughts.

The Discipline of Application

Unlike secular counseling, biblical counselors use God's Word not only to confront sinfulness but to teach the application of God's truth. A counseling appointment isn't over until the counselor gives some direction for changing behavior. The Apostle Paul put it this way: "Throw off your old sinful nature and your former way of life…Put on your new nature, created to be like God—truly righteous and holy" (Ephesians 4:22, 24). It's easy to understand someone's dilemma, offer a word of encouragement, and conclude the session with a word of prayer. However, people seeking your counsel want direction through the discipline of application.

Effective biblical application doesn't happen automatically, and it's often time consuming. As a counselor, you see people's problems through "fresh eyes," and you have the responsibility to tell them both what God has to say about changing their situation and how they can start making changes. To maximize the results of helpful application, you'll probably suggest homework or follow-up assignments. I use a variety of assignments, such as having people do word and topical studies in the Bible or reading resources I provide.

These suggestions will help you be more effective with application:

• **Get familiar with the book of Proverbs.** Many appropriate passages provide help for many emotional and situational problems.

• **Study epistles that have application sections.** For example, the first 11 chapters of Romans deal with doctrines. But in chapter 12, Paul begins applying that truth. The first three chapters of Ephesians teach theology, but the last three chapters tell how to apply that theology in everyday situations. Look for similar patterns in other New Testament letters.

• **Ask God to give you practical wisdom.** Not everything is answered directly in the Bible, so we must strive after wisdom to see answers that apply.

• **Application requires follow-up.** Make sure the people you're counseling have a plan for following through with life changes. Then come alongside them during the process to acknowledge how difficult change can be. Follow up using e-mail or a phone message to offer an encouraging word before the next counseling appointment.

The Discipline of Follow-Up

The Apostle Paul provides a great example for the discipline of follow-up. When he planted a church, he evangelized an area, ministered the Word, provided shepherding, grew the church, and then left. But upon his departure, he appointed elders or assigned others to look after the people in his absence. He sent people with specific gifts and encouraged the use of other Christians in the community. He wrote letters and gave instruction, even from distant locations. He wept and cared for people long after he had been in their midst physically. These same principles also work in your counseling ministry.

Here are a few suggestions for follow-up:

• **Move the people you counsel to mentors.** For example, after you've counseled a married couple for a period of time, urge them to connect with a mentor couple. Help the mentor couple choose appropriate study material, and arrange for the two couples to get together. The mentoring couple gets to use their gifts, while the mentored couple receives long-term marital discipleship.

• **In January, call the people you counseled the previous year.** You'll enjoy hearing of their progress and offering a word of encouragement. On occasion, you might create more work for yourself if someone needs to begin counseling again. Yet in the long run, it's a good way to say, "I care about you."

• **Follow up using e-mail.** Just a brief note provides encouragement.

• **Stay in touch with birthday greetings.** I call everyone on my birthday list every year. I don't need to do this, but it's another way to let people know I'm interested in their continual growth.

The Discipline of Compassion and Empathy

This discipline wraps itself around all the other disciplines. It's the spirit of counseling we see in the life of Jesus Christ. His life was marked with compassion for the needy and empathy for people whose hearts were broken. When he "saw the crowds, he had compassion on them because they were confused and helpless, like sheep without a shepherd" (Matthew 9:36). Jesus not only saw with his eyes but with his heart. Every counselor needs to pray for this spiritual quality. The Apostle Paul asked, "Is there any encouragement from belonging to Christ? Any comfort from his love? Any fellowship together in the Spirit? Are your hearts tender and compassionate? Then make me truly happy by agreeing wholeheartedly with each other, loving one another, and working together with one mind and purpose" (Philippians 2:1-2).

When people come to you in their brokenness, you should respond with the spirit of true compassion. This requires discipline because compassion and empathy aren't natural tendencies. In fact, they're supernatural—empowered only by the Holy Spirit.

Try these suggestions to help practice this discipline:

• **Try to relate to the situation of the person you're counseling.** Identify with their hurts as if they were your hurts. Paul urged us to "be happy with those who are happy, and weep with those who weep" (Romans 12:15). When you put yourself in others' shoes, you'll enhance your sensitivity and compassion for the sorrows and hardships they're dealing with.

• **Don't be unnecessarily harsh.** That won't help anyone. Confronting sinful behavior doesn't negate compassion and empathy. Learn to be lovingly honest. Don't speak in judgmental tones as if you're exempt from suffering or temptation. Speak with true compassion.

• **Listen compassionately.** Listen silently, but when the time is done, make sure you *hear* the fear, hurt, or suffering of the people you're counseling. Practice not having an answer to all of life's sufferings. Humanly speaking, some difficulties make no sense. Sometimes, you might simply confess, "I don't know what to say…I'm so sorry." Don't spiritualize all pain and suffering. If you do, you minimize it for those you're desperately trying to help. Jesus didn't say to suffering people, "Pull yourself together!" He wept and responded with compassion knowing that God had a wonderful plan for their lives.

I hope these practical disciplines will add to your counseling success. Each counselor is different, and the people we counsel have a vast variety of needs. But some general "rules of thumb" at least provide a place to start. Pick and choose as you see fit, and use what suits your counseling style. Through your discipline as a counselor and the work of the Holy Spirit, you'll bless couples to draw closer to Christ. And that's what it's really all about.

Doyle Roth, a pastor at Littleton Bible Chapel in Littleton, Colorado, has been involved in counseling ministry for more than 30 years. He's the author of *OOPS! I Forgot My Wife: A Story of Commitment as Marriage and Self-Centeredness Collide* and *OOPS! We Forgot the Kids: A Story of Relationships as Parenting and Self-Centeredness Collide.*

appendix

RESOURCES AND FORMS FOR MARRIAGE MINISTRY

The eHarmony Marriage Program
by Drs. Les and Leslie Parrott

Imagine you're a floor manager at a bicycle manufacturing plant. It's your responsibility to make sure that the bicycles you produce are a quality product and ready for distribution. However, for some time now you've realized that more than half of the bicycles your plant is producing are coming off the lines unable to work properly. In fact, many fall apart after very little use. And the other bikes that last longer are not as stable as they first appear.

No doubt you'd be desperate for a better way to build a bike. You'd be frantic, in fact, wouldn't you?

Well, we're guessing you might be feeling the same way about the marriages in your church. You're looking for a new way to build better marriages. And we believe that we can tell you about something that just might be what you've been looking for.

Why Are We Using the Same Old Tools?

If you're like most people ministering to couples, the tools you have in your ministry tool box probably include two essentials: (1) counseling, for both premarital couples as well as couples in pain; and (2) marriage retreats and seminars, for reaching as many couples at one shot as you can. In our survey of more than a hundred churches, we found these two tools to be the most common. After that, some churches put a special emphasis on small groups or classes for couples or a special sermon series. And then, we find that a small but growing number of churches are also doing "marriage mentoring" (see "The Sleeping Giant in the Church" beginning on page 187).

So, with these same old tools, used for decades, all of us interested in building healthier marriages have been trying to turn around the divorce rate, alleviate pain for couples in distress, curb destructive habits (like anger, reckless spending, and so on) in the home, eradicate the poison of pornography and other addictions, and launch new couples for lifelong love. But it's not working. Like the frantic floor manager at a malfunctioning bicycle plant, we need a new system.

A New Tool for Marriage Ministry

We believe that the eHarmony Marriage Program *is* that system. It works by having couples in your care take an online assessment that provides them (and you) with the most accurate clinical snapshot of their marriage available. In other words, by spending less than an hour answering a series of questions online about their marriage, a couple (or one spouse, if answering alone) will be provided with a one-page summary of relational strengths as well as their personal opportunities for growth. This single page often puts into words what couples have been trying to express for months. As one recent user said, "The summary page that showed us the specific areas in our relationship that we needed to focus on was worth it all—it helped us set our marital compass to know which direction we needed to go."

> To use the eHarmony Marriage Program, simply log on to www.eHarmony.com and click the "Married" tab for more information or to get started.

We couldn't agree more. That's exactly what we designed the summary page—what we call the "Marriage Action Plan"—to do: (1) raise awareness of where a couple is at, (2) provide encouragement by pointing out what's going well, and (3) give specific direction for a concrete and doable plan to make the marriage better.

Following the Marriage Action Plan, the couple receives more than three dozen pages of personalized feedback in 10 important areas. These areas include:

1. Dreams
2. Communication
3. Sex
4. Commitment
5. Wellness
6. Trust
7. Home
8. Family
9. Companionship
10. Values

Each of these 10 sections provides the couple with unique and detailed comments and recommendations on their relationship.

Going Deeper—Much Deeper

While the eHarmony Marriage Profile is a true eye-opener for couples, the greatest blessing of this program comes when couples take the next step by following a customized plan for improving their marriage. We provide couples with a fun and interactive system for gaining the insights and skills they need most—and it's done in a time-efficient manner. In other words, couples can no longer use the excuse of "we just don't have the time." Why? Because all we need from them is 20 minutes a week. That's it!

Here's how it works. Once they've reviewed their Marriage Profile (on their own, with you as a pastor or counselor, or with another facilitator like a marriage mentor), a couple receives a series of online sessions to complete in the privacy of their own home. They do one interactive online video session per week, and it takes just 20 minutes.

These interactive sessions are done at their computer—together or individually. They then receive a friendly e-mail (to both of them) containing a brief activity to do together.

How You Fit In: Three Major eHarmony Marriage Ministry Models

As you can see, this new tool for ministering to couples is *very* flexible. Pastors, marriage ministry leaders, lay counselors, small group facilitators, classroom leaders, and marriage mentors can all choose exactly how involved they need to be with a couple, based on the detailed feedback from the eHarmony Marriage Program.

You don't need to complete any certification or training program to use this ministry tool. You can use it starting today. Just have a couple in your care go to the eHarmony Marriage Web site, and you're off and running.

Here are some proven interaction models and typical ministry scenarios you'll identify with. You can think of these as different ministry models to follow with the eHarmony Marriage tool in your toolbox:

1. The Kick-Off Model. This is most appropriate for relatively healthy couples looking to enhance their marriage. In this model you'll probably meet with the couple just to get them started, encouraging them to do the program on their own and inviting them to touch base as appropriate.

• *The Typical Scenario:* A couple you know to be relatively functioning but hitting a tough patch asks you for guidance in the church foyer or on the phone.

• *You Say:* "I'm so glad you are asking for help, and I know just what I'd like you to do. I want you to go online together and complete the eHarmony Marriage Program. It's easy and you'll love it. Once you've got your marriage profile in hand, come in and see me for a few minutes. The program will help us chart your course, and it will show you what to do next. Of course, I'd love to know how it's going along the way."

• *Your Time:* Perhaps just a few minutes, but it's up to you. This is designed to be low maintenance with a high impact. It can be as formal or informal as you like.

• *Your Role:* In this model, you become the catalyst for helping this couple get exactly what they need, but you don't have to fill your schedule with trying to figure that out. eHarmony Marriage does the work for you. You might or might not choose to review their profile with them. Either way, they'll know what Interactive Video Exercises to complete.

2. The Milestone Model. This is appropriate for relatively healthy couples and for couples grappling with a significant issue or two in their relationship.

• *The Typical Scenario:* A couple tells you they're struggling because the husband has a problem with anger, or the wife has a money management problem, or they don't agree on their parenting approaches.

• *You Say:* "I've got a tool for helping you get through this issue, and I want to meet with you once a week (or every two weeks) for the next couple of months. First, however,

I want you to go online together and complete the eHarmony Marriage Profile. It takes less than an hour to answer the questions. I want you to bring your marriage profile to our first session."

• *Your Time:* This requires a moderate commitment of your time—typically three to five hours over three months or so.

• *Your Role:* In this model, you meet with the couple at particular milestones—after they've completed the questionnaire and after completing each online video session. You debrief the eHarmony video sessions they've completed before coming to see you. This keeps them accountable and will help them take the information to an even deeper level by talking about it with you.

3. The Intensive Model. This is most appropriate for distressed couples struggling with a serious threat to their marriage and even those on the brink of divorce.

• *The Typical Scenario:* A couple tells you they are barely talking, or that they don't know what to do because he's admitted to a pornography addiction, or that she's had an affair, or that they are considering separation.

• *You Say:* "You've done the right thing to come to me, and I want to help. Let's meet this week and devise our plan. First, however, I want you to go online and complete the eHarmony Marriage Profile. You don't have to do this together, but I'd like both of you to complete it and bring it in when we meet."

• *Your Time:* This requires a significant commitment of your time—typically one hour a week over several months.

• *Your Role:* In this model, you make a commitment to the couple to meet regularly—as long and as often as you deem necessary to help them get through their crisis. You'll use the results of their profile to point out what's going right for them, even though everything feels wrong. And you'll want to take full advantage of the online video sessions to augment the personalized attention you're giving this couple.

So there you have it—three proven ways to most effectively use the eHarmony Marriage Program in your church. Keep in mind that these are the general models for using this tool. You might find an effective way that's uniquely your own. Again, the program is designed to be as flexible and creative as you are. And the program is constantly improving as a result of feedback from people just like you. So don't hesitate to make your suggestions known.

Drs. Les and Leslie Parrott are co-founders of RealRelationships.com and co-creators of eHarmony Marriage. Their books include *Your Time-Starved Marriage, Love Talk,* and *Saving Your Marriage Before It Starts.*

Marriage Ministry Event and Activity Feedback Form

	YES	NO
1. Did you like this event?	❑	❑
2. Would you enjoy doing this event again?	❑	❑
3. Did you meet someone new?	❑	❑
4. Was the cost reasonable?	❑	❑
5. Would you invite a friend next time?	❑	❑
6. Did you learn something new about yourself?	❑	❑
7. Did you learn something new about your marriage relationship?	❑	❑
8. Did you learn something new about God?	❑	❑
9. Did you get to know other couples in the group better?	❑	❑
10. Are you glad you came?	❑	❑

11. On a scale of 1 to 10, how would you rate this event?_____

12. If you had to describe this event in one word, what would it be?_____

13. What did you like about this event?_____

_____

_____

_____

14. What did you not like about this event?_____

_____

_____

_____

15. What would you change about this event?_____

_____

_____

_____

_____

16. What did you learn during this event?_____

_____

_____

_____

Marriage Ministry Retreat Schedule

Friday

6:00 p.m.–7:00 p.m.	Registration
7:30 p.m.–8:00 p.m.	Refreshments and Fellowship (Icebreaker)
8:00 p.m.–8:30 p.m.	Praise and Worship
8:30 p.m.–10:00 p.m.	Session 1/Couple's Breakout Time*
10:00 p.m.	Fellowship and Game Time—Informal

Saturday

7:00 a.m.–7:30 a.m.	Morning Prayer Meeting
8:00 a.m.–8:40 a.m.	Breakfast
8:40 a.m.–9:00 a.m.	Praise and Worship
9:00 a.m.–10:30 a.m.	Session 2/Couple's Breakout Time*
10:30 a.m.–11:00 a.m.	Refreshment Break
11:00 a.m.–12:00 p.m.	Session 3/Couple's Breakout Time*
12:00 p.m.–5:30 p.m.	Lunch and Free Time
5:30 p.m.	Dinner
7:00 p.m.–7:30 p.m.	Praise and Worship
7:30 p.m.–9:00 p.m.	Session 4/Couple's Breakout Time*
9:00 p.m.	Saturday Night Campfire/Fellowship

Sunday

8:00 a.m.–9:00 a.m.	Breakfast
9:15 a.m.–9:30 a.m.	Praise and Worship
9:30 a.m.–10:00 a.m.	Message
10:00 a.m.–10:30 a.m.	Communion Service
10:30 a.m.	Check Out of Rooms and Departure

*For some great ideas to help participants experience spiritual renewal personally and in their marriages during these breakout times, use the "Spiritual Retreat Ideas" beginning on page 26.

Serving Survey

Here are some areas in the church where you can serve together as a couple. Please check all the ways you might be willing to pitch in and lend your helping hand.

Don't worry! Checking a box doesn't mean you're committed. This just allows the church to know what kind of resources we have among us. Someone will contact you about each service opportunity, and you can choose to sign up or graciously decline.

Name:_____

Address:_____

_____

Phone number:_____

E-mail address:_____

❑ Lead a Bible study

❑ Be a mentor

❑ Write or design publicity pieces

❑ Do general office work

❑ Serve meals

❑ Plan and prepare meals

❑ Bring treats

❑ Speak at an event

❑ Facilitate a small-group discussion

❑ Be greeters or ushers

❑ Be on a planning committee

❑ Teach a Sunday school class

❑ Shop for supplies

❑ Organize supplies

❑ Work in the church library

❑ Organize volunteers

❑ Provide transportation

❑ Contact church visitors by phone

❑ Visit church visitors in their homes

❑ Be on a welcome team

❑ Sing or play special music

❑ Lead group singing

❑ Work at a registration table

❑ Host an event in my home

❑ Serve as lay counselors

❑ Provide child care

❑ Work in the church nursery

❑ Other:_____

❑ Other:_____

❑ Other:_____

Traditional Wedding Service Order

Prelude
(Option: special music during seating of grandparents and parents)
Grandparents seated
Parents seated (groom's parents, then bride's parents)

Music change when wedding party enters
Pastor enters
Groom and groomsmen enter: groom, best man, groomsmen
Bridal party enters: bridesmaids, maid of honor, flower girl, and ring bearer

Music change when bride enters
Bride enters escorted by father or both parents
Opening comments and prayer by pastor
"Who gives this woman" question and father-of-the-bride's response
Groom steps forward to take bride; bride and groom take positions on
platform (bride hands bouquet to maid of honor)
(Option: special music)

Message by pastor
"I do" vows
"Repeat after me" vows
"Ring" vows
Pronouncement of husband and wife
(Option: special music)

Pastor explains the unity candle, and couple lights it
(Option: special music)

Prayer
Groom kisses the bride (bride gets bouquet from maid of honor)
Introduction of "Mr. and Mrs." to congregation

Recessional music
Bride and groom exit, followed by wedding party
Parents exit, following the wedding party

Ushers return to usher out guests

Wedding Information

Date and time of wedding: _____

Location: _____

Date and time of rehearsal: _____

Bride's name: _____

   Bride's parents: _____

   Bride's address: _____

   Home phone: _____ Work: _____ Mobile: _____

   Date and place of birth: _____

   Religious background or affiliation: _____

   Maid/Matron of Honor: _____

   Bridesmaids: _____

Groom's name: _____

   Groom's parents: _____

   Groom's address: _____

   Home phone: _____ Work: _____ Mobile: _____

   Date and place of birth: _____

   Religious background or affiliation: _____

   Best Man: _____

   Groomsmen: _____

Wedding Planner: _____

   Wedding planner's address: _____

   Work phone: _____ Mobile: _____

Photographer: _____

   Photographer's address: _____

   Work phone: _____ Mobile: _____

   Wedding photos taken:

   Before ceremony: _____ During ceremony: _____ After ceremony: _____

Florist: _____

   Florist's address: _____

   Work phone: _____ Mobile: _____

Musicians: _____

Location of reception: _____

   Reception open to all wedding guests: _____ By invitation only: _____

Dates placed on church calendar: Rehearsal: _____ Wedding: _____

Approximate number of guests: _____

Special Requests: _____

_____

_____

Time for the wedding party to arrive: _____

Date of counseling: _____